Chicken Soup 心灵鸡汤 for the Soul

温暖心灵的幸福瞬间
True Love II

Jack Canfield（杰克·坎菲尔德）
［美］Mark Victor Hansen（马克·维克多·汉森）/ 编著　南溪 / 译
Amy Newmark（艾米·纽马克）

CS 湖南文艺出版社
HUNAN LITERATURE AND ART PUBLISHING HOUSE　博集天卷
CS-BOOKY

图书在版编目（CIP）数据

温暖心灵的幸福瞬间：汉英对照／（美）坎菲尔德（Canfield,J.）等编著；南溪译. — 长沙：
湖南文艺出版社，2012.6
（心灵鸡汤）
书名原文：True Love
ISBN 978-7-5404-5457-9

Ⅰ.①温…　Ⅱ.①坎…　②南…　Ⅲ.①英语—汉语—对照读物②故事—作品集—美国—现代
Ⅳ.① H319.4:I

中国版本图书馆 CIP 数据核字（2012）第 046598 号

著作权合同登记号：图字 18-2012-34

上架建议：心灵励志·英语学习

Chicken Soup for the Soul: True Love
101 Heartwarming and Humorous Stories about Dating, Romance, Love, and Marriage
by Jack Canfield, Mark Victor Hansen, Amy Newmark
Foreword by Kristi Yamaguchi and Bret Hedican
Published by Chicken Soup for the Soul Publishing, LLC www.chickensoup.com
Copyright © 2009 by Chicken Soup for the Soul Publishing, LLC. All Rights Reserved.

Chicken Soup for the Soul, P.O. Box 700, Cos Cob, CT 06807-0700, Fax 203-861-7194

心灵鸡汤：温暖心灵的幸福瞬间

作　　者：（美）坎菲尔德 等
译　　者：南　溪
出 版 人：刘清华
责任编辑：丁丽丹　刘诗哲
监　　制：蔡明菲　潘　良
特约编辑：沙玲玲
版权支持：辛　艳
封面设计：吕彦秋
版式设计：崔振江
出版发行：湖南文艺出版社
　　　　　（长沙市雨花区东二环一段 508 号　邮编：410014）
地　　址：www.hnwy.net
印　　刷：三河市华东印刷有限公司
经　　销：新华书店
开　　本：880mm×1230mm　1/32
字　　数：310 千字
印　　张：11
版　　次：2012 年 6 月第 1 版
印　　次：2020 年 9 月第 2 次印刷
书　　号：ISBN 978-7-5404-5457-9
定　　价：32.00 元
（若有质量问题，请致电质量监督电话：010-84409925）

目录
Contents

Chapter 2　Lessons in True Love

第二部分　真爱课程篇

Chapter 3　Happily Ever Laughter
第三部分　欢乐篇

前言
Foreword

Kristi: Everyone enjoys a great love story, so we were excited about being part of the *Chicken Soup for the Soul family* for this wonderful book of true love stories. This is not my first time in a Chicken Soup for the Soul book. I had a story about my early years as an athlete in *Chicken Soup for the Preteen Soul 2* and my mom had a story about my skating career in *Chicken Soup for the Sports Fan's Soul*.

Skating is great, but true love is even better! After all, it's something we all strive for and most of us achieve it at some point in our lives. Bret and I are fortunate to have it all—great careers, a strong marriage, and a wonderful family. But it almost didn't happen...

Bret: We met at the 1992 Olympics when I was playing for the U.S. hockey team and Kristi was figure skating for the U.S. She won a gold medal that year.

Nancy Kerrigan and Kristi were walking around meeting some of the other American team members. Kristi made an impression on all of us—she was just excited to be there and happy to be watching the hockey team and the players and be a part of it.

Kristi: There were about twenty-five hockey players and I remembered a few of them, but not Bret. When we met again a few years later in Vancouver, he told me that we had met at the Olympics. I had to go back to look at the photos to see if he was really there.

A hockey player was the last type of athlete I thought I would ever date. Hockey players are just a different breed from figure skaters. We always competed with the hockey players for rink time when I was a kid.

Bret: We had no class.

Kristi: It was pretty funny, because when we were reintroduced, one of my choreographers was with me, and he said there was this cute guy who kept looking over at me. I was so embarrassed, as if I was transported back to grade school.

We dated for about three years before Bret proposed. Bret was playing for the Vancouver Canucks and I was based in the Bay Area so we were only going to see each other over Christmas for a day and half, actually only forty hours! Bret called me and said he had missed his flight. I was not happy. There had been a snowstorm in Vancouver, and Bret's car wasn't working, and there were no cabs available since they are not accustomed to heavy snow in Vancouver.

Bret: We were spending Christmas Day with Kristi's family so I wanted us to have a nice quiet Christmas Eve dinner, just the two of us, so I could propose. But when I arrived, I discovered that Kristi had said that her sister and brother-in-law could join us. I pulled her sister aside and told her I had the ring in my pocket, and that she needed to leave right after dinner.

Kristi: He was still in trouble with me for being late, so it took me a while to figure out what was going on, and then I thought, "Don't do it because I've been so nasty all night." But we ended up at the top of the Marriott in downtown San Francisco, with a 360 degree view of the city, and he proposed. Of course I said yes.

Our parents were thrilled and excited and we decided to have a nice intimate family wedding in Hawaii. My extended family had a tradition of vacationing on the Big Island of Hawaii—25 or 30 of us at the Orchid Mauna Lani. We loved it and thought a small wedding would be nice.

You can guess what happened. We gave everyone more than a year to plan, so they could plan their family vacations around the wedding, and almost 100% of our invites said yes. Over 300 people came. We took over the whole hotel. It was awesome. It turned into a five-day wedding because everyone came early and by the time we had the ceremony on Saturday, everyone knew each other.

Bret: At the reception I scored points by serenading my bride with the Bob Dylan song "Make You Feel My Love." I saw Scott Hamilton quoted in People Magazine saying that every single woman in the room was crying.

Kristi: That was in 2000, and three years later we had our first child, Keara, and two years after that we had Emma. Our daughters are our proudest accomplishments. The minute you become a parent, you become so much closer and it reinforces the bond you have with each other. You become more conscious of the values you want to instill in your family. You also have a better understanding of your own parents—it's a lot of work!

While our marriage is still young compared to many out there, we feel a real affinity to the stories in this latest Chicken Soup for the Soul volume about true love. It's a lot of fun to read about dating, proposals, and weddings and remember our own years of long distance dating and our own wedding. And we love the stories written by long-time couples about how they keep their marriages fresh and their relationships healthy. Some of the stories are so funny, and a few will make you tear up. There is something in here for everyone, even you guys out there. We wives know that you secretly enjoy a good love story too, right Bret?

Bret: Yes, dear.

~Kristi Yamaguchi and Bret Hedican

· · · · · · · · · ·

克丽斯蒂：人人都喜欢伟大的爱情故事，所以能够参与《心灵鸡汤：温暖心灵的幸福瞬间》一书的编辑，我们感到十分荣幸。这不是我第一次为《心灵鸡汤》写作，一个关于我早年作为运动员的故事曾在《心灵鸡汤：儿童成长2》中发表。母亲也曾在《心灵鸡汤：体育迷》中，讲述过我的滑冰生涯。

滑冰是很棒的运动，但是真正的爱情更加美好！毕竟，我们每个人对爱情都有强烈的渴望，并希望在生命中的某一时刻收获爱情。布雷特和我是幸运的。我们婚姻幸福，事业顺利，家庭美满。但是，有可能这一切都不会发生……

布雷特：我们是在 1992 年的奥运会上相遇的，当时我在美国冰球队，克丽斯蒂在美国女子花样滑冰队。那年，她赢得了金牌。南希·克里根（冬奥会花样滑冰明星）和她一起，在赛场上走来走去，和其他的美国队成员打招呼。克丽斯蒂给我们所有人留下了深刻的印象——她非常兴奋，很高兴能观看冰球比赛和认识其他球员，并成为团队的一员。

克丽斯蒂：那时大概有 25 名队员，我记得其中一些人，但对布雷特没有什么印象。几年后，我们在温哥华再次相遇。当他告诉我，我们曾在 1992 年奥运会上见过面时，我非常惊讶，还回去翻了以前的照片看他是不是真的在那里。

我从没想过自己会和一名冰球队员交往。要知道，冰球和花样滑冰不过是冰上运动的不同种类罢了。当我还是个孩子的时候，我们就经常和冰球运动员抢冰场场地。

布雷特：我们冰球运动比较没地位了。

克丽斯蒂：说来挺逗的，我们再次遇到的时候，我的编舞导演和我在一起。他跟我说："有个很可爱的家伙一直盯着你看呢。"我当时觉得特别尴尬，就好像回到了小学时代一样。

我们交往了三年左右，布雷特向我求婚。当时，布雷特在温哥华加人队，而我在旧金山训练。所以我们只有在圣诞节期间——大约一天半的时间才能见对方。只有 40 小时！所以布雷特打电话告诉我说他错过航班的时候，我特别伤心。那天温哥华下了很大的雪，他的车子发动不了。而且因为大雪的原因，他也打不到出租车。

布雷特：我们原本打算同克丽斯蒂的家人一起过圣诞节。所以，在圣诞前夜，我希望我们两个能一起吃一顿浪漫、温馨的晚餐。然后，我可以借这个机会向她求婚。但是，我到达之后克丽斯蒂告诉我，她的妹妹和妹夫也要和我们一起吃晚餐。于是，我把她妹妹拉到一边，告诉她我的口袋里揣着戒指，希望她能在晚餐后离开。

克丽斯蒂：我当时还在为他的迟到而生气，所以，我花了一点时间才弄明白究竟发生了什么事情。我的第一反应是："不要啊，我今天晚上表现得那么恶劣。"但是当我们站在旧金山市中心万豪酒店顶层俯瞰全城的时候，他真的向我求婚了。当然，我答应了。

父母听到我们订婚的消息都替我们感到激动和兴奋。我们打算在夏威夷举办一场甜蜜的家庭婚礼。我们家族有在夏威夷度假的传统——家族里有 25到 30 个人都会选择夏威夷大岛马纳拉尼海岛的兰花酒店。我们很喜欢那里，觉得在那里举办一个小型婚礼会很不错。

你可以想象得出后面发生了什么。我们给所有亲朋好友一年多的时间来准备，让他们的家庭休假安排在我们的婚期前后。几乎所有受到邀请的亲朋都同意这么做。结果，我们的婚礼来了三百多位宾客，几乎占用了整个酒店。那场面真的太壮观了。我们的婚礼持续了五天，因为每位宾客都是提前到达的，等我们周六举行仪式的时候，他们彼此间早都认识了。

布雷特：在婚宴上，我为我的新娘唱了一首鲍勃·迪伦的《感受我的爱》，这给我加分不少。斯科特·汉密尔顿（萨克斯风手）引用《人物》杂志上的话说，房间里的每一个单身女子都感动得哭了。

克丽斯蒂：在 2000 年，也就是结婚三年后，我们有了第一个孩子琪拉。两年后，我们有了艾玛。两个女儿是我们最大的骄傲，是孩子让我们两个紧紧地连在一起。有了自己的孩子之后，你会更注重培养家庭价值观，也会更加理解自己的父母。为人父母，实在不简单呢！

相比其他人，我们的婚姻还很年轻，但是我们的确在《心灵鸡汤：温暖心灵的幸福瞬间》中找到了共鸣。这些有关约会、求婚和婚礼的故事，读起来非常有意思，也让我想起自己坠入爱情时的那段时光和我们的婚礼。我们喜欢那些老夫老妻写的文章，他们教会我们如何让婚姻健康、富有活力。有的故事让人忍俊不禁，有的则让你泪流满面。每个人都能从故事中有所收获，即使男人也一样。我们做妻子的知道，背地里你们也很喜欢看爱情故事的，对吗，布雷特？

布雷特：呵呵，亲爱的，确实如此。

——克丽斯蒂·亚玛古驰和布雷特·赫迪坎

引言
Introduction

My very thoughtful son, who is a college senior with a long-time fabulous girlfriend, has a wonderful metaphor for relationships. He views a relationship as a machine— a box full of intermeshed gears working together. When the machine is new, the gears are shiny and sharp. They work together, but there is some roughness around the edges and a little resistance as they mesh. Over time, the gears lose some of their shininess, and their edges become a little rounded, but they work together more and more smoothly. A little dirt gets in the machine from time to time, and it must be cleaned out diligently in order to keep the gears working well and avoid permanent build-up.

Once in a while, a major problem may occur, and a piece of metal may fall into the works. But a well-maintained machine with well-matched gears will survive this. The gears will keep moving and the stray piece of metal may get thrown against the side wall of the machine, leaving a permanent dent that mars the machine but doesn't impair its performance. Or the piece of metal may actually damage a gear, bending it or breaking it, but the machine soldiers on, and the gears still mesh better and better over time, albeit with one missing tooth.

Our relationships are like that metaphorical machine. Over time, our gears may darken with age and wear down, and even show some breakage, but if we tend to them they should mesh more and more smoothly. If the machine really suffers irreparable damage, and we break up or divorce, we look to start over with new machines.

Chicken Soup for the Soul: True Love is an inspiring collection of stories about dating, romance, love, and marriage. You will find stories about everything from first dates and falling in love, to proposals and weddings, to second chances and love later in life, to making relationships work over the years. Whether you are looking for new love, basking in the glow of a successful relationship, or working on a relationship that needs a little polishing, you will find fundamental wisdom in these pages, from real people sharing their personal stories with you.

Our Assistant Publisher, D'ette Corona, and I had so much fun reading the thousands of stories submitted for this book. After all, who doesn't enjoy a great love story? We laughed and cried, nodded our heads in recognition, shook our heads in disbelief, and were disappointed when it was all over and the book was finished!

So now it is your turn. "Gear up" for a great read. We hope these stories will help your relationship "machine" work as well as ours, or give you faith that your next box of gears will be the one that operates smoothly for the rest of your life!

~Amy Newmark

Publisher, Chicken Soup for the Soul

· · · · · · · · · ·

　　我的儿子是名大四学生，他有个很优秀的女朋友，对恋爱也有着独到的看法。他曾将恋爱中的两人比喻为一台由啮合齿轮构成的机器，刚开始的时候，齿轮是崭新锐利的。它们刚开始一起工作，由于齿轮太锐利，它们啮合的时候偶尔会出现摩擦或阻力。但是随着时间的推移，齿轮失去了些许光泽，边缘也更加圆润，但它们的配合却越来越好。偶尔，它们也会沾染上一些灰尘，这时候就需要及时清除，保持机器正常工作，避免造成永久性损坏。

　　一段时间后，机器也可能出现一些小故障，比如某个部件不能正常工作。但是如果进行精心保养和护理，它们也能够渡过难关。齿轮运转过程中，被甩出机器侧壁的金属部件可能会在机器上留下永久性凹痕，但却不会损害其性能，部件也有可能会弄弯或折断一个齿轮，但是机器维修工会修好损伤的部分。机器上哪怕缺少一个齿牙，齿轮还是能够很好地啮合在一起。

　　恋爱中两个人的关系也正如这个比喻中的机器。随着年岁增长，我们的齿轮可能也会变暗和磨损，甚至有一定的损坏，但只要细心呵护，这台机器便能运转得越来越顺畅。如果机器真的遭受无法弥补的损害，我们就会分手或者离婚，期待着能同新齿轮更好地啮合。

　　《心灵鸡汤：感悟真爱》一书收录了有关约会、恋爱、婚姻的各种感人故事：从初次约会到坠入爱河，从求婚策划到婚礼举行，从和好如初到新的爱恋。品味这些故事的同时，相信你能找到让爱情经久不衰的秘诀。无论渴盼下段恋情的成功，还是需要给多年的爱情打磨抛光，这些真实的人和事都会对你有所裨益。

　　出版助理德·卡罗娜和我在审阅无数来稿时，收获了巨大的快乐。毕竟，谁不喜欢动人的爱情故事呢？我们开心地笑，感动地哭，既会认同地点头，也会微微摇头表示怀疑。当这本书的编辑工作完成时，我们的内心则感到深深的不舍和失落。

　　现在，轮到你了。"加大油门"开始愉悦的阅读之旅吧。希望这些故事能让你们的爱情"机器"更加良好地运转，或是帮你找到同你默契啮合一生的齿轮。

　　　　　　　　　　　　　　　——《心灵鸡汤》出版人艾米·纽马克

第一部分 婚姻相处篇

Chapter 1
Keeping the Love Alive

A successful marriage requires falling in love many times, always with the same person.

~Germaine Greer

成功婚姻需要你一次次地坠入爱河，不过总是和同一个对象。

——杰梅茵·格里尔

Destiny in the Desert
沙漠中的命运

Everyone says you only fall in love once but that's not true,
every time I hear your voice I fall in love all over again.

~Author Unknown

"We never do anything fun together anymore,"
I bellyached to my devoted and doting husband Ilan.
So Ilan started bombarding me with e-mails and
flyers offering "weekend getaways" and other exotic
and not-so-exotic "events" all over the country and
abroad. "Romantic log cabin with Jacuzzi," screamed
one flyer. "Visit Costa Rica," enticed another. But
when I noticed a small advertisement for a "midnight
walk in the desert," not far from the Dead Sea,
I knew I had stumbled on just the right activity
which would combine Ilan's affinity for the rugged
outdoors with my romantic nature. We bought the
tickets online and marked the date in our calendars.

We live in Israel, about 150 miles from the
Dead Sea. Because of the narrow, winding, poorly-
lit roads as you move farther away from the center
of the country, this adds up to a three-hour car ride.

Each way. With three young daughters at home, taking a "midnight walk" in the desert required much more logistical planning than a simple stroll in the park.

After dropping our daughters off at the homes of various friends and relatives for the night, we headed south for our rendezvous. We briefly considered detouring into Tel Aviv for a romantic candlelight dinner (which Ilan assured me would be cheaper than paying for the gas we were about to burn), but since we had already purchased our "midnight walk" tickets, we felt that our destiny was sealed in the desert.

We spent the drive listening to music, catching up on the week and enjoying the fact that there was no bickering coming from the backseat to distract us. When we finally arrived at the winding snake path that was meant to guide us to our midnight walk's starting point, we hit a traffic jam resembling that of rush hour in the city. We managed to piece together from other drivers that a semi-trailer had jackknifed somewhere down the road and was blocking the path. I wondered to myself if the semi-trailer driver's wife had also complained that they never did anything fun together anymore and if this was her just reward.

Ilan, who never leaves home without his "coffee kit" (essentially a tool box filled with a small gas burner, six glasses, coffee, tea, sugar and non-perishable milk) decided to make us hot drinks—in the car—while we were waiting. Spicy cinnamon tea never tasted so good. Still, we grew impatient after sitting in the exact same spot for forty-five minutes along with groups of other would-be midnight walkers who were congregating near their cars. So we decided to change the course of our destiny. Ilan knew of a lovely public beach (called, incidentally, Public Beach) where, because we had the forethought to throw our bathing suits in the car "just in case," we could take a swim. The changing rooms were locked so we boldly swapped our hiking clothes for bathing suits right there on the beach! With the moonlight as our guide, we stepped into a warm, comforting, Dead Sea bath. Our midnight walk had turned into a midnight swim.

Holding on to each other as we gently floated in the saltwater under the moonlit sky, we talked about philosophy, astronomy, history, the secrets of a good marriage and changing destinies. We talked about how to get our money back for those unused tickets for a midnight walk in the desert.

And then, at just about midnight, we reluctantly got out of the water, showered ourselves off on the beach, changed clothes, and started the long drive back to the city. Without any effort or preparation, we had spent one of the most pleasant evenings we'd had in a long time. And I realized that my destiny wasn't waiting for me in the desert after all; he's been right beside me for the past twenty years.

~Gayle Danis Rinot

都说一个人只可以爱一次，但这不是真的，每次听到你的声音时，我再一次坠入爱河。

——佚名

"我们再也不能一起做有趣的事了。"我向对我百依百顺的亲爱的丈夫伊兰抱怨说。因此伊兰的邮件和传真狂轰滥炸地向我袭来，提出各种"周末休闲游"，具有异国情调和本土气息的旅行。一封传真上写着"带有按摩浴缸的浪漫小木屋"。另一封写着"哥斯达黎加之旅"，充满诱惑，让我惊叹。但是当我在广告上看到离死海不远处的

"沙漠午夜漫游"时，我知道我正好找到一个能把伊兰热衷户外运动和我的浪漫本性结合起来的好方法。我们在网上买了火车票，也在日历上标明了出发日期。

我们住在以色列，离死海大约241公里。由于离市中心很远，道路变得很窄，蜿蜒崎岖，而且路灯也不太亮，所以无论从哪条路上走，开车到死海都得需要三小时的路程。比起在公园里遛弯，把三个年纪尚小的女儿们留在家里，去沙漠中"午夜漫游"需要精心策划一下。

我们把女儿们放在几个朋友和亲戚家，拜托他们照顾一晚之后，就一路向南，奔赴我们的约会地点。我们一开始想绕道去特拉维夫享用一顿浪漫的烛光晚餐（伊兰向我保证过这要比在路上烧的油钱便宜得多），但是因为我们已经买好了"午夜漫游"的票，我们都觉得这是命中注定，一定要在沙漠中度过。

一路上我们听着音乐，聊着过去一周发生的事，我们很高兴车的后排没有发出任何吵闹声来打扰我们。最终我们到达了蜿蜒如蛇般的道路，这条路将引导我们开启午夜漫游之旅，我们遇到了交通堵塞，和在城市的高峰时刻出现的拥堵一样。我们从其他司机零星话语中得知一个半挂车在路上弯折了，挡住了道路。我在想是不是半挂车司机的妻子也抱怨他们再也不能一起做有趣的事了，这是不是就是她想要的乐趣呢。

每次出门，伊兰都不会忘记带他的"咖啡工具"（就是一个工具箱，里面装有一台燃气炉灯、六个玻璃杯、咖啡、茶、糖和不易变质的牛奶），趁我们在车里等着的时间，他决定给我们煮点热饮。香辣肉桂茶一向都不怎么好喝。我们和其他一些要去午夜漫游、可现在却聚在车旁的人在同一个地方坐了45分钟后，变得越来越不耐烦。因此，我们决定改变我们命运的轨迹。伊兰知道有一块美丽的公共海滩（名字恰巧就叫公共海滩），我们为了以防万一在车上放了泳衣，因此就可以游泳了。更衣室锁住了，我们就大胆地在沙滩上脱下远足的衣服，换上泳衣。借着月光，我们跳进一个温暖舒服的死海浴池。我们的午夜漫游变成了午夜游泳。

月光清亮的晚上，我们手牵着手，轻轻漂浮在盐水中，讨论着哲学、天文学、历史，以及维持一段幸福婚姻的秘密和命运的多变。我们商量着怎么样才能把那两张没有用过的沙漠午夜漫游的票换成钱。

大约在午夜的时候，我们依依不舍地从水里出来，在沙滩上冲了个澡，换上衣服，踏上了返回城市的漫长道路。毫无疑问，这是我们一起生活这么久以来，度过的最美妙的一个夜晚。我意识到等待我的并不是沙漠中的命运；有他陪我度过这二十年才是我的命运。

——盖尔·丹尼斯·瑞诺特

"We never do anything exciting anymore... but at least we aren't doing it together!"

"我们再也不做让人激动的事了……但至少我们两个人都没有做！"

The Runner
逃跑者

I'd like to run away from you, But if you didn't come and find me... I would die.

~Shirley Bassey

I'm a runner. I'm not a runner in the traditional sense. I run from love. It scares the crap out of me, and I don't know why. There's something about feeling that good which instills fear in me like nothing else. It's impossible to feel that good without knowing you're going to end up getting hurt. It's the way it's always been for me.

It's anyone's guess how I became a runner. Maybe not having a father figure around the house when I grew up had something to do with it. It's possibly nothing more than a simple phobia, induced by something completely untraceable. It could be nothing more than a small part of a much bigger mental illness, which I too would acknowledge, then attempt to do nothing about. Acceptance has never been a problem with me. But taking action, well, that's a whole different story. All this aside, I have this problem—I'm a runner.

We've all been taught to embrace our fears, as do I. I've even been known to search for love, sometimes to even run after it, but the results have always been the same. Find someone, begin a relationship, let love blossom, and when things start getting good, run like a river after spring rains. As I said before, I'm a runner.

Strangely, one of my biggest hopes in life is to settle down with that one special someone. The person who makes you feel like you're home, just because you're with them. The person who can make your heart melt with a simple look. The person who understands I'm a runner, and she waits patiently for me to get tired, and turn to face what she's already faced—that love only gets better with time.

And with the right person, love can blossom into something beyond our wildest dreams.

True love, when allowed to take its course, is grander than the grandest of fairy tales. It is the essence of life, and all which encompasses our existence as humans. Everything else is just life's complements.

Runners never get the opportunity to experience this secure faith in love. It's the initial Wow, and then it's off to the races. There is help for runners, but you would have to want help, more than you want love, because you can't experience one without eliminating the other.

Something happened a few years ago to change my life forever. I met her. The one. The love of my life. For awhile, at least. I mean, I do have some run still left in me.

She seems to recognize this, and from time to time she gives me space. No leash. No restrictions. When I come back around, she takes me in, feeds me, and gives me a heart to lean on. She forgives, but she doesn't forget. For this, I'm grateful. I need the reminder, although she could be a bit more subtle sometimes. Then again, when I step back and look through her eyes, which is easy to do when you're in love, I see the pain I cause her.

This is enough to make me want to run away forever, because the last thing I want to do is cause someone else pain. Especially someone I love as much as I love her. But if I did run away from her with intent not to return, and I tried once, then we both lose.

You see, I learned something about running away from true love. You can't. It follows you wherever you go. True love is inside you. It is a part of you, and it consumes you. It's supposed to. It is, after all, the essence of life.

In a nutshell, true love makes hope look like a distant cousin. When it comes to things which drive us, and hope, for many, is the grandest of things, love is still the grand master.

As the years have passed, I now run less and less. When I run, I never stray too far from home, because deep down, I know I love her too. She's special. She understands my mental illness like none before. She accepts me as I am, to a point. I'd be disappointed if she didn't want to change me a little. I do have flaws which could use some mending.

Today, we share a unity of life's spirit. I've never felt this before. Hell, I never would have even said anything like that before, but she brings this out in me. Love can be so many things, but in the end, it's what you allow it to be—not what you make it.

I now live to make her happy, as she has done so many times for me. The past is the past, and the future will surely bring many surprises. But for today, I'm happy to be where I'm at in life. I still hope for many things, but none of those hopes compare to the love I feel for this woman.

She fills my heart with joy. She gives me new hope. There's no place to run when you've found where you were going, and that's a good thing. Because, for the record, I'm tired of running.

~Jay Rylant

我想要逃离你，但是如果你没有来找我，我将会死去……

————雪莉·贝西

　　我是一个逃跑者。我不是传统意义上的逃跑者。我逃离的是爱情。爱情总是让我毛骨悚然，我也不知道这是为什么。关于爱情的美好事情带给我的只有恐惧，别无其他。我感觉不到美好的爱情，只知道最终爱情将死亡，你也会受伤。对我来说，爱情就是这样的。

　　大家都想知道我是怎么变成一个逃跑者的。这可能和我在一个缺少父爱的家庭中成长有点关系。原因很简单，这都源于我对那些难以捉摸的事情所产生的恐惧感。这只不过是正在恶化的精神疾病的一点征兆，这个我也很清楚，但是从未想过去做些什么。对我来说，接受从来都不是一个问题。但是要采取行动却是另外一回事了。除此之外，我还有一个问题——我是个逃跑者。

　　我们都被教导过要直面恐惧，我也是如此。我曾经一直在寻求爱情，甚至有时候还勇敢地去追逐，但是结果总是一样。找到一个人，开始了一段感情，然后热恋，当事情有眉目的时候，我就像春雨过后的河流一样，匆匆而逃。就像我之前说的，我是个逃跑者。

奇怪的是，我人生中最大的理想就是能和那个特别的人一起过安定的日子。那个人能让你感觉自己像是在家里，因为你和她在一起。那个人只要你看一眼，就能让你的心融化。那个人理解我是个逃跑者，她会耐心地等着我疲倦的那一天，让我面对她早已领悟的东西——经过时间的洗涤，爱情会越来越甜蜜。

跟合适的人在一起，爱情将超越你最疯狂的想象。

顺其自然的真爱比最美的童话还要美好。它是生命的本质，是人类生存下去的全部依靠。其他东西只是对人生的补充。

逃跑者永远不会感受到爱情的坚贞。这是最初的誓言，然后要用一辈子去遵守。有帮助逃跑者的方法，但是你可能渴望得到这种帮助更甚于渴望爱情本身，因为你无法经历一场不会伤害到对方的爱情。

几年前发生的一件事从此改变了我的人生。我遇到了她，命中注定的人。我生命中的爱情。至少也维持了一段时间。我的意思是我还是想逃跑。

她似乎注意到了这一点，时不时给我空间来思考，不会束缚我，不会限制我，当我回去找她的时候，她让我进来，给我吃的，还有一颗可以依靠的心。她原谅了我，但是她没有忘记。对此，我很感激她。我需要她的提醒，虽然有时候她的提醒不太明显。然后又一次，我退缩了，看着她的眼睛，当你爱上一个人的时候，很容易做到，我看到我给她带来的痛苦。

这足以让我一去不复返，因为我最不愿意做的事就是给别人带来痛苦。尤其是让我足够倾心的人。但是如果我离开了她，执意不回来会怎么样呢，于是我试了一次，最后我们失去了彼此。

你看到了，我从逃离真爱中学到了一件事——你无处可逃。无论到哪里，它都会跟随着你。真爱就在你的心里。是你生命的一部分，而且一点点地吞噬着你。只能如此。这就是生命的本质。

总而言之，真爱让梦想变得遥不可及。尤其是那些让我们痴情的东西，梦想对很多人来说是最美好的事物，但是爱情才是美丽的主宰。

随着时间的流逝，现在我逃跑的次数越来越少了。当我逃跑的时候，再也不会离家那么远了，因为在我的内心深处，我知道我也爱她。对我来说，她是个特殊的人。和之前的人不同，她知道我有精神疾病。她完全能接受我这样一个人。如果她一点也不想改变我的话，我会很沮丧。我也有瑕疵，需要修补。

今天，我们共同拥有生命之魂。我从来没有这种感觉。我也从来没有说过像这样的话，是她帮助我说了出来。爱情可以是很多方面的，但是最终你只能顺从它——而不能改变它。

现在我活着的意义就是让她高兴，就像她曾经多次为我做的那样。过去的都已逝去，未来肯定充满许多惊喜。但是今天，我很高兴拥有现在的生活。我仍旧对很多事情心存梦想，但是任何一个梦想都不能和我对这个女人的感觉相提并论。

她让我的内心充满喜悦。她给了我新的希望。当你知道前进的方向后，就不需要再逃跑了，这是件好事。因此我郑重声明，我已经厌倦了逃跑。

——杰·瑞兰特

"In the race of life... true love is the finish line!"

"在人生的长跑中……真爱才是终点！"

He's a Keeper
他是我的守护神

Even for two people who are very much in love, learning to live together is full of challenges. How comforting is it to discover that the conflicts we face are not unique to our own relationship!

~Marilyn McCoo

The cleaning service had barely backed out of the driveway, our pine floors still damp from the Murphy Oil Soap. Yet, the bathroom mirror displayed smudges along the beveled right edge. Only one other person shared my home with me—my handsome husband of just two months.

"Rob, I want you to come here right now. I have something to show you."

When I was thirty-four, this seemingly perfect man danced into my life. As a health care administrator, I was expected to attend the semi-annual management gatherings at the luxurious Peabody Hotel. That spring night, my suitable escort sat glued to his chair as I stood on the edge of the dance floor, tapping time with open-toed silver slippers. Rob, another manager, motioned me to the dance area and showed me how to rock. Instantly the party livened up as I submitted to the rhythm of the blues, twirling in my handkerchief-hem periwinkle party dress. The night passed quickly as Rob and I danced every number until the band packed up.

"That was fun, thanks," I told Rob, gasping for cool air and appropriate words.

"See you back at the old salt mines," he responded and waved goodbye.

My group of friends and courtesy date waited patiently for me at the hotel exit. No one asked any questions and I offered no explanations. No doubt this had been the best work party ever. I told myself that I might have danced with "the one" that night.

Within a few days, Rob invited me on our official first date—another dance. After almost two years of courtship, I married my own Fred Astaire.

I knew that marriage was not easy, so I had delayed this commitment until my thirties. Friends endearingly chided me, saying "You are too stuck in your ways to marry." As the only daughter in our family, I had grown up with my own room, my own clothes, my own phone, and later my own car, my own apartment, my own everything.

Now married, I had to share everything. The simplest daily happenings that broke with my personal routines caused me frustration at home. However, Rob patiently embraced my idiosyncrasies with gentleness and compassion. He mostly accepted whatever came his way with an easygoing personality. Repeatedly he calmed any stress I created in our new home.

Rob understood that he had married a woman who had been single her entire life. For me, everything stayed in its assigned place, planned for my convenience. Rooms went untouched and my few dishes remained clean and put away in the kitchen cabinet. The cleaning service arrived monthly to deep clean my home, though it was never really dirty.

Now, there were two of us. Admittedly Rob was neat but less obsessed with order. How could marriage change my environment so quickly? Why did I find socks under the sofa and used dishes in the sink? Before marriage, my mirrors stayed clear and shiny. Now I found smudges on the bathroom mirror, only minutes after the cleaning service performed its magic.

"Honey, I have something to show you," I repeated. Rob released the TV changer and ambled into the bathroom. I pushed my chin forward, planting my feet firmly before the bathroom sink.

"Yes?"

"Do you see this mirror?"

"Yes."

"Do you see the fingerprints all over this clean mirror?" Rob came closer to inspect the mirror from several angles.

"Yes."

"Do you know whose fingerprints those are?" Again he leaned over to peer at the smudges.

"Yes."

"Well, whose fingerprints are all over this clean mirror?" I demanded. He paused and looked straight into my soul.

"Honey, those are the fingerprints of the man who loves you."

I stood speechless for a few seconds. All resentment melted as I gazed into his kind brown eyes. This was the man who had chosen to marry a fussy old maid, a spinster, who had trouble coupling. He was the man who loved me.

Rob reached for a towel to clean the mirror, but my hand stopped him. "And what beautiful fingerprints they are," I responded. "I just love those fingerprints—and the man who made them."

Yes, being married meant I had to share; and yes, there would be more to clean. The house would not stay systematized, nor would Rob use my organizing key rack at the back door. But this man loved and accepted me just like I was. Now I had his unique fingerprints on my mirror, a testimony to the fact that I had married "the one" and would not be alone any more. Everyone was right: marriage meant trade-offs, but for me, Rob was a keeper.

~Marylane Wade Koch

即使是两个彼此深爱的人，也要学会面对共同生活中的挑战。值得
欣慰的是，并不只是我们在面对关系中的冲突。

——玛丽莲·麦库

　　清洁服务人员刚刚开车走了，沾着墨菲石油
香皂的松木地板还是很潮湿。而且浴室镜子的右
角到处是污迹。和我一起住的只有一个人——刚
和我结婚两个月的英俊丈夫。

　　"罗伯，我想让你现在过来一下。我要给你
看点东西。"

　　在我 34 岁那年，这个看起来几乎完美的男
人闯入了我的生活。我是一名医疗保健行政人员，
要参加在豪华的皮博迪酒店每半年举行一次的管
理人员聚会。在那个春天的夜晚，我的舞伴一
动也不动地坐在他的椅子上，而我站在舞池的外
围，用露着脚趾的银色拖鞋拍着拍子。罗伯，另
一位管理人员，把我推向舞池里，并教我怎么跳
舞。我跟着蓝调的节奏，转动着我那镶着常春花
图案的晚礼服，顿时整个派对活跃起来了。那个
夜晚过得太快了，我和罗伯每支舞都跳了，直到
乐队收工。

　　"我玩得很高兴，谢谢你。"我绞尽脑汁找了

些适当的词语，倒吸一口冷气对他说。

"辛苦你了，再见。"他一边说着一边挥手告别。

我的朋友们正礼貌而又耐心地在酒店出口等着我。没有人问我任何问题，我也没有做任何解释。这次聚会无疑是最好的一次。我对自己说我有可能还会和那天晚上的"他"一起跳舞。

过了几天，罗伯邀请我参加我们的第一次正式约会——也是跳舞。在他追求我差不多两年之后，我嫁给了属于自己的弗雷德·阿斯泰尔。

我知道婚姻生活不会那么轻松，所以一直延迟到我30多岁才结婚。朋友们都温和地指责我说"在结婚的看法上，你太固执己见了"。作为家里唯一的女儿，在我的成长岁月中，我睡自己的房间，穿自己的衣服，用自己的电话，到后来开自己的车，住自己的公寓，所有的东西都是我一个人享用。

现在结婚了，我要和别人一起分享。日常生活中最简单的小事也总会打乱我个人的习惯，让我在家里感觉很不自在。但是罗伯耐心地用他的绅士风度和怜悯之心对待我的怪癖习性。他随和的性格几乎每次都能包容我。就这样他不断地缓解着这个新家对我造成的压力。

罗伯知道他娶了一个一直过着单身生活的女人。对我来说，每一件东西都应该为了我的方便摆放在一个固定的位置。房间应该一尘不染，餐具应该干干净净地放在厨房的橱柜里。清洁服务人员每个月都到家里来做彻底清扫，虽然屋子从来都不会特别脏。

现在我们两个人在一起生活。我承认罗伯很爱干净，但是对整理内务不怎么放在心上。婚姻怎么会在这么短的时间里就改变了我的生活环境呢？为什么沙发底下会有袜子？为什么水槽里会有没洗的盘子？结婚前，我的镜子一向是干干净净，闪闪发亮。可现在，清洁服务人员刚刚像变魔法一样让浴室的镜子焕然一新，马上就被弄得到处是污迹。

"亲爱的，我要给你看个东西。"我又说了一遍。罗伯放下电视遥控器，踱着步子慢慢走进浴室。我伸着下巴，在浴室的水槽前稳稳地站着。

"怎么了？"

"看见这面镜子了吗？"

"嗯。"

"看见干干净净的镜子上弄得全是手指印吗？"罗伯走近点，从各个角度检查镜子。

"看见了。"

"你知道这是谁的手指印吗？"他又一次靠过来，盯着这些污迹看。

"知道。"

"嗯，这干干净净的镜子上弄的是谁的手指印呢？"我问他。他怔住了，然后直视着我的灵魂。

"亲爱的，这些手指印是爱你的那个男人的。"

我站在那儿，沉默了几分钟。当我凝视着他那温柔的棕色眼睛时，所有的怨愤都融化了。是这个男人选择娶一个挑剔的老姑娘，一个总是找麻烦的老处女。他就是那个爱我的男人。

罗伯拿来一条毛巾要擦镜子，但是我的手抓住他的手。"这些手指印多美啊，"我对他说，"我是太喜欢这些手指印了——还有那个弄手指印上去的男人。"

是啊，结婚就意味着要分享；是啊，需要擦拭的东西会更多。屋子不再有条不紊，罗伯也不会把钥匙挂在门后面。但是这个男人能够接纳我，爱我。现在镜子上留下了他独一无二的手指印，证明我嫁对了人，我不再孤独了。大家说的是对的：结了婚就要作出取舍，但是罗伯是我的守护神。

——玛丽·韦德·科赫

"We're a perfect match...
Once you eliminate all
our imperfections!"

"只要你忽略了我们身上所有的瑕疵，我们两个就是最完美的一对。"

Little Things Matter
琐事也重要

> You cannot plough a field by turning it over in your mind.
> ~Author Unknown

Last year my husband, Bob, and I stopped celebrating many special occasions, including Valentine's Day. We were busy and neither of us felt like going out just to buy cards and chocolate. Usually, I decorate the house with special candles and heart-shaped ornaments that I've had for over twenty years. But I didn't bother. So the day came and went with nothing more than a "Happy Valentine's Day" peck on the cheek.

During a plain omelet supper, I looked over at Bob and said, "I feel badly we didn't do anything special." He did too. It seemed like we were two people who'd been married for many years, and these little things just didn't matter anymore.

But they do.

After supper, we snuggled together, recalling wonderful memories of how we met.

Over thirty years ago, I taught a class called

"Life After Divorce" . Bob, a handsome blond blue-eyed man, who looks no different to me today, was a student.

Back then, I was crazy-in-love with a fellow I'll call Michael. But I was always unlucky in the love department. That was because I picked guys who were commitment-phobic. I believed I could change them. Finally, I realized I was the one who needed to change.

Michael was "perfect"—funny, handsome, and smart. The problem was that he wasn't in love with me.

The more Michael would get close, then back off, the harder I'd try to win him over. But I failed. With each "failure" I felt more undesirable, which eroded my selfesteem.

While dating Michael, I started hanging out with Bob. But we were just buddies. We had a blast—biking, swimming, hiking. I never worried about what I said or if my apartment was messy. With Michael, I'd berate myself for everything I thought I'd said wrong. I'd usually run words through my "Is this clever and smart?" filter before saying them.

There was no filter with Bob. I never felt self-conscious. We confided our inner secrets and spent most times in joyous laughter. If I dripped mustard on my chin from my hot dog, I didn't care. Had that happened with Michael, I'd have been mortified.

It was such a shame that I wasn't crazy-in-love with Bob.

I can recall a pivotal moment as vividly as an earthquake. I was home, waiting for Bob. I was wearing my baggy shorts and gray T-shirt. It was the only outfit I had put on, which was such a contrast to trying on outfit after outfit before seeing Michael.

Then it hit me. I had a smack-bang revelation. I said out loud, "What are you doing?" It was at this most crucial instant, like Dorothy with her slippers, that I realized that what I had been looking for had been there all along.

Someone who loved me as I was, make-up or not, clever repartée or not. In other words, I had found my best friend.

I can still picture looking up at him and taking the first step. I kissed him… and you can probably take it from there.

It was thrilling to change my never-going-anywhere dating path and wise up to what's really important. To me, true love means being each others' best friends.

And now, after so many years of marriage, we still are.

But last month we learned that relationships can't lie still. They need to be nurtured.

After Valentine's Day, I put out our St. Patrick's Day ornaments and candles. Bob came home with a three-dollar heart-shaped cake from the "day old" bin. As he presented it to me, his eyes were brimming with happy tears. He said, "Every day is Valentine's Day with you." I looked up and kissed him… and you can probably take it from there.

And so we vowed we'll never be too busy to make trips for just a card. Little things do matter.

~Saralee Perel

田地不是靠一遍一遍的想象就能耕好的。

——逸名

从去年开始，我和丈夫鲍勃再也不搞很多特殊节日的庆祝活动了，包括情人节在内。我们都很忙，忙到都懒得出去买卡片和巧克力了。这二十年来，通常我会用一些特别的蜡烛和心形装饰物来装饰屋子。但是现在为了省事，不想麻烦了。所以节日来临之际，只有在脸颊上轻轻地来一个"情人节快乐"之吻，仅此而已。

在一顿只有普通煎蛋的晚饭上，我看着鲍勃说："我们没有做任何特殊的事情，我觉得很糟糕。"他也是这么想的。我们两个好像是一对结婚很多年的夫妻，这些琐事再也无关紧要了。

但是琐事也很重要。

吃晚饭后，我们依偎在一起，回想起我们相遇时的美好回忆。

三十年前，我开了一门课，叫"离婚后生活"。鲍勃，一个金发碧眼的帅小伙（在我看来至今也没有什么变化）还是个学生。

那个时候，我疯狂地爱上一个叫迈克尔的人。但是在情场上，我总是很不幸。因为我爱上的都是一些害怕作出承诺的男生。我坚信我能改变他们。最终我意识到我才是那个需要改变的人。

迈克尔是个完美的男人——幽默、英俊、聪慧。但问题是他不爱我。

迈克尔越是每次靠近我、然后退缩的时候，我就越是努力地想赢得他的心。他每一次对我疏远都让我感觉到他越来越讨厌我，也渐渐地侵蚀着我的自尊。

在和迈克尔约会的那个时候，我开始和鲍勃交往，但我们只是好哥们儿。我们在一起玩得很开心——骑单车、游泳、徒步旅行。我从来不会担心自己说了什么，也不用担心我的公寓是不是很乱。但是和迈克尔在一起的时候，如果我觉得自己说错了，就会痛斥自己的一切，总是在说话之前，脑子会先进行反问"这样说明智吗？"

和鲍勃在一起说话不用顾忌，都是无意识说出的话。我们向对方吐露内心的秘密，大多数时候都是在欢声笑语中度过的。如果吃热狗的时候，我不小心把芥末沾在下巴上，根本不会在意。如果是和迈克尔在一起，我肯定会感到羞愧。

遗憾的是，我没有疯狂地爱上鲍勃。

我能清楚地记得那个重大时刻，就像发生地震的情形一样。我在家里等着鲍勃。穿着一件宽松的短裤和一件灰色衬衫。这就是我的全套装束，和在见迈克尔之前一套一套地换衣服形成鲜明对比。

突然我犹如醍醐灌顶一般。我大声喊道："你在做什么？"在这个最关键的时刻，就像桃乐丝找到了她的鞋一样，我意识到我一直寻找的东西就在我的身边。不管我是否化妆，是否聪明，有一个人就是爱这样的我。换句话说，我找到了最好的朋友。

我还记得我抬头看着他，大胆迈出第一步。我亲吻了他……剩下的大家就自己推测吧。

我很高兴能改变自己一直坚信的约会路线，去做一些真的很重要的事。对我来说，真爱就是成为彼此最好的朋友。

现在，结婚这么多年之后，我们依旧是最好的朋友。

但是我们在上个月意识到我们之间的感情不能总在原地不动。我们需要用心去经营。

情人节过后，我拿出圣帕特里克节的装饰物和蜡烛。鲍勃回家的时候，从一个老掉牙的箱子里拿出一块 3 美元买的心形蛋糕。他拿着蛋糕，面对着我，眼睛里闪烁着幸福的泪花。他说："和你在一起，每一天都是情人节。"我仰起头，亲吻着他……剩下的大家就自己推测吧。

我们发誓再也不会因为忙就懒到不愿意跑个腿去买张卡片。琐事也同等重要。

——萨拉莉·佩雷尔

Connecting
交流

The difference between try and triumph is a little umph.
~Author Unknown

Ray and I glide around the ballroom floor to the strains of "The Tennessee Waltz" . Ray is handsome in a black silk shirt open at the throat and khaki slacks. He smells of a musky aftershave, and his lead is gentle as he lifts his arm to turn me under. I look into his hazel eyes and my heart skips two beats.

I haven't felt this way in a while. Just this morning I was grousing to Annie, my Golden Retriever, that a second marriage isn't what it's cracked up to be. Too many complications with joint and personal accounts, blended families, and difficult exes. Plus, after ten years of marriage, we seem to be falling into patterns that are more comfortable than romantic.

Ray turns me under his arm again, and once more we lock eyes. My spine actually tingles, sparking memories of younger days and first kisses. As we move with the rhythm of the band, I feel the swell of Ray's bicep under my left hand, and sense the warmth of his body when he pulls me close for a pivot turn.

Driving home, we talk about what a great time we've had. We agree that the eye contact was the thing, even more than dancing, that made us feel truly connected. We vow to look lovingly at each other more often.

How hard can it be?

The next morning, I set the stage. I float two lush, red rhododendron blooms in a bowl and set it in the middle of the table, then turn on soft jazz. We make a veggie scramble and settle across from each other.

"Nice," Ray says, but he doesn't even glance my way. He reaches for the morning paper just to the left of the flowers.

"Eye contact?"

"Right." He pushes the paper away and looks at me, smiling his fabulous, crooked smile that still stirs me after a decade together. I return the smile and blow him a kiss.

Then we pick up our forks and dig in. The scramble is delicious. I've downed a third of mine when I remember to look at Ray again.

He's reading the sports section.

I sigh and take the front page.

As we rinse the breakfast dishes and load them in the dishwasher, I invite Ray to chat for a few minutes in the family room before we go to our respective home offices. Surely we'll fix our gaze on each other as we talk.

Ray dries the frying pan, puts it away, and settles into an overstuffed chair, no newspaper in sight.

I head for the couch across from him, thinking I'll tell him how nice the front yard looks since he deadheaded the last of the daffodils and cleared out last year's growth from the ferns. I've taken three steps when Naomi, our little black kitty, crosses my path. With a gravelly meow she reminds me that I've forgotten to give her breakfast. I return to the kitchen and fill her bowl with kibbles. While I'm at it, I fill our dog Annie's bowl with her kibbles, and add a vitamin, a glucosamine chew, and two tiny spoonfuls of a Chinese herb for her arthritis.

As I pass the phone table on my way to the couch, I notice the button on the answering machine blinking red. It will take just a minute to check messages. One is for Ray. I turn to hand him the phone.

He's not there.

A wave of guilt washes over me. I blew it. Did he leave while I fed our pets, or while I picked up the messages? He's probably in his office now, paying bills. I might as well go work on a story.

I'm at my computer, fingers flying, when Ray wanders in. "Sorry I didn't wait," he says sheepishly. "Do you want to talk now?"

"It was my fault. Rain check?" I want that intimate chat, but right this minute I have an idea flooding the page. I know from experience that if I take a break I'll lose it.

And so the day goes. We both down hastily-made sandwiches in our offices. Midafternoon we shift gears and go out to the garden, working side by side, weeding and pruning.

When it's time to tie up a bundle of branches spread across a wheelbarrow, I see an opportunity for a romantic interlude.

I gather the branches in my arms and he pulls the twine taut. We're facing each other and I catch his eye. He winks. An electric spark jolts me.

"Hi," I say, considering the idea of abandoning the garden for a more intimate setting.

But Ray turns back to his job, tying a careful knot. I don't even get a sweaty hug.

Maybe if we'd held each other's gaze while we counted to ten.

"Missed my chance in the garden, didn't I?" Ray asks as he seasons chicken breasts to grill and I wash spinach leaves for a salad. "Want to watch a movie after dinner?" At least he's been thinking about all our misses. Watching a movie is sitting side by side, like gardening, except for that moment tying the branches. Still, we'll be together.

"I need ten minutes," I say when we've eaten and cleaned up. "Got a quick read for someone in my critique group."

I disappear into my office and work furiously. One e-mail leads to another. I don't know how long Ray has been standing at my desk when I realize he's there. I check my watch. How can an hour fly by so fast?

"Morgan Freeman, Hillary Swank. That movie you've been telling me about." He shrugs his shoulders. "Never mind. We can watch it another time."

Finishing my work as fast as I can, I go in search of Ray. I find him in the bedroom propped against a mound of pillows reading *A. Lincoln: A Biography*. His evening ritual just before he turns out the light. I've botched it yet again. And I wish Ray had tried harder too. Who would expect connecting to take so much conscious effort?

In the bathroom, I lift my leg to the counter to stretch my hamstring, thinking maybe we'll try again tomorrow. Or next week. Or next year. As I turn on my electric toothbrush, I feel Ray's arms reach around my waist.

There he is, in the mirror.

In the mirror, we lock eyes.

He turns me to face him and I melt into his arms. Yes, this marriage is on a better track.

~Samantha Ducloux Waltz

尝试和成功只有一步之遥。

——佚名

　　我和雷随着"田纳西华尔兹"的旋律在舞厅地板上翩翩起舞。雷穿着那件露出喉结的黑色丝绸衬衫和卡其色休闲裤，英俊极了，闻起来有一股麝香润肤露的香味。当他举起手，让我在手臂下面旋转的时候，显得极具绅士风度。我看着他那双淡褐色的眼睛，心脏仿佛突然停止了跳动。

　　我已经有很长时间没有这种感觉了。就在今天早上我还跟安妮——我的金毛猎犬，发牢骚说第二段婚姻并不像表象那样如意。共同账户和个人账户，混合家庭和难以计算的各种费用，存在的问题太多了。除此之外，结婚十年后，我们似乎陷入一种更加舒适而不是浪漫的生活模式。

　　雷又让我在他的手臂下转了个圈，我们的目光再一次锁定对方。我的脊柱甚至感觉到了刺痛，突然回想起我们年轻时和第一次亲吻时的情形。我们随着乐队奏出的旋律舞动着，我的左手摸到雷鼓起的二头肌，当他把我拉近，绕着他旋转时，我感受到他那温暖的身体。

　　在开车回家的路上，我们讨论着刚刚度过的

美好时刻。我们都认为眼神交流非常重要，甚至比跳舞本身还重要，它让我们紧紧相连。我们都发誓要花更多时间深情地望着对方。

这是有多难做到呢？

第二天早晨，我作好充足准备。我把两朵开得正艳的红色杜鹃花插在花瓶里，放在桌子中间，然后播放着柔美的爵士音乐。早餐是黄油炒蛋，我们坐在桌子的两头。

"不错啊。"雷说一句，甚至看都没看我一眼。在鲜花的左侧翻找着早报。

"眼神交流呢？"

"好啊。"他把报纸放在一边，看着我，露出他那迷人而带有一丝狡黠的微笑，一起生活十年了，他的笑仍让我心潮澎湃。我对他报以同样的微笑，吻了他一下。

然后我们拿起刀叉开始吃饭。鸡蛋炒得美味极了。我吃到第三口的时候，突然想起来，又看了看雷。

他在读体育新闻。

我叹了口气，拿起头版报纸。

在我们去各自的办公室工作之前，趁着收拾早餐碗筷、并把它们放进水池的时间，我邀请他和我在家里聊会儿天。当然谈话的时候，我们的眼睛要望着彼此。

雷把煎锅擦干，放好，没有看见报纸，就坐在软垫坐椅上。

我从他前面经过，朝沙发走去，心里想着我要告诉他，在他拔掉草坪里最后枯萎的几朵水仙和去年长的杂草后，前院看起来多美啊。我走了三步，突然内奥米——我们的小黑猫挡住了我的路。发出一声嘶哑的"喵喵"声，提醒我忘了给它早餐了。我回到厨房，给它的碗里倒了点猫食。同时，又给我们家的狗安妮的碗里倒上狗食，还放了一粒维生素片、一粒葡萄糖咀嚼片和两小勺治疗关节炎的中草药。

当我经过放电话的桌子回到沙发上去的时候，我注意到答录机上的红色按钮一直在闪烁，我花了一分钟时间看了看留言，一条是给雷的。我转身把电话给他。

他已经不在了。

我心中感觉到一阵内疚，都是我搞砸了。他是在我喂宠物的时候，还是在我看留言的时候走的呢？他现在可能已经在办公室支付账单了吧。我还是去写我的小说吧。

我坐在电脑前，飞舞地敲着键盘，这时雷慢慢走了进来。"对不起，刚才没有等你，"他不好意思地说着，"现在可以谈话吗？"

"这都是我的错。改天再聊，好吗？"我想和他亲密地聊天，但现在我在写作上突然有个好构思，经验告诉我如果我停下来，就会失去灵感。

日复一日。我们在各自的办公室吃着简易三明治。下午3点左右，忙完工作后我们到花园里一起铲草修枝。

在把手推车上的树枝捆成一束时，我看到了一个上演浪漫插曲的好机会。

我双手抱着树枝，他把绳子拉紧。我们面对着面，我看了看他的眼睛，他向我眨了眨眼。我仿佛被电火花击中一样。

"嗨。"我想着把花园变成一个更加温馨的场景，便对他说。

但是雷转过身继续干活，想把绳子系得更紧些。我甚至连一个汗淋淋的拥抱都没有得到。

也许如果我们能一直盯着对方，数到十就好了。

"在花园里我错过了一次机会，是吗？"当雷给要烧烤的鸡胸肉调味、我在洗做蔬菜沙拉用的菠菜时，他问道，"吃完晚饭后我们去看个电影怎样？"至少他一直在想我们错过的机会。和在花园干活一样，看电影就意味着要并排着坐在一起，只是不需要捆树枝了。但是，我们还是能在一起。

"我需要十分钟，"在吃晚饭收拾的时候我说，"我得马上看看评论组里的一个人发的邮件。"

我消失在我的办公室里，拼命工作。电子邮件一封接着一封。当我意识到雷就站在桌子旁边的时候，我不知道还要让他等多久。我看了看表。一小时怎么这么快就过去了？

"摩根·弗里曼，希拉里·斯旺克。你一直跟我提这个电影来着。"他耸了耸肩，"没关系。我们可以换个时间再看。"

我尽可能快地完成了我的工作，然后去找雷。我看见他在卧室里靠在一堆枕头上读《亚伯拉罕·林肯传》。这是他晚上关灯睡觉前的习惯。我又一次把事情搞砸了。我希望雷能像我一样知难而进，多作些努力。谁能想到需要如此多刻意的努力才能换来交流？

在浴室里，我把腿放在台子上舒展筋骨，心里想着也许我们明天可以再试一次。或者下个星期。或者明年。当我启动电动牙刷时，我感觉到雷的胳膊搂住了我的腰。

在镜子里，我看见见了他。

在镜子里，我们四目相对。

他让我转过身来对着他，我依偎在他的怀中。是啊，我们的婚姻会越来越美好的。

——萨曼塔·杜克鲁·华尔兹

Sleepless Nights
不眠之夜

Hearing is one of the body's five senses, but listening is an art.

~Frank Tyger

No question, when I look back on life with eyes tempered by advancing age and growing wisdom, I readily admit I got married too young. I was barely seventeen when that handsome young fellow (a man nine years my senior) walked into my life.

We met on a warm summer's eve. Our meeting was probably more of an observation event than it was an actual meeting. He and a friend were sitting at a drive-in café laughing at me and my friends trying to ditch a carload of guys we had no interest in meeting. A couple of days later, I met that laughing college boy and by summer's end, the smallest seed of a romance had begun to sprout. But then he returned to his university studies 500 miles away, and I returned to high school.

Time passed. We wrote letters back and forth. He finished up at the university and found a job while

I trekked off in the opposite direction to business college in another state. On occasion, we arranged to meet up for a day or two but marriage never seriously entered into our conversations until nearly three years had passed. By then, we had to admit we were in love and perhaps were old enough to settle down. Oh, how little we knew!

I had barely turned twenty and he was twenty-nine when we married. We settled down in a small apartment hours away from either of our families. Perhaps that was a good thing since we had only each other to turn to during the tough times. Being young and in love made us oblivious to the practical things in life—such as living within our means. If social activities were happening around town, that's where we had to be, no matter the cost. Then came baby number one followed by baby number two. That's when the real struggling from paycheck to paycheck began. On top of the money stress, my fastidious nature kept me picking up behind him and the kids, doing laundry in the bathroom sink, wrestling with two busy toddlers, and cooking meals made from meager selections of groceries, while he, tired after a long day's work, simply flopped down in a chair and read the newspaper. Tired and irritated, I took to pouting over the smallest infractions, but he didn't notice—or pretended not to notice, I'm not sure which. A distinct chill factor settled over our apartment.

We decided to fix a bad situation. The solution seemed simple enough. We vowed to never again go to sleep angry at one another. If something bothered us, we would talk it out before going to sleep.

Sounds easy, right? Wrong! Here's why. When a bone-tired person is ready to slip into bed, the last thing that person wants is to get caught up in is a midnight heart-to-heart airing of grievances. Here's how it plays out. First come the tears, then the indignant denials, then more tears, followed by apologies and concessions. Finally, somewhere near dawn, comes remorse and forgiveness followed by the good stuff—cuddling together until sleep comes at

0-dark-thirty in the morning. Exhaustion has a way of making seemingly-huge disagreements seem trivial.

Truth is… the decision to never again go to sleep angry was a good one. We spent a lot of sleepless nights but we never again woke up angry at each other.

This year, we celebrate our forty-seventh year together and still agree that little resolution probably saved our marriage a dozen times over. Back then, it planted itself into our lives as a type of Golden Rule and remains there to this day. By choosing harmony, we allowed a new and deeper type of love to grow. We've seen other love stories fade and slip away because of hurt feelings and unresolved arguments, but we chose to protect our love, even at the cost of surrendering a good night's sleep. Or was it ten or twenty nights, or maybe more? I've lost count. But, no matter, the price was worth it then and it's still worth it today.

~Jean Davidson

听觉是人体的五感之一，但倾听是一门艺术。

——弗兰克·泰格

毫无疑问，随着年龄的增长和智慧的积淀，蓦然回首，我承认自己结婚太早了。当那个英俊的年轻小伙子（一个比我大9岁的男人）走进我的生活的时候，我刚满17岁。

我们是在一个夏天的傍晚相遇的。与真正的会面相比，我们的见面更像是在互相观察。他和一个朋友坐在一个免下车的咖啡厅里，一边看着我和朋友们挣扎着摆脱一群我们不想看到的男生，一边不停地笑着。过了几天，我遇到了那个爱笑的大学生，在那个夏末，一粒小小的浪漫种子渐渐发芽了。但是之后他又回到 800 多公里远的大学学习，我也返回了高中。

时间飞逝。我们来来回回地给对方写信。他大学毕业后找了一份工作，而我朝着相反的方向辗转到另一个州商学院念大学。偶尔我们会安排一两天见上一面，但是从来没有严肃地讨论过结婚这个话题，直到差不多三年过去了。那个时候，我们都得承认彼此是相爱的，也许我们已经到了能够定居的年龄了。哦，我们是多么的无知啊！

我们结婚的时候我刚过完 20 岁生日，而他已经 29 岁了。我们住在一所小公寓里，距离各自的家都只有几小时的路程。也许这是件好事，因为在困难时期，我们只有彼此可以依靠。

因为我们都还很年轻，而且在热恋中，所以对现实生活——例如量入为出还没有什么概念。如果市中心有什么社交活动，我们从不考虑费用，一定会参加。后来第一个孩子出生了，接着又生了第二个孩子。这时我们才真正开始在靠薪水生活的日子里挣扎。由于金钱造成的压力，天性挑剔的我总是因为他和孩子们生气，我在浴室的水槽里洗衣服，照顾两个淘气的小孩，到商店买菜做饭。而他呢，上了一天的班，累了就软绵绵地瘫坐在椅子上读报纸。我又累又气，开始因为他的一丁点小错误就板着脸，但是他没有注意到——或者假装没有注意到，我不知道究竟是前者还是后者。屋子里充满了冰冷的气息。

我们决定改善一下这个糟糕的现状。解决的方法看起来很简单。我们发誓再也不带着怒气睡觉了。如果有让我们烦心的事，就在睡觉前一起讨论。

听起来很简单吧？你错了！因为当一个筋疲力尽的人准备上床睡觉的时候，最不想做的就是在大半夜和别人谈心，讨论各种抱怨。结果呢？无外乎是哭，然后因为忽视自己的愤怒哭得更伤心，再接着就是道歉和妥协。最后，天快亮的时候，想到了好的一面又开始后悔并原谅另一方——拥抱在一起，直到 0 点 30 分才睡着。疲倦的力量在于能够将干戈化玉帛。

事实是永远不要在生气的时候睡觉是一个正确的决定。我们度过了很多不眠之夜，但是醒来的时候再也不会对彼此生气。

今年，我们庆祝了一起度过的第 47 个年头，我们一致认为这个小决议可能挽救了十几次的婚姻危机。回想那个时候，它就像我们生活的黄金法则，一直保留到今天。我们选择和谐相处，这样能够更新并加深我们之间的爱。我们曾经看到过因为受伤和未解决的争议导致其他爱情故事转瞬即逝，但是我们选择去保护彼此之间的爱情，甚至不惜牺牲一晚好觉、或者是十晚、二十晚，甚至更多。我已经记不清楚了，但是没有关系，这是值得的，到今天也是值得的。

——吉恩·戴维森

The Value of a Good Husband
一个好丈夫的价值

Love doesn't sit there like a stone, it has to be made, like bread; remade all of the time, made new.

~Ursula K. LeGuin

I'm one of those old-fashioned women who love the idea of a good, strong marriage. My dream of staying home to take care of the house and put dinner on the table has finally come true. Yikes! How did I get to be such a dinosaur?

My blossoming years coincided with those of the feminist movement in the mid-1960s. I'd seen my parents' marriage end badly. So by my freshman year in college I was already part of the bra-burning crowd, telling dates not to open the car door for me and vowing to trample all men on my way up. I promised myself not to get married unless I was a total failure at any desirable career by age thirty, which seemed terrifyingly old at that time.

Unfortunately, that promise lasted about two minutes—I met a guy in college and was swept off my feet. We got engaged when I was nineteen and married two years later. We thought our common interests would enhance the pursuit of our goals. Instead, it created immense competition and jealousy between us. By the mid-1970s, in the throes of "me-ism," we expected way more than any two self-centered people were capable of giving each other. We went our separate ways.

Other guys came along who fit the stereotype of what women were fighting against: irresponsible, wishy-washy, noncommittal and over-the-top macho. They were good for fun and easy to say goodbye to. But casual intimacies left me with an empty yearning. It was like giving a piece of me away that could never be replaced.

I soon began to avoid dating altogether, concentrating on work and taking care of myself. But it eventually began to sink in that I had no one to turn off the lights with at night, or wake up to in the morning, no one with whom to share exciting news and late-night TV. Was I weak? Don't think so. Lonely? Not in a desperate way. There was just an awareness that there might be more in store for me than my ego allowed. I yearned for a touch, a steadiness, an affection that I thought didn't exist in relationships anymore.

Just when it seemed there would never be anyone for me, along came Mr. Beige.

We met at a disco on a night when my girlfriend, Ellie, was shopping for a new boyfriend. When we walked in, we immediately noticed two men in gorgeous suits sitting at the bar. Ellie was attracted to the tall one in the black suit. I thought the shorter one in the beige suit was more handsome, but looked sort of somber.

Since Ellie was too shy to approach them and I didn't care about meeting anyone, I went right up there and asked Mr. Black Suit to dance with her. Their relationship lasted two weeks. I'm still with Mr. Beige after nearly thirty years.

It turned out Mr. Beige—now known as Jerry—had accompanied Mr.

Black Suit that night for much the same reason I had accompanied Ellie. But he was determined to counter the culture. He made me enjoy having doors opened. He liked getting dressed up. He was on time, dependable, financially viable, entertaining, resourceful and interested in what I was doing. My growing feelings for him made me want to reciprocate his kindnesses. Besides—he was a great disco dancer.

Both of us were gun-shy from previous marriages, so we initially went the ever-growing route of living together. Six years and one cold feet separation later, he proposed and we walked down the aisle.

Our marriage takes a lot of work, compromise, sacrifice and that new dirty word, "submission" sometimes. Do we butt heads? Sure we do. It's human nature to want our own way. Sometimes I hate the decisions he makes, other times we make them together, and yet other times it's a relief to hand off the responsibility. We've learned that true love goes deeper than seeing flowers and butterflies every time you look at someone, or making the other person ecstatically happy every day. Sometimes we disappoint each other, because nobody's perfect. But our determination to serve one another holds our relationship together during tough times.

I'm happy to mention that allowing God to play a role in our marriage has added to its longevity. It's taken both of us further toward shedding "me"—not losing our identity, but learning to be less self-absorbed and more giving. We have a commitment to be up for the challenge. You have to get brave and take risks to make love last.

~Sheryl Young

Chapter 1 Keeping the Love Alive
第一部分 婚姻相处篇

爱不是一块石头，一动不动地坐在那里；对待爱，要像做面包那样——反复揉搓，不断翻新。

——厄休拉·K.勒瑰恩

我是一个墨守成规的女人，向往美好而又坚韧的婚姻。我的梦想就是待在家里操持家务，准备好晚餐放在桌子上，现在终于梦想成真了。呀！我怎么会变成这么一个思想守旧的人呢？

我的青春时光正值 20 世纪 60 年代女权主义运动的兴起。父母悲惨的婚姻结局我历历在目。刚上大学的第一年，我就加入了为解放妇女而游行示威的大军，让我和约会彻底"绝缘"，而且发誓要无视遇到的所有男人。我向自己保证不结婚，除非到了 30 岁，我渴望的职业生涯彻底失败，在那个年代，这种想法简直太迂腐了。

不幸的是，这份承诺只维持了大约两分钟——我在大学里遇到一个男生，他踩了我一脚。我 19 岁那年，我们订婚了，两年后，我们结婚了。我们觉得共同的兴趣爱好能提高我们追求的目标。但是恰恰相反，我们之间竟产生了激烈的竞争和猜忌。到 20 世纪 70 年代，"个人主义"膨胀泛滥，我们渴望的生活方式是两个以自我为中心的人远远不能给予的。于是我们各奔东西了。

后来认识的几个男人都是女人极力反抗的那种类型的：不负责任、优柔寡断、态度暧昧、大男子主义。和他们在一起时很开心，但也很容易分手。这种不牢靠的亲密关系只给我留下虚无缥缈的幻想。就像丢了魂一样，再也回不来了。

不久后，我就开始逃避任何约会，一心一意地工作和照顾自己。但是后来我意识到晚上没有人给我关灯，早上没有人叫我起床，没有人和我一起看精彩的新闻和午夜电视。是我太软弱了吗？我觉得不是。是寂寞了吗？那也没到寂寞难耐的地步啊。我感觉有更多内心所不允许的东西蕴藏在我的体内。我渴望温暖、安逸的生活，我渴望爱情，以前我总觉得我的感情生活中再也不存在这些东西了。

就在我觉得再也没有人爱我的时候，米色先生出现了。

我们是晚上在一个迪斯科舞厅相遇的，那时我的女朋友艾丽要给她新交的男朋友买礼物。我们走进舞厅的时候，很快就注意到有两个穿着华丽西服的男人坐在吧台上。艾丽被那个穿着黑色西服的高个子男人吸引了。而我觉得那个子稍微矮一点、穿着米色西服的男人更英俊，但是他看起来有点忧郁。

因为艾丽太害羞了，不敢和他们搭讪，而我觉得和陌生人认识一下没什么大不了的，就走到他们跟前，让黑色西服先生和她跳舞。他们的交往只维持了两个星期。而将近30年后，我依旧和米色先生在一起。

原来那天晚上米色先生——那时还不知道他叫杰瑞——是陪黑色西服来的，跟我陪艾丽一样的原因。但是他决定逆文化主流而行。他让我觉得敞开心扉很愉快。他喜欢装扮自己，还是个守时、可以信任的人，他生活富裕，喜好娱乐，足智多谋，而且他对我的工作十分感兴趣。渐渐地我也对他有了好感。而且，他还很会跳迪斯科舞。

婚姻都让我们闻之色变，所以最开始的时候我们不断调整一起生活的方式。就这样一起过了 6 年，中间有一次分手，之后他就向我求婚了，我们一起走上了婚姻殿堂。

我们的婚姻经历了多道磨难，有妥协，有牺牲，有时候还有那新的不雅之词"投降"。我们会发生争吵吗？当然。固执己见是人的天性。有时候我很讨厌他作的决定，有时候我们一起作决定，有时候甩掉责任也是一种解脱。真正的爱情不只是看到某个人的时候心花怒放，或让一个人每一天都充满欢乐。有时候我们也会让对方失望，因为人非圣贤孰能无过。但是我们彼此真心的相待帮我们度过了苦难时期，让我们的爱情坚如磐石。

我很想说的是多亏上帝从中穿针引线，使我们的婚姻更加持久。让我们进一步认清自我——同时又没有失去我们的个性，而是学会无私奉献。我们承诺要一起面对挑战。要想获得一份持久的爱情，必须要接受并勇敢迎接所有的风险。

——雪莉·杨

Breakfast and a Movie
早餐加电影

> The secret of love is seeking variety in your life together,
> and never letting routine chords dull the melody of your
> romance.
>
> ~Source Unknown

Breakfast and a movie. How in the world did it come to this?

It seems that every other issue of every women's magazine on the planet has an article about saving your marriage. And the number one piece of advice in these articles is to make time for you as a couple. But if you have young children, you know as well as I do that "couple time" is pretty much an imaginary concept.

Life wasn't always like this, of course. Back in our childless days, my wife and I would frequently go out. One of our favorite activities was dinner and a movie.

Then baby arrives and things change. No one's got the energy to go out at night. If baby is sleeping, that's a good time for both of you to also catch a few zzz's.

But thanks to all those magazine articles, we worried about our relationship. If there was no "us time", surely our marriage was at risk.

So we occasionally summoned up the courage to have a night out. We'd call up a babysitter and take a stab at that old standby, dinner and a movie.

Big mistake. If we weren't nodding off during dinner, we definitely had a hard time staying awake through the movie. And even if we did manage to remain conscious, the only topic of conversation during our precious couple time was our infant daughter, Sarah, who was at home doing exactly what we should have been doing: sleeping.

We soon realized that dinner and a movie was no longer for us. All it meant was the outlay of extra money for a babysitter, the loss of a good night's sleep, and a disrupted routine.

But we didn't want to give up on this concept of couple time. After all, lots of magazine writers (probably single and childless) were urging us on and we didn't want to disappoint them.

So we came up with a new approach: something we called movie and a dinner. We hired a babysitter for the afternoon and early evening and headed out to a matinee performance followed by the early bird special at a local eatery. This option worked surprisingly well.

Not only did we get to spend time together when we were both conscious and reasonably coherent, we also never had a problem getting a babysitter. After all, we were usually home by 7 P.M., long before the sitter's own social life commenced.

But once our daughter passed the toddler stage, the movie and a dinner option didn't work so well. Sarah had weekend activities and obligations. Or she wanted to have a friend over. Or she just wanted to spend more time with Mommy and Daddy.

Chicken Soup for the Soul 温暖心灵的幸福瞬间
心灵鸡汤 True Love II

As a consequence, we forgot about movie and a dinner. We were too busy with family time and kids' activities. Once again, couple time became the lowest priority.

But we hadn't forgotten our magazine writer friends (probably sadistic and divorced). So we searched for a new option.

Now that Sarah was in school and life was more normal, we thought maybe the old dinner and a movie approach would work. It turns out it didn't.

Although life had returned to something approaching normalcy, it turns out that we had gotten older in the process. The thought of staying up past 10:00 no longer had any appeal.

But surely there had to be some way to find time to spend together. According to our writer friends (probably rich with two nannies), our marriage depended on it. There had to be something we could do on a regular basis. Something that would allow us that precious "us time" without costing a fortune or disrupting our sleep.

Finally, this year we hit on the ultimate couple time solution: breakfast and a movie. With Sarah in school, every so often we take a weekday to ourselves. And what do we do? You guessed it.

We go out for a nice leisurely breakfast where we can listen, communi-cate and, best of all from my perspective, eat. And then it's off to the local multiplex which just so happens to start showing movies at ten or eleven in the morning.

We pick out a first-run feature we'd like to see, put up our feet and enjoy two hours of uninterrupted movie viewing. Sometimes we even get the entire theater to ourselves.

After the movie is over, we have a whole array of options. We can go out for lunch, go to a coffee shop or browse in a bookstore. We can do a bit of shopping, watch another movie or, my personal favorite, go home and have a nap.

I think this is an option with legs. So long as Sarah is in school, we can continue to do breakfast and a movie. The only potential problem I see is that everyone reading this piece is going to start doing the same thing and the breakfast restaurants will be crowded and the morning shows at the cinemas will be sold out. Oh well, if that happens, there's always takeout breakfast and a rental movie.

~David Martin

爱情的秘密在于一起寻找生命中的变化，绝不要让千篇一律的和音破坏了浪漫的旋律。

——出处不详

早餐加电影。怎么想到把这两个搭配在一起的呢？

仿佛世界上每份女性杂志都会谈论到如何挽救婚姻这个话题。这些书中提出的第一点建议就是营造一个"二人世界"。但是如果你有小孩，可能知道"二人世界"只不过是一个虚构的概念。

当然，生活并不总是如此。在我们还没有生孩子之前，我和妻子经常出去约会。我们最喜欢的活动就是吃晚餐，然后去看电影。

有了孩子之后，情况就变了。谁也没有精力在大晚上跑出去玩。如果孩子睡着了，我们才能趁机打个盹儿。

但是，多亏了这些杂志上的文章，我们也开始担心起来。如果没有了属于我们两个人独处的时间，婚姻肯定会出现危机的。

所以，我们会时不时地鼓起勇气，出去玩一晚上。我们打电话找个保姆来家里照顾孩子，然后我们重温往事、吃晚餐、看电影。

可是我们大错特错了。要不是在吃晚餐的时候打了个盹儿，真的很难在看电影的时候保持清醒。即使我们努力让自己保持清醒，但在这宝贵的独处时间里，我们讨论最多的话题就是我们的小女儿莎拉，她正在家里睡觉，平常的这个时候我们肯定也在睡觉。

我们很快意识到晚餐和电影再也不属于我们了。这些事只不过意味着要付额外的钱给保姆，睡不成好觉和扰乱作息。

但是我们还是不想就此放弃我们的二人世界。而且，很多杂志的作者（可能是单身和没有孩子的）都鼓励我们继续加油，我们不想让他们失望。

所以我们想出一个新办法：我们称它为电影加晚餐。我们雇了一个保姆在下午和傍晚照顾孩子，我们去看日场电影，然后在当地的餐馆吃一顿早到客人优惠餐。这个想法真是太好了。

我们不仅能在保持清醒和理智的状态下共度美好时光，而且再也不用愁找不到保姆了。因为我们通常在晚上 7 点前就回家了，离保姆夜生活的开始还有好长一段时间。

但是，我们的女儿学会了走路以后，电影加晚餐的效果就不太理想了。莎拉周末有自己的活动和计划。有时候想叫个朋友过来玩，有时候想花更多的时间和爸爸妈妈待在一起。

就这样，我们忘了电影和晚餐。既要照顾家又要照顾孩子，我们俩忙得不可开交。二人世界再一次被抛到九霄云外。

但是我们没有忘记那些杂志作家朋友们（可能是有虐待倾向和离婚的）。所以我们又想出一个新主意。

莎拉已经上学了，我们的生活也恢复到正常状态了，我们想以前的晚餐加电影计划也许还有效，但结果并非如此。

虽然我们的生活已经恢复到接近正常的状态，但我们的生理机能也渐渐退化了。再也没精力熬夜到晚上10点了。

但肯定还有办法让我们独处。据我们的作家朋友们（可能是有钱请得起两个保姆的）所说，我们婚姻的保证就在于此。我们一定能在某个固定时刻一起共同度过。能让我们享受宝贵的"二人世界"，同时又不必破费或影响到睡觉。

最后，在今年我们想到一个共度二人时光的终端计划：早餐加电影。因为莎拉在学校上学，所以有很多工作日可以由我们自己支配。我们会做什么呢？或许你猜出来了。

我们一起出去吃一顿悠闲自在的早餐，这时我们互相倾听、交流，让我最高兴的是可以一起吃饭，然后去当地的多厅电影院，在早上10点或11点正好开始放电影。

我们选一个喜欢的首场电影，然后就坐下来享受两小时不间断的电影观赏。有时候我们两个人独享整个电影院。

看完电影后，我们还有很多选择。我们可以去吃午餐，去咖啡店里喝杯咖啡，还可以去书店里看看书。我们也可以去购物，再看一场电影，或者做我更想做的——回家睡个午觉。

我想这是一个两全其美的好办法。在莎拉上学的日子里，我们可以一直像这样吃早餐、看电影。唯一可能存在的问题是在读这篇文章的人也开始做同样的事，到时候供应早餐的餐厅将挤得水泄不通，电影院早上放映的电影票也会被抢购一空。嗯，好吧，如果出现这种情况，我们可以吃外卖早餐，租影碟回家看。

——大卫·马丁

Date Night
午夜约会

Reflect upon your current blessings.

~Charles Dickens

"Bye guys," I say, kissing my two girls in the church hallway before heading outside to the car. "Have fun."

It's Wednesday evening—church choir night for my daughters. I have two hours until pick-up time, and like a teenager, I am giddy with anticipation.

"Where do you want to meet?" my husband asked at breakfast. "It's Wednesday, you know."

As I drive to the neighborhood café, I find myself singing along to the radio. Free from my usual dinner-making routine, (thanks to a church choir program that serves my children nuggets and noodles, along with a hefty dose of praise and song) I am carefree. I park the car, then rummage through my purse for some lip gloss. Glancing in the visor mirror, I fluff my hair, tucking a pesky white strand under my (mostly) brown locks. It's silly, I know:

primping and fussing for a dinner date with my husband of thirteen years. But, as I walk in the restaurant, I know it's worth it.

"You look nice," my beloved smiles, handing me a dinner menu.

For the next hour, we feast on pizza and salad, swapping family and work stories between bites of pepperoni and cheese. My usual calorie-conscious self, lost to the revelry of the day, eyes a glass case full of cheesecakes and brownies.

"Want to get dessert?" I surprise myself by suggesting such decadence.

My turtle cheesecake, a tower of chocolate and caramel topped with pecans, is sweet and indulgent—just like this evening.

"Can I taste a little of that?" I say, poking my fork deep into my husband's peanut butter pie.

After dinner, we linger over cups of hazelnut coffee. I am full—of good food, companionship, and the comfort in knowing that my spouse is still my very best friend.

I glance at my watch. "We still have a half hour," I say, hopeful to go for a walk or do some window shopping.

Holding hands, we cross the street and enter the public library. I head straight to my favorite section—nonfiction, and give thanks for time to peruse the newest releases without being pulled into the children's room. My husband flops into an armchair and relaxes with a newspaper.

Thirty minutes pass in a flash.

"It's time to go," I reluctantly announce, peering over the top of my spouse's paper. In my arms I hold a stack of books—souvenirs reminding me to return again next week.

"I can pick up the girls if you want," my husband says. "You take your time. We'll meet you at home."

I sigh a bit, sorry to see the evening come to a close. At home, it will be the usual routine: baths and bedtimes, stories to read and lunches to pack. I love motherhood, but I relish this respite.

Despite conflicts and commitments, (I do, after all, have to take a turn as parent helper at children's choir) I will do my best to continue dating my spouse. Although my girls are jealous when they hear tales of cheesecakes and pizzas, deep down I know they benefit. Secure in the knowledge that Mom and Dad love each other, they are free to grow up in confidence, surrounded by the very real possibility that romance can last forever.

Although marriage may be made in heaven, I think its maintenance must be done here on Earth.

Thank goodness for Wednesday choir night: an opportunity to fine-tune the most sacred of bonds.

~Stefanie Wass

对当前幸福的深思。

——查尔斯·狄更斯

"再见，孩子们，"在上车之前，我在教堂的走廊上亲吻着我的两个女儿告别，"祝你们玩得高兴。"

那是个星期三的傍晚——我的女儿们晚上要去参加教堂唱诗班活动。两小时后我去接她们，像个十几岁的孩子一样，我充满无限期望。

"我们去哪里见面呢？"在吃早餐的时候，我的丈夫问我，"你知道，今天可是星期三啊。"

我开车来到附近的咖啡厅，不由自主地随着收音机里的音乐哼了起来。不用再像平常一样无聊地做晚饭（多亏教堂唱诗班的安排，我的孩子们不仅有饭吃，还能唱歌，并获得赞美），我感觉轻松自在极了。我停好车，在钱包里翻找唇彩，照着遮光板镜，撩起我的长发，把一撮让人生厌的白发卷进（几乎全部）棕色的卡子里。我知道这有点幼稚：精心打扮、小题大做，就为了和结婚13年的丈夫约会吃个晚饭。但是当我走进餐厅的时候，我知道这一切都是值得的。

"你看起来真美。"我的爱人微笑着说，把晚饭的菜单递给了我。

接下来的一小时，我们尽情享用着比萨、沙拉，一边嚼着腊肠和奶酪，一边津津有味地聊着家里和工作中的故事。一向对卡路里抱有警戒之心的我，此时也沉浸在狂欢之夜，眼睛盯着满满一杯的乳酪蛋糕和巧克力蛋糕。

"想吃点甜品吗？"我自己都惊讶竟会提出这么一个让人堕落的建议。

龟形蛋糕——它在顶部点缀着核桃仁的巧克力和焦糖就像这个夜晚一样甜美而又纵情。

"我能尝一尝吗？"我一边说，一边拿起叉子一把插入丈夫的花生奶油馅饼。

吃过晚饭后，我们又喝了几杯榛子咖啡。美食，温情和深入了解我的配偶——仍然是我最好的朋友带来的抚慰，让我的胃和心都感觉满满的。

我看了看手表。"我们还有半小时的时间。"我对他说想出去走走或逛逛街。

我们手牵着手穿过马路，走进公共图书馆。我径直走向我最喜欢的陈列区——非虚构小说，为有时间仔细阅读这些最新出版的著作而不用被孩子们拉入她们的卧室心存感激。我的丈夫一屁股坐进扶手椅里，拿起一份报纸悠闲地读着。

一眨眼的工夫，30 分钟过去了。

"该走了。"我看了一眼丈夫的报纸，依依不舍地对他说。我的手里抱着一堆书——提醒我下周回来还书的纪念品。

"如果你想的话，我可以去接女儿们，"我的丈夫说，"你慢慢看，我们回家见。"

我轻轻叹了口气，看到这个晚上马上就要过去了，心里很不是滋味。回到家里，又要例行公事了：洗澡、睡觉、讲故事、准备午餐便当。我很喜欢做母亲的感觉，但是我也很享受能让我喘口气的机会。

尽管自己很抵触这份要尽的责任（我要轮着在孩子们的唱诗班上当一次父母帮手），我还是会继续和丈夫约会的。虽然女儿们听到蛋糕和比萨晚餐的故事后都很嫉妒我们，但是我心里知道这也是为了她们好。爸爸妈妈深爱彼此，她们也有安全感，这个"浪漫可以永恒"的事实也让她们能够充满自信地自由成长。

虽然天堂里的婚姻可以天长地久，但是我觉得必须在人间精心呵护它。

感谢星期三晚上的唱诗班活动：让我有机会再次回味那最神圣的感情。

——斯蒂芬妮·沃斯

浪漫的每一天

Marriage is a book of which the first chapter is written in poetry and the remaining chapters in prose.

~Beverly Nichols

"What's the most romantic thing your spouse has ever done?" the MC asked the three couples. My husband Scott and I were attending a wedding for one of our friends where a family rendition of *The Newlywed* Game was taking place.

"I don't know how I would answer that," Scott leaned over and whispered.

"Oh, you're plenty romantic," I whispered back and then promptly forgot about the incident as dinner was served and we talked and laughed with the other guests at the table.

A few days later I noticed that Scott seemed somewhat subdued.

"What are you thinking about?" I asked.

"It still bothers me that I can't think of anything romantic that I have done for you," he replied.

I reminded Scott of several occasions that were

romantic, but he didn't feel any better.

As I got into bed that night I began to reflect, "What is romance anyway?" Most people think of weekend getaways or vacations to exotic places. Candlelight dinners and flowers for special occasions might top the list. But those moments, as wonderful as they are, are few and far between the things that take place every day. I thought back to our life together. Maybe true romance is more in the daily happenings of life than in the occasional moments.

Maybe romance is in the way Scott says "Hi Gorgeous" when he greets me, even though after three children, and more than twenty-five years of marriage, I hardly recognize the young bride in our wedding album. Maybe romance is in the daily walks where we talk about the trivial and momentous parts of our day and of our life together. Maybe it's the way we still hold hands and show our displays of affection, ignoring our teenage daughters' cries of "Get a room!"

Maybe romance is the way Scott encouraged me to be a teacher when I shared with him my dreams of teaching children with special needs. We had very little money at the time. And even though it meant Scott had to squeeze childcare duties into an already tight ministry schedule, Scott never complained. In fact, he was my biggest cheerleader.

And he did it all over again when I said I wanted to go back to school for my Master's degree. I thought of how I never tire of spending time with Scott, how even a trip to the grocery store is somehow special, simply because I'm spending time with this man I love so much.

"Maybe," I said to Scott the next evening as we sat down to dinner as a family, "Romance isn't as much about the occasional candlelight dinner or a romantic weekend getaway, as it is about the hundreds of ways you show me you love me every single day."

With that said, I reached over and gave him a big hug and kiss and grinned as a familiar chorus of "Get a room!" reverberated throughout the kitchen.

~Deb Stanley

Chapter 1 Keeping the Love Alive
第一部分 婚姻相处篇

婚姻是一本书，第一章是诗，其余章节是散文。

———贝弗利·尼克尔斯

"你的爱人为你做过的最浪漫的事是什么？"
主持人提问三对夫妻。我和丈夫斯科特正在参加
朋友的婚礼，在那里正好在录一个叫"新婚游戏"
的电视节日。

"我真不知道该怎么回答。"斯科特低着头，
小声说着。

"哦，你是一个很浪漫的人。"我轻声回答他，
吃饭的时候，我们和同桌的其他客人有说有笑，
早已把刚才的事抛到九霄云外了。

几天后，我发现斯科特好像有点忧郁。

"你在想什么呢？"我问他。

"我竟然一件也想不起来为你做过的浪漫的
事，我觉得心里很烦。"他回答道。

我提醒斯科特几次浪漫的场合，但并没有让
他感觉好一些。

那天晚上我睡觉的时候，开始思索"浪漫到
底是什么呢"。大多数人都会想到周末约会或者
异地休闲度假。首先想到的可能是在特殊场合准
备的烛光晚餐和鲜花。这些时刻虽然美好，但是

却并不常有，而且也与日常生活截然不同。我回想起我们在一起的日子，也许真正的浪漫更多地体现在生活中每天发生的平凡小事，而不是某个特殊时刻。

也许浪漫就是斯科特见到我时说的"嗨，美女"，即使在有了3个孩子、结婚25年后的今天，我已经认不出结婚相册里那年轻貌美的新娘了。也许浪漫就是在每天散步的时候谈论两个人一天或一生中发生的琐事和大事。也许浪漫是我们仍然手牵着手，表达我们对彼此的爱意，而不必理会我们十几岁的女儿大声叫着"到你们的卧室去"！

也许浪漫就是当我告诉他我的梦想是教那些有特殊需要的孩子时，斯科特鼓励我成为一名教师。那时我们生活很拮据。即使这意味着斯科特要腾出时间来照顾孩子，他也从来没有抱怨过。事实上，他是我最大的支持者。

当我说我想回到学校攻读硕士学位时，他依旧如此。我想到和斯科特在一起，我从来没有感觉到厌倦，即使是到杂货店买个东西也具有特殊意义，这都是因为我和深爱的男人在一起。

"也许"，第二天晚上一家人坐下来吃饭的时候，我对斯科特说，"浪漫不在于某顿烛光晚餐，也不是某次浪漫的周末约会，而在于你用上百种方式表明每一天你都爱我。"说完后，我伸出手臂给了他一个大大的拥抱，亲吻着他，听到厨房里回荡的那熟悉的声音"到你们的卧室去"，我咧着嘴笑了。

——戴坡·斯坦利

Isn't It Romantic
浪漫的周末

The essence of pleasure is spontaneity.

~Germaine Greer

"Want to meet me for lunch on the 20th?" Tom asked.

Something about that date bothered me. I glanced at the calendar and dropped the phone. I quickly picked it up; the call was too expensive to waste minutes. I put the receiver to my ear and managed to get out, "Huh?"

"I said meet me for lunch on the 20th."

"But... but that's the day you are returning from Japan!"

"I know," he laughed. "Get a sitter for the weekend and meet me for lunch in San Francisco. I've already booked your flight."

Now I held the phone in a death grip. A romantic weekend away! In California! He didn't have to ask again. Our first vacation alone without the boys in five years.

After we hung up, I felt like I was walking on

clouds. He'd been gone for almost two weeks, and I'd been feeling lonely and overburdened. The house was in total disarray, the kitchen without a floor, the refrigerator in the living room, and the powder room toilet in the foyer. I'd been so upset when he had to take this business trip in the middle of renovations, it just added to the stress of married life with children and responsibilities. But now we were meeting in San Francisco for an entire weekend, just the two of us, with no kids, no household disasters to fix, no worries at all except maybe where to eat dinner.

Then I heard the school bus pull up in front of the house and I realized that I was going to have to do one of the world's biggest juggling acts. I spent hours that night on the phone calling everyone several times until all the schedules lined up. My younger son, who was still in preschool, was going over my girlfriend's house for Thursday and Friday nights. My older son, who was in elementary school, needed to spend Thursday night with my parents who lived two blocks away so he could catch the school bus. Friday afternoon my sister was going to pick him up after school and keep him Friday and Saturday nights. In the meantime, my parents were meeting my friend at the mall to pick up my younger son Saturday afternoon. Then both boys were to get home Sunday to spend the rest of the day with a babysitter. I was exhausted just making those plans and then I realized it was Tuesday and I was leaving in two days. I rushed around buying some new clothes and getting one of the worst haircuts I'd ever had.

Friday morning, I got up at 5:00 A.M. and drove to the airport for a 7:30 flight to independence, freedom and, of course, romance. I never got to fly by myself and I was nervous and a little scared, but when I arrived in California, my heart started racing and I was so excited about seeing my husband that I bought him a bouquet of flowers from an airport vendor.

I only had to wait twenty minutes and then we were together hugging and kissing and after ten days apart, it felt so good to be back in his arms. We never got that lunch I'd flown out there for. Instead, we went to our hotel on the Wharf, watched the seals barking and sunning from our balcony and relaxed for a few hours. Tom must have been so happy to see me that he didn't even mention my haircut for hours. We were both exhausted, me from rushing everywhere making sure the kids had everything they needed, and Tom from traveling halfway across the world.

But we didn't give in to our tiredness because we only had a weekend to enjoy San Francisco. We did all the tourist things—a tour of the city, a stroll in the Japanese Garden, walking up and down those famous steep streets, dinners at Fisherman's Wharf, a boat tour of the bay and Golden Gate Bridge and shopping for souvenirs for the kids.

It was wonderful, rejuvenating, and romantic. That is until we got to the airport. Tom's ticket was first class, and alas, mine wasn't. We had hoped to upgrade my ticket, a prospect I was looking forward to, but the flight was overbooked. The best we could do was move my seat all the way up front, right behind the first class section.

I blinked back tears. I didn't want Tom to see how disappointed I was. What a way to end our weekend getaway, in separate sections of the plane.

After everyone boarded, Tom approached the man sitting next to me and asked, "Would you mind trading seats with me so I can sit with my wife?"

The guy looked at the first class seat Tom had just abandoned and agreed in a heartbeat. Only a fool would have said no!

The flight attendants couldn't believe it. Tom had traded down so he could sit with me. They kept coming up to us and saying, "I can't believe you gave up first class to be with your wife. It's just so romantic!"

In fact, they thought it was so great they catered to us the entire flight. They gave us the movie headsets for free, gave us each a glass of wine, and even served us the first class dessert.

Before the plane landed, the three flight attendants, a man and two women, came up to us and asked us how long we'd been married. I said twelve years. After we landed they stood together and handed me two pink carnations and Tom a bottle of champagne. "Wow, even after twelve years," one of them sighed. "This is because you are a really romantic couple," they gushed.

On the drive home from the airport I held my flowers, smiled and said, "Those flight attendants didn't understand how right they really are. I know you sat with me because I am your wife. After all, you have to live with me for the rest of your life."

Tom laughed and didn't deny it, but I know he really sat with me because he wanted us to be together. Whatever the reason, it was a romantic weekend and a flight that I still remember fondly even after another twelve years together.

~Dina A. Leacock

自然是快乐的真谛。

——杰曼·格里尔

"20 号和我共进午餐好吗？"汤姆问我。

约会的事情让我很困扰。我瞥了一眼日历，扔下手机，又赶紧捡起来。话费太贵了我不想浪费时间。我把耳朵放在听筒上，回过神来说："啊？"

"我说，20 号和我一起吃午饭。"

"可是……那天你不是刚从日本回来吗？"

"我知道"，他笑了，"周末雇个保姆，然后和我去旧金山吃午饭吧，我已经帮你预订机票了。"

我紧紧地握着电话。一个浪漫的周末！在加利福尼亚！他没必要再问一遍了。这是五年来我们第一次没有带孩子一起去的旅行。

挂了电话后，我感觉仿佛腾云驾雾。他在外出差近两周，我感到很孤独，有种被遗弃的感觉。整个房子乱七八糟的，厨房没有地板，冰箱在客厅里，卫生间在门厅里。当他要在房屋装修期间出差的时候我就一直很心烦，孩子和责任已经使婚姻生活充满了压力，他的出差让这种压力更加重了。但是现在我们整个周末都要在旧金山度过，这是我们两个人的二人世界，没有孩子，无须处理房屋装修的各种混乱，不用担心任何事情，可能只需考虑去哪里吃饭。

接着我听见校车停在屋前，这才意识到我要去做世上最麻烦的事。我花费好几小时给好多人打了好几个电话，直到安排好所有的事情。我还在上学前班的小儿子，周四、周五晚上要去我一个朋友的家里。正在读小学的大儿子，周四晚上要去我父母家，因为离我家只隔着两条街，他能赶上校车。周五下午，我姐姐去接大儿子放学，周五、周六晚上他就在我姐姐家里。同时，周六下午，我父母跟我朋友在商场见面，接上我的小儿子。之后他俩周日回家和保姆一起在家。仅仅做完这些计划我就感到筋疲力尽了，忽然我意识到今天是周二，我两天后就要去旧金山了。我匆忙出去买了些新衣服，还剪了世上最难看的发型。

周五早晨，我五点起床，开车去机场赶七点半的航班。去找寻我的独立、自由，当然，还有浪漫。我从未自己一个人乘坐过飞机，我很紧张还有点害怕，但是当我到达加利福尼亚的时候，我的心跳开始加速，要见到丈夫了，我好激动，还在机场给他买了一束鲜花。

我只等了 20 分钟，然后我们就在一起拥抱接吻了。跟他分开 10 天，又回到他的怀里感觉是如此美妙。没有吃饭，我们就直接去了码头的宾馆。宾馆的阳台可以沐浴到温暖的阳光，还能看到喊叫的海豹。我们好好地放松了几小时。汤姆见到我也很高兴，他甚至都没有提我失败的发型，我们都很筋疲力尽，我奔波了各个地方安顿好孩子们，而汤姆则环绕了大半个地球。

但是我们都战胜了疲劳，因为我们在旧金山只能享受一个周末。我们在这里尽情地游览，环游了整个城市，在日本公园漫步，在那些著名的陡峭的街道上上下下，在渔夫码头吃晚餐，乘船游览海湾和大金桥，为孩子们选购纪念品。

直到我们到了机场都感觉是那样奇妙、振奋、浪漫。汤姆的机票是头等舱，可我的不是。我们期望把我的机票也升级为头等舱，可航班都预订满了。我只能把我的座位一直往前移，紧挨着头等舱。

我的眼睛闪着泪花。我不想让汤姆看到我的失落。我们浪漫的周末就这样结束了。

所有人都登机后，汤姆跟我身边的人说："你介意跟我换个座位吗，我想跟我妻子坐在一起。"

那人看到汤姆是从头等舱过来的，就很激动地同意了。傻瓜才会说不呢！

空服们简直不敢相信。汤姆为了我放弃了头等舱的座位。他们一直过来跟我们说："我简直不敢相信你为了你妻子放弃了头等舱，太浪漫了！"

其实，他们感觉整个旅程能为我们服务很高兴。他们给我们免费的电影耳机，给了我们每人一杯酒，甚至还给了我们只有头等舱乘客才有的点心。

飞机着陆之前，三名空服人员——一位男士两位女士，向我们走来，问我们结婚多久了，我说结婚 12 年。飞机着陆后，他们站在一起送给我两朵粉色的康乃馨，送给汤姆一瓶香槟，其中一个惊叹道："哇，都 12 年了还如此亲密！"他们脱口而出道："你们真是一对浪漫的神仙眷侣。"

开车回家的路上，我捧着花，笑着说："那些空服人员不明白，其实是他们误会了。我知道你跟我坐在一起是因为我是你的妻子。毕竟，你的下半生要跟我生活在一起啊。"

汤姆笑了，没有否认，但是我知道他跟我坐在一起是因为他不忍与我分开。不管什么原因，这是一个浪漫的周末，又是一个 12 年过去了，我依旧清晰地记得这次旅行。

——迪娜 A. 里柯克

Three Little Words
简单的三个字

To the world you might be one person, but to one person you might be the world.

~Author Unknown

It was on an ordinary wintry evening after many years of marriage that I realized how much I meant to my husband. On that particular evening he said three little words that sent me into a euphoric spin and made my heart swell with the beat-skipping, pitter-pat feeling usually reserved for puppy love or a new romance.

Oh, he told me often that he loved me, never forgot our wedding anniversary or my birthday, and was a considerate mate in every way. We had settled comfortably into an uneventful, unexciting, drama-free existence, which was fine with me.

He had worked late, as he often did, and his dinner waited for him in the oven as our three boys, who had been fed and bathed, were sprawled in their usual places between the fireplace and the television set with our two dogs and two cats.

I was in the basement, transferring clothes from washer to dryer, when I heard the front door open and close. When I was almost to the top of the stairs, he hung up his raincoat, and surveyed the wall-to-wall array of little boys and pets before him. Then I heard him say three little words, "Where is everybody?"

~Jackie Fleming

对于世界来说，你只是一个人；但对于一个人来说，你可能是整个世界。

——作者不详

　　在冬季一个平凡的晚上，结婚许多年后，我才意识到自己对丈夫有多重要。在那个特别的晚上，他说了简单的三个字，让我快乐得眩晕，我的心就像初恋般扑通扑通地跳个不停。

　　哦，他经常告诉我他爱我，从来不会忘记我们的结婚纪念日或者我的生日。在各个方面他都是一个体贴的伴侣。我们舒适地过着平静、平凡、平淡的生活，我觉得这样很好。

　　他跟平常一样，工作到很晚，我把晚餐放在烤箱里，三个孩子吃完饭洗完澡，一如既往地在壁炉和电视机之间的地方躺着和两只小狗小猫玩。

　　当我听到门开关的声音时，我在地下室，把衣服从洗衣机里拿出来放到烘干机里。我就要走到楼上了，他挂起他的雨衣，看了看墙上的摆设、眼前的孩子和宠物们。接着我听到他说了三个字："大伙呢？"

——杰姬·佛莱明

第二部分 真爱课程篇

Chapter 2
Lessons in True Love

Remember, there are no mistakes, only lessons. Love yourself, trust your choices, and everything is possible.

~Cherie Carter-Scott

记住，没有错误，只有教训。爱自己，相信自己的选择，一切皆有可能。

——谢丽·卡特·斯科特

Snitterfield
斯特拉特福镇

> The more you invest in a marriage, the more valuable it becomes.
>
> ~Amy Grant

In July of 1994 my husband Bill and I were enjoying a vacation in England. While driving north along the east coast we saw several road signs pointing to the nearby town of Snitterfield. We chuckled at the name and at one point I said, "Perhaps that is where I ought to send you whenever you get into a snit." To this day we use the word Snitterfield as a synonym for being in a grouchy mood.

In December of 2006, Bill had several major "snits" within a short period of time. I was feeling very uncomfortable about his frequent outbursts, which were often misdirected toward me. Early one morning I woke up crying and when Bill asked me what was wrong I told him how uneasy I was feeling, not knowing when or where he was going to have another "snit." I asked him to think seriously about what he could do to change that behavior.

Suddenly Bill bolted out of bed saying, "I'll be back shortly!" He disappeared into his study and an hour later he emerged with a freshly printed document which he posted on the refrigerator. He announced to me that he had created a Snitterfield Scorecard.

"A what?" I asked, half asleep.

Bill explained that he wanted me to help him monitor his moods by giving him some daily feedback about his behavior.

"And how can I do that?"

"Put a mark on my calendar at the end of each day. You're a teacher. You can figure out a good system."

"Are you serious?"

"Yes, very!"

So I came up with the following symbols:

+ no snits

? a few grumbles

- serious grouchiness

! run for your life

For the first week of our plan, every day was marked with a +. In twenty-three years of marriage I had never known Bill to be so even-tempered and patient with himself and with me. As he gained more self-control, I relaxed more. I could hardly believe the changes we were experiencing.

Once in a while Bill would revert to his old ways. When I put a "?" on his calendar, he expressed genuine regret that he had spoiled his record and he often apologized.

At the end of January I let him know how much I appreciated the effort he was making and told him I thought we could now let go of the scorecard idea.

"Marti, you have no idea how important it is for me to look at that calendar every day. Please continue to help me make progress."

I thought to myself, "Small price to pay for such a big payoff!" And so we continued using the scorecard through February, through March, through April. We talked about changes in his temperament and about how much happier we were in our relationship and daily life together.

Once in a while I would sense that an outburst was pending. When I started singing softly, "Do you know the way to Snitterfield...?" Bill would laugh and his energy would change immediately. At the end of April I sent Bill an e-mail with "prospective tourists" as the subject:

"The mayor of Snitterfield wishes to inform all prospective tourists that the residents of Snitterfield have recently voted to change the name of their town to Summerfield. So if you are planning a trip to Snitterfield, please note that it is no longer on the map."

Bill laughed out loud when he read the e-mail. Then I told him that after four months I had decided to resign from my position as his scorekeeper since my job was no longer relevant.

And that's the end of the story. We had found a seemingly silly way to address a serious long-term problem and it worked! Now, two years later, we continue to lead an (almost!) snit-free life together, full and love and laughter.

By the way, next time we go to England we are planning to visit the real village of Snitterfield, which is, in fact, a lovely rural village of 1,400 people in the West Midlands. There is a church there dating from the thirteenth century. Snitterfield was the home of Shakespeare's father. The name Snitterfield was originally Snytenfeld which meant a "meadow for birds."

~Martha Belknap

你对婚姻投资得越多，它会变得越有价值。

——艾米·格兰特

1994年7月，我和丈夫比尔在英国旅行。当车沿着东海岸线向北行驶的时候，我们看见一些路标指向附近的斯特拉特福镇。看着这个名字我们都咯咯地笑了，当时我说："以后你情绪崩溃的时候我就把你送到这儿。"直到今天我们还用"斯特拉特福"这个词来比喻不好的心情。

2006年12月，比尔在短期内有几次严重的情绪崩溃。我对他频繁的情绪爆发感到特别不舒服。有一天早晨，我哭着醒来，比尔问我怎么了，我告诉他我不安的心情，不知道他何时何地就又"崩溃"了。我让他好好想想怎么去改变。

比尔突然起床匆匆离开，说："我一会儿就回来！"他去了书房，一小时后，他拿着一份刚打印的文件出现了，他把这些纸贴在冰箱上，并且对我宣布说他制作了一个斯特拉特福积分卡。

"什么？"我半睡半醒地问。

比尔解释说他想让我帮他控制他的情绪，每天对他的行为打分。

"我怎么做？"

"每结束一天前在我的日历上做个标记。你是个老师，你能想出好的计分方法。"

"你是认真的？"

"是啊，非常认真！"

然后我就起来做了以下标记：

＋没有情绪崩溃

？发一些小牢骚

－严重发牢骚

！逃命吧

执行计划的第一周，每天都是"＋"，在23年的婚姻生活中，我从未看到比尔情绪如此稳定，对他自己和对我都是如此有耐心。随着他自控能力的增强，我的心情感到更轻松了。我简直不敢相信我们经历的这些变化。

有时比尔也会重蹈过去的覆辙。当我在他的日历上画"？"的时候，他会真诚地报以悔意，后悔破坏了良好的纪录，并为此道歉。

1月底，我告诉他我对他所作的努力感到很欣慰，我觉得他现在可以不必再用积分卡了。

"马蒂，你不知道每天看着这个日历对我有多重要，请继续帮助我进步。"

我独自思忖："这么小的付出竟换来了如此大的回报！"所以2月、3月和4月我们还是继续用积分卡。我们谈论他性格的变化以及我们现在在一起的生活有多么幸福。

有时我会感觉到他就要情绪崩溃了。当我开始轻声唱歌的时候："你知道去斯特拉特福的路吗？"比尔就会大笑，他的情绪马上就变了。4月底，我给比尔发了一封邮件，标题是"未来的游客"：

斯特拉特福镇的市长希望通知所有未来的游客，所有斯特拉特福镇的居民近期已投票将镇的名字改为萨默菲尔德。所以如果你计划去斯特拉特福镇旅行，请注意它已经不在地图上了。"

比尔读邮件的时候大声地笑了。接着我告诉他再过四个月，我要辞去我记分员的职位，因为已经没有工作可做了。

故事到此结束了。我们用了一种看起来很愚蠢的方式来解决这个长期存在的严重问题，而且还奇迹般地解决了！现在，两年过去了，我们继续在一起过着一种（几乎）零崩溃的生活，充满爱和欢乐。

顺便提一句，下次我们去英国，打算去参观一下真正的斯特拉特福镇，这其实是威斯特米兰一个非常可爱的小乡村，有 1400 名居民。镇上有一个 13 世纪遗存下来的教堂。斯特拉特福镇是莎士比亚父亲的故乡，它的名字起源于斯尼特福镇，意为"鸟类的草场"。

——玛莎·贝尔纳普

Aged to Perfection
岁月的完美

If you live to be a hundred, I want to live to be a hundred minus one day, so I never have to love without you.
~Winnie the Pooh

Looking through my old yearbook I came across a comment by one of my girlfriends. She wrote, "May you find your prince charming, tall, handsome and rich." We used to talk about our "perfect" loves at high school slumber parties in between painting our toes and dancing the twist. In college I added intelligence, compassion, and a sense of humor to the list of attributes that included broad shoulders, narrow waist, thick head of hair and, of course, treating me like I was the most beautiful creature walking the planet.

Now, as a member of AARP, I get magazines with updates on who is keeping it together and still glamorous at age sixty (most likely with a few nips and tucks) and I find it takes a lot longer to lose the pounds that I used to shed by just thinking about it. And what ever happened to the "perfect love" of my youthful dreams?

In the chair next to mine lies the object of my thoughts. Mouth open, he snores to his own private chorale, his abundant belly rising and falling in time with the cadence. Sigh. Where did I go wrong? I glanced at the thinning hair and lines around the eyes of the man I have been with for almost twenty years. Where did the narrow waist go and what happened to the glorious thick, golden hair and… I stop myself. "Go back to your list, Linda, and take another look." There were other attributes just under all those meaty physical ones. I went over them one by one.

1. Sense of humor: Oh yes, he is always ready to laugh at my jokes (even when he has heard them before) and especially at himself. That's where those cute little wrinkles around his blue eyes came from.

2. Compassionate: The man will cry at a sad movie, sharing tissues with me. He would give his heart to anyone in pain, especially any of our kids. Together we held our old tabby cat and sobbed when we had to put him down.

3. Intelligence: Yes, he is definitely an intelligent man. He built his own business from nothing and earned the respect of his employees and his clients. And he can fix things—saving us a considerable amount of money on minor home repairs. That man knows a thousand ways to use a wire coat hanger to create some widget to repair some thingamajig.

4. He treats me like I'm beautiful: Okay, so now I am blushing, and not a little humbled. He still tells me I look great and is not shy about telling others how beautiful or how funny he thinks I am. He rarely walks by me without touching me. He always kisses me before going out. As my waistline

expands and contracts in true menopausal form, he has never once complained, especially about my mood swings. He listens and he holds me when I need to be held. And, hey, his shoulders are still broad enough for me to cry on or rest my head. He tells me he loves me.

5. He cooks: If I buy the food and plan the meal, he will cook it better than I could. He actually likes cooking and has a family recipe for homemade lasagna that makes me salivate just thinking about it. It is a two-day process. When we had a little competition over who could make the best chicken soup he won, hands down. He has this knack for combining just the right spices.

Oh my. A small lump forms in my throat. Humility is hard to swallow sometimes. My list could go on and on, with nary a slender waist or full head of hair in the lot. So what if he is barely an inch taller than me? He loves it when I wear heels that take me to a lofty 5' 10". I look over at my man again.

He wakes himself up with a particularly loud snort to find me staring at him. I must have this stupid grin on my face because he says, "Okay, what's going on? What did I do? Was it something embarrassing?" I smile at him. "You know, I was thinking." He gives me a wary look that means, "Uh oh, she's been thinking again; this can't be good."

I lean over and whisper, "How about I take you out to dinner, my treat?" His eyes narrow. "Uh, okay, but what is it going to cost me?"

Hmmm. Have I been that shallow? I lean in closer. "Nope. Let's just call it an appreciation dinner—long overdue." At that he grins hugely and says he will take a quick shower and change.

As he gets up, he brushes by me patting my backside in that sweet, absent-minded way he always does. I grab his arm. "Don't ever stop doing that." He stops and looks at me. "Stop doing what?" I feel my face turning red and it is not a hot flash. "You know, the way you always grab my, um, well, you know." He looks more closely at me smiling from ear to ear. "Why, I do believe you are blushing. Woman, you still surprise me. And, as far as that other 'you know' thing, you can count on it."

I giggle, little bubbles of laughter that make me feel almost adolescent. Yep, things are definitely as they should be. Now, where did I put that cologne he likes?

~Linda Leary

如果你要活到 100 岁，那我想活到 100 岁的前一天，这样我就永远都不会失去你。

———小熊维尼

翻着过去的年鉴，看到一个朋友给我写的评论，"祝你找到一个高大、潇洒、富有、魅力无穷的白马王子。"我们曾在高中的睡衣舞会上憧憬完美的爱情，一边跳舞一边盘点着我们心中的白马王子应该有哪些特征。上了大学，我又加了一些特征：睿智、有同情心、幽默，而且肩宽腰细、头发浓密，当然，要把我当做世界上最美丽的人来对待。

现在，作为美国退休人员协会的一员，我总是看一些讲年届六十仍魅力不减而恩爱如初（或多或少还是有水分的）的杂志。我也发现减肥比以前花费的时间更长了，过去我只要想想就瘦了。难道年轻时代对于"完美爱情"的梦想变了吗？

我思考的对象就在我旁边的椅子上。口微张、有节奏地打鼾、圆滚滚的肚皮跟着节奏起起伏伏。我叹了口气。我到底哪里做错了？我瞥了一眼他稀疏的头发和眼角的皱纹，我跟他在一起将近20年了。那曾经平坦的腹部去哪儿了？那浓密的金发又去哪儿了？我掐断了自己的思绪——"琳达，再看看别的特征吧。"除了形象特征，下面还有很多别的特征。我一个一个重温着。

1. 幽默感。是的，他听到我讲的笑话总是会大笑，尽管有些他已经听过了，他也总是会自嘲，这就是那蓝色眼睛旁眼角纹的来源吧。

2. 同情心。他会为一部伤感的电影而流泪，和我一起分享纸巾。他关心每一个身在苦痛中的人，尤其是我们的孩子。我们一起抱着那只年迈的虎斑猫，它去世的时候我们一起抽泣。

3. 智慧。是的，毫无疑问，他是一个睿智的人。他白手起家，赢得员工和客户的敬重。他自己也会修理坏掉的东西，为我们省下一笔可观的维修费。他还用钢丝衣架做成无数种小部件来修理各种东西。

4. 他觉得我很美丽。好吧，我现在脸红了，并且一点也不谦虚。他依然对我说我看起来很美，而且不羞于告诉别人他认为我多么美丽、有趣。他每次经过我都会抚摸我。在出门前总是会给我一个甜蜜的吻。我的腰身变粗并且进入更年期，他从来没有抱怨过我强烈的情绪波动。他总是倾听，在我需要拥抱的时候搂着我。他的肩膀还是那样的宽阔，让我可以靠在上面尽情地哭泣。他总是对我说他爱我。

5. 他厨艺很好。我买了一些食物准备做饭，他做的总是比我做的好吃。他很喜欢做饭，还有一本自制意大利面的家族食谱，我光想象就馋得流口水了。做意大利面大约要两天的准备时间。我们曾经比赛过看谁做的鸡汤好喝，他总是赢得轻而易举。他有做厨师的天分。

　　我的天哪，我的喉咙好像有什么东西卡住了。有时候谦卑是很难做到的。我的名单可以不断地继续，但是却没有了纤细的腰或者浓密的头发。如果他只比我高几厘米呢？我穿上高跟鞋后足有177厘米，但他还是很喜欢我穿高跟鞋。我低下头又看了看他。

　　他醒了，鼻子里发出很大的哼哼声，发现我正盯着他看。我一定笑得很傻，因为他说："发生什么事了？我做了什么？是做了什么难堪的事吗？"我笑着对他说："没有，我刚刚在思考。"他小心翼翼地看着我，意思是，呃，她又思考了，情况不妙。

　　我侧过身来对他低语："我带你去吃晚饭，我请客，怎么样？"他的眼睛眯起来："嗯，好啊，但我要付出什么代价啊？"

　　呃……我有那么肤浅吗？我靠近他说："不用，我们就叫它'迟来的感恩大餐'吧。"他笑得更大声了，然后说他去洗澡换衣服。

　　他起来后，轻轻地抚摸着我的背，温柔而又心不在焉，如往常一样。我搂着他的胳膊。他停下来看着我说："永远不要停止这样做。""停止做什么？"我感到我的脸红了。"就是你搂我的方式，嗯，你懂的。"他在我耳边细语，"你脸红了？我简直不敢相信。你这女人总是能给我惊喜。刚刚说的'你懂'的那个，你可以永远依靠它。"

　　我咯咯地笑了，笑声就像一个热恋中的少女。是的，事情就是这样。我把他喜欢的古龙香水放哪儿了？

——琳达·利里

More than Red Roses
胜似红玫瑰

> Love is the condition in which the happiness of another person is essential to your own.
>
> ~Robert Heinlein

How does a man show a woman he loves her? I used to think he bought her a dozen red roses and dinner at a cozy restaurant along the Willamette River. I've seriously revised my thinking.

My husband shows love, or at least a great deal of tolerance, by sharing our white-carpeted home with a large dog that gravitates toward mud puddles whenever outside, and sharing our bed with a cat that likes to hog all the covers. He gardens alone when I go to the barn to see my lovely Arabian mare.

I, in turn, show my love by partnering in household tasks, helping him manage his commercial properties, and opening my heart to his adult children and their families.

Generally our routines work well, and we've been moving quite happily toward our tenth anniversary. But there are times when he is convinced that I love

Naomi the cat, Annie the dog, or Vida the horse more than I love him. Naomi, Annie, and Vida are getting older, right along with Ray and me. If Naomi, an eight-pound black kitty, starts losing too much weight, I obsess about every kibble she eats. If Annie, an eighty-pound Golden Retriever, starts limping too much from the arthritis in her right shoulder, I rush her to the vet. If Vida, my Arabian mare, flattens her ears when I put her into a trot, I postpone all household tasks and spend extra hours at the barn massaging knotted muscles. At those times my relationship with Ray gets a bit ragged.

I'd been in an obsessing-about-kitty phase, and Ray was already feeling unloved and unappreciated, when my horse suddenly got so ill I thought I might lose her. She spiked a fever, dropped liquid stools, and her heartbeat nearly double-timed with a worrisome "whoosh" added to the beat. She grew so weak within a matter of a few days that when the vet came out Vida literally fell over twice as he examined her.

I sobbed my worries to Ray while I waited for the results of the blood work. Ray isn't fond of horses. In seventh grade he rode a horse called Little Buck at a friend's birthday party. Though the horse never even crow-hopped, Ray expected with every lurching step that it would live up to its name, and the fear settled deep in his cells. He would rather eat glass than go to the barn with me. But he did care that I was upset, and listened to me babble about Vida for hours.

I could think of nothing else. Talk of nothing else. Vida is my dream come true. Growing up, I saved every dime I could find to ride the electric horse at the grocery store, and read every book about horses in the library. I handled turning forty by buying my own horse, and turning fifty by riding her on the beach. I couldn't lose her.

Blood work confirmed that Vida had a serious infection, probably staph. A daily intravenous injection of antibiotics seemed our best hope of saving her.

I considered giving Vida the shots myself to reduce vet bills, and set up a training session with the vet to learn to give them. My face must have been as white as Vida's blaze when he showed me a syringe as long as my forearm and explained the things to avoid so I didn't endanger my horse's life.

I went home to Ray, terrified and babbling even more.

He put his book and glass of wine aside, listened as I told him what I was feeling, then said, matter-of-factly, "I'll help you."

I dropped into a chair, speechless. When I found my voice I said, "We're talking every day. You'll help me?"

"I can do it."

"We're talking the barn a half hour away. A thousand-pound horse. Foot-long shots into a vein near her heart."

"I'll do it. I used to give myself shots every day."

Shots every day? He'd never told me that. I eyed him dubiously. Ray panicked when he had to wash gravel out of my shoulder after a cycling accident. "Why did you give yourself shots?" I asked.

"For my allergies."

He did have allergies, so I supposed he might actually have given himself shots. If so, maybe he could help me with Vida. I drew my chair closer to his. "How old were you?"

"Twelve."

A smile broke through my worry. He'd given himself shots more than fifty years before. He sounded supremely confident, and terribly earnest. "Let me make sure I have this right," I said. "You gave yourself shots every day."

"Well, my mother did it most of the time."

My chest hurt from holding in a burst of laughter. "You gave yourself shots every day except that your mother did it most of the time? How many shots do you think you actually gave yourself?"

"I don't know. At least one. They hurt."

Now I had to hold my sides not to double up. "How long did this shots thing go on?"

"A couple of weeks. They didn't work that well."

I got up from my chair, climbed into his lap, and gave him a huge hug. "You would have really done it for me, scary horses, scary needles and all, wouldn't you."

"I would have."

He wrapped his arms around me and I rested my head against his chest. Our conversation had helped me relax enough to see what I needed to do for myself and for Vida. Tough as it was for me to pull out my plastic, the vet accepted credit cards. I'd still need to go to the barn every day, but I'd worry about Vida a lot less and so be able to talk with Ray about something else, at least for a while.

Now I know how a man shows a woman he loves her. It's far more than red roses and dinners alongside the river. He surrenders his personal interests, packs up his courage, and goes wherever she needs him. That's true love.

~Samantha Ducloux Waltz

爱一个人就是他的幸福比自己的更重要。
——罗伯特·海因莱因

　　一个男人怎样表达对一个女人的爱？我曾认为爱就是在威拉米特河惬意的饭馆里，男人送给女人一束美丽的红玫瑰。后来我彻底地改变了这种想法。

我丈夫表达爱的方式，至少是宽容的，他会和一只在外玩耍沾满泥土的大狗一起坐在家里白色的地毯上；他会和一只猫同床共枕，把床单都拱起来。我去马厩看我心爱的阿拉伯母马时，他会独自享受地种植花草。

而我呢，表达爱的方式就是共担家务，帮他管理商业财产，对他已成年的孩子和家人敞开心扉。

一般情况下我们这种模式运转得很好，我们就这样幸福地一起度过了十年。但是有时候他觉得我爱猫咪内奥米、小狗安妮、小马维达胜于他。内奥米、安妮、维达、丈夫雷和我一样都在慢慢变老。如果 3 公斤多重的黑色猫咪内奥米，体重开始不断减轻的时候，我会检查她吃的所有食物。如果 3 公斤多重的金色猎犬安妮，因为右肩的关节炎而步履蹒跚时，我会飞快地带着她去看兽医。如果我带着心爱的阿拉伯母马维达慢跑的时候，发现她的耳朵耷拉下来了，我会放下所有的家务去马厩多花几小时帮她按摩僵硬的肌肉。这些时候，我和雷的关系就变得有些僵了。

我有段时间特别迷恋猫咪，雷觉得自己备受冷落。我的爱马突然生病时，我怕我会失去她。她发高烧还拉肚子，心跳是平时的两倍，每跳一下就会发出焦虑的"嘶嘶"声。她在短短几天就变得如此脆弱，我请了兽医过来，兽医给她诊治的时候她都摔倒了两次。

在等验血结果的时候，我抽泣着对雷诉说我的担忧，雷对马没有兴趣。七年级的时候他在朋友的生日聚会上骑过马，那匹马叫"小巴克"。尽管那匹马没有跳也没有叫，但是雷骑得摇摇晃晃，每一步都感觉要掉下来了，他身上的每个细胞都充满深深的恐惧。他宁愿吃玻璃也不愿跟我去马厩。但是他理解我的烦恼和沮丧，耐心地倾听我絮叨维达几小时。

我想不到我们还能聊什么。维达实现了我的梦想。小时候，我积攒下每一分钱，为的就是能骑一下杂货店电动木马，还读了图书馆所有有关马的书籍。40 岁的时候，我为自己买了一匹马，50 岁的时候我骑着她去了海边。我不能失去她。

验血结果确认了维达患有很严重的传染病，可能是葡萄球菌。我们能做的就是每天给她静脉注射抗生素，希望能救她。

我曾想过亲自给维达注射，以减少医疗费用。我跟着医生学了一段时间。当医生给我前臂一样长的注射器，跟我解释着怎样注射才不会伤害到维达的性命，我的脸一定跟维达身上的白斑一样惨白。

我吓坏了，跑回家找雷，絮叨了更多。

他把书和酒放到一边，倾听着我的感受，然后面无表情地说："我来帮你。"

我坐在椅子上，说不出话来。好不容易挤出几个字："这样的事每天都要做，你确定要帮我？"

"我能做到。"

"我们说的是开车半小时到马厩。一匹将近半吨重的马。用一英尺长的注射器注射到离她心脏不远的静脉血管。"

"我来做。我以前天天给我自己打针。"

天天注射？他从来没跟我说过那些。我怀疑地看着他，他有点惊慌失措。我问他："你以前为什么要给自己打针？"

"因为过敏。"

他是有过过敏症，所以也是有可能给自己打针的。如果是这样，那他真有可能帮我给维达打针。我拉着椅子靠近他说："你那时几岁了？"

"12 岁。"

微笑化解了我的担忧。他五十多年前给自己打过针，听起来他很自信，也极其认真。我说："我确定我没听错吗？你每天给自己打针？"

"好吧，大部分是我妈妈打的。"

我强忍着不笑出来，憋得胸口都有点疼了。"除了你妈妈给你打的以外，你还每天给自己打针？你每天给自己打几针啊？"

"我不知道，至少一针，挺疼的。"

现在我不能再弯着身子了，我捧腹大笑："打了多长时间？"

"几个星期。效果不是很好。"

我从椅子上起来，坐到他的膝盖上，给了他一个大大的拥抱，说："你真的愿意为我做这些吗？恐怖的马、恐怖的针等，你真的愿意？"

"我愿意。"

他搂着我，我把头靠在他的胸膛上。我们的对话让我无比放松，我明白了我需要为我自己、为维达做什么。虽然对我来说很难，但我还是拿出我的信用卡给了医生。我还是需要每天都去马厩看维达，但是我不再那么担心。我可以和雷谈论一些别的事情，哪怕只是一会儿。

现在我知道男人怎样向女人表达他对她的爱了，远不仅仅是红玫瑰或河边的烛光晚餐。他能够放弃个人的利益，鼓起勇气，当女人需要的时候他就一直陪在身边。这才是真正的爱情。

——萨曼塔·杜克鲁·华尔兹

Stronger Together
在一起更坚强

Snowflakes are one of nature's most fragile things, but just look at what they can do when they stick together.

~Fay Seevers

"I promise to love and cherish you in sickness and in health, for better or worse, as long as we both shall live." Like most couples, Nolan and I spoke these vows in 1972 never realizing what the future would hold for us as a married couple.

"Your baby has cystic fibrosis and probably will die before the age of thirteen. But don't get your hopes up because most kids with CF do not even live that long," cautions the young intern. He promptly walks out of the dismal hospital room. The news is incomprehensible. Our precious baby is only three months old… how can a doctor talk about her death? Nolan and I caress our infant and wonder what the future will hold for our little girl. How long will Rebekah live? Tears are uncontrollable.

The next day a counselor advises that our attitude toward this devastating disease will determine how Rebekah deals with cystic fibrosis. Also she warns, "The majority of couples who have a child with an incurable disease get a divorce. The financial burden and emotional stress is just too great." Nolan and I assure the counselor that our marriage will last. The counselor says, "I hope you are right and that your marriage will not be another divorce statistic."

Distraught over the counselor's information, we talk about the importance of communication to keep our marriage alive. Daily, Nolan and I discuss situations and make each decision together. Together, our determination and commitment will help fight this deadly disease. We know we are stronger together than apart. The wedding vows we made to each other five years earlier were for better or for worse. This event certainly is "the worse" in our marriage. We are determined to survive this disease as a family committed to loving one another.

During the hospitalization, we learn the effects of this progressive disease. We must administer breathing treatments to our baby to prevent lung congestion. Doctors, nurses and counselors are available at the hospital to answer questions and help us learn more about the deadly disease. But we wonder, "What will happen once we take our little girl home?"

Finally, the day arrives and we leave the hospital. A breathing machine and numerous medications are necessities we take with us. We are determined to enjoy our beautiful daughter for as long as she lives. Nolan and I believe that we can handle the daily stress associated with CF because we have each other's love and strength.

Our family settles into a routine. We want to keep things as normal as possible for our daughter and two-year-old son, Bryant. But each time Rebekah coughs repeatedly, fear engulfs us. The responsibility for her health is overwhelming.

Constant hospitalizations do put a strain on our relationship. Sometimes, we are on an emotional roller coaster. We are more determined than ever to make every moment count. Rebekah's health is always a great concern. We know that our marriage must remain strong. So, we decide to consciously make a time for each other every evening to talk. As soon as the children go to bed, we turn off the television and share the events of the day. We discuss and solve problems one at a time. Our home is a place of calmness and loving acceptance.

Years pass quickly. Rebekah enters a private school where teachers commit to understand CF. It is extremely difficult for a parent to leave a child with a critical illness anywhere, especially for long periods. I seek an activity to keep me busy while Rebekah is at school. My husband suggests enrolling in college. So, I do. While my children are in school, I attend classes to pursue my lifelong dream of teaching. Often I say to Nolan, "I don't think I can handle college and house chores in addition to all of Rebekah's special needs." My husband is adamant and encourages me. Nolan helps both children with homework and administers Rebekah's breathing treatments. After the children are in bed, he helps me with my homework until after midnight.

Our hard work pays off! Finally, my dream comes true. I am a college graduate at age forty. I apply to teach at the Christian school my children attend and they hire me to teach second grade. So, I am fulfilling my lifelong ambition to teach.

At times, our life seems almost normal. Rebekah amazes us with her determination to succeed. She participates in sports, drill team and cheerleading. But, she battles constant fatigue and chronic lung infections. But even with all of my daughter's accomplishments, often I am frightened that the doctor's predictions will come true. Will Rebekah die soon?

To our amazement, Rebekah lives past the age of thirteen. Our daughter has a dream of teaching and wants to attend college after high school. But to our distress, she develops diabetes, a frequent complication for adults with cystic fibrosis. Now, in addition to CF and two to three hours of daily breathing treatments, Rebekah must control blood sugar levels by exercise and insulin. The disappointment is great! Nolan and I struggle to deal with an additional disease. But our amazing daughter says, "This is no big deal! What's another disease! I have learned from the two of you that our family can handle anything together. We love each other and we are a team! You and Dad have taught me that!"

Our team seems to be challenged often. The death of my beloved dad is overwhelming. Nolan helps me through the grieving process. We take walks and I pour out my emotions. We visit the gravesite together and remember my dad and his influence on my life. Nolan and I face another challenge together… two teenagers. We experience the joy of success with good grades, awards, and winning teams. Rebekah participates in dance recitals, volleyball teams, and an award-winning cheerleading squad. She receives a national cheerleading award. Bryant pursues soccer, baseball, and varsity football. We also encounter the frustration of two teen drivers with speeding tickets and car wrecks. But we survive the teen years. Our marriage is strong because we are committed to tackling each problem together with love.

Our son has even noticed a difference in our marriage. Bryant says, "Lots of my friends' parents divorced, thinking that would solve all of their problems. I know it took extra efforts for you two to stay together. I don't know how a separated family could handle problems like CF. I appreciate how our family focuses on God and has always worked together as a team."

Our daughter graduates from high school and takes college courses with a fierce determination to succeed. Hospitalizations occur every six months. Rebekah is finally a college senior but the last semester is physically demanding and her body is ravaged by pneumonia. At age twenty-three, she is sicker than she has ever been. The fear of losing our beloved daughter is ever constant. The counselor was right. The stress is great with a chronically-sick child. However, when Nolan and I pray together, God enables us to overcome the fear.

After ten days of hospitalization, Rebekah's physical strength returns and her lungs are clear. She gets to go home in time for Christmas. Amazingly, she continues college. A miracle happens! Rebekah graduates from UNT with a degree in education. On that day, tears flow freely as Nolan and I marvel at the accomplishments of our daughter. Rebekah hugs us and says, "Thanks so much for supporting and believing that I could achieve my goal of a college degree."

Our theory of stronger together is proven true year after year! We praise God for the power to conquer the daily effects of our daughter's disease. Stress, fear, financial obligations, and even dealing with medical insurance frustrations… we can handle together. Now, the average life span for an adult with CF is the mid-thirties. But, we've met adults with CF who are fifty and researchers claim a cure for CF in the future is realistic. We believe that our daughter will continue to accomplish her dreams.

Our marriage is stronger now than when we first made the wedding vows. The reason is simple: we love each other, pray constantly, communicate daily, and have faith in God. What a team! And after thirty-seven years of marriage, "I promise to love and cherish you in sickness and in health, for better or worse, as long as we both shall live" is a vow that still endures. We can definitely say, "Our marriage will last for better or worse as long as we both shall live ."

~Marilyn Phillips

雪花是自然界最脆弱的物质，但是看看如果它们凝结在一起会变成什么样。

——费伊·西弗斯

"无论健康还是疾病，顺境还是逆境，在我有生之年，我发誓我会爱你、珍惜你，直至死亡把我们分开。"像所有的夫妻一样，在 1972 年，从未想过婚后生活会如何的我和诺兰发表了婚誓。

"你的孩子患有囊肿性纤维症，可能只能活到 13 岁。但是不要抱太大的希望，因为大多数患有这种疾病的孩子活不到那么久。"实习医生劝告道。他迅速离开这沉闷的病房。这个消息犹如晴天霹雳。我的宝贝只有 3 个月，医生怎么就能说到她的死亡呢？诺兰和我抚摸着这个小婴儿，疑惑着我们小女儿的将来会怎样呢？利百加能活多久？我们的眼泪无法抑制地流了下来。

第二天，一位医师说，我们对这种不治之症的态度，将决定利百加囊肿性纤维化疾病的发展状况。她也警告我们说："对于大部分的夫妻来说，如果孩子得了不治之症，最后都会离婚，经济负担和感情的压力实在是太大了。"诺兰和我向医师保证我们不会离婚。医师说："我希望你们是对的，希望你们的婚姻不会以离婚告终。"

被医师这么一说，我们心里很烦乱。我们探讨着沟通对婚姻来说是多么重要。每天，诺兰会和我讨论目前的现状，然后一起作决定。我们在一起的决心和对彼此的承诺帮我们对抗这致命的疾病。我们知道我们在一起比分开更坚强。五年前我们结婚时，对彼此发誓：无论顺境逆境，都要互相关爱，直至死去。目前显然是婚姻的"逆境"，我们下定决心战胜疾病，因为承诺过要互相关爱彼此。

住院期间，孩子病情渐渐好转。我们必须管理好孩子的呼吸治疗仪，防止肺充血。医生、护士和医师们帮我们解答了各种问题，让我们更加了解这疾病。我们在想："我们带女儿回家会怎么样？"

我们终于离开了医院，带着呼吸仪器和很多必备药品回家了。我们决定女儿活多久就爱她多久。诺兰和我相信我们能很好地应对疾病带来的压力，因为我们拥有彼此的爱和力量。

这个家很快步入正轨。我们想让一切都恢复正常，无论是我们的女儿，还是对我们两岁的儿子布莱恩特。可是每次利百加咳嗽不止的时候，我们内心总是充满恐怖。我们肩上最大的责任就是她的健康。

持续的住院治疗的确让我们的关系变得紧张。我们的情感跌宕起伏，仿佛坐在过山车上一样，时而满怀希望，时而无比绝望。我们的决心比以前更大了，决定要让每个时刻都过得有意义。利百加的健康是我们最关心的事，我们知道婚姻必须很牢固。所以，我们决定在每天晚上抽出时间与对方交谈。孩子们睡了以后，我们关掉电视，分享当天发生的事情。我们一次只讨论和解决一个问题。家中充满平静和爱。

转眼间，许多年过去了。利百加去了一所私立学校上学，那里的老师了解囊肿性纤维症。对于每一对父母来说，把一个身患顽疾的孩子放到别的地方是极其困难的，尤其是长期分隔。利百加去上学的时候，我就找些别的活动来让自己忙碌起来。丈夫建议我去上大学。我去了。孩子们在学校的时候，我就去上课，去追求我毕生的梦想——教学。我经常对诺兰说："又要上课，又要做家务，又要照顾利百加，我觉得自己应付不过来了。"丈夫总是坚定不移地鼓励我。他给孩子们辅导功课，料理利百加的呼吸仪器。孩子们睡了以后，他帮我补习功课，直到深夜。

功夫不负有心人！最终，我的梦想实现了。在 40 岁的时候，我成为了大学毕业生。我申请在我孩子所在的基督教学校教书，他们录用了我，让我教二年级的学生。我实现了毕生的夙愿。

我们的生活恢复了正常。利百加立志要成功的决心让我们很惊讶。她参加体育运动——钻探队和拉拉队。但是她还得和持续的疲劳以及慢性肺感染作斗争。尽管女儿取得了这么多的成绩，我经常会害怕医生的预言有一天会变为现实。我的女儿不久后就会死吗？

令我们惊喜的是，利百加活过了 13 岁。我女儿的梦想是当一名老师，她想高中毕业之后上大学。但是让我们不安的是，她得了糖尿病，这是患有囊肿性纤维症的成年人常见的严重并发症。现在，除了针对囊肿性纤维症需要进行的两到三小时的呼吸治疗外，利百加必须通过运动和注射胰岛素来控制血糖。我们都感到异常沮丧！诺兰和我努力去应对这个新疾病，然而我们神气的女儿说："什么新疾病啊，这没什么大不了的！你们让我知道没有团结一致战胜不了的困难。我们互相关爱对方，我们是一个团队！这是你和爸爸教我的！"我们这个团队似乎遭遇到各种挑战。我最心爱的父亲去世了，我几乎崩溃。诺兰帮我走出痛苦。我们出去散步，我向他倾吐我的情感。我们一起去墓碑前，缅怀父亲和他对我一生的影响。

诺兰还和我一起面对着另外一个挑战——两个青春期少年。我们经历了很多成功的喜悦，优异的成绩、奖励和胜利。利百加参加了舞蹈演奏会、排球队，还有一个获奖的班级拉拉队。她获得了国家拉拉队奖。布莱恩特喜欢足球、棒球，参加了大学足球竞赛。我们也会经历一些很沮丧的事情——两个年轻驾驶员超速开车的罚单、损坏的汽车。但是我们幸存了下来。我们的婚姻很牢固，因为我们一起用爱来应对每一个困难。

我们的儿子甚至发现了我们的婚姻与别人的不同之处。布莱恩特说："我很多朋友的爸妈都离婚了，觉得离婚就能解决所有的问题。我知道你们在一起肯定作了很多努力。我不明白如果家庭破裂了，还怎么能应付像囊肿性纤维症这样的难题。我真的很感激我们的家人，一心追随上天，总是像一个团队一样一起解决所有的事情。"

我们的女儿高中毕业后，怀着必胜的信念上了大学。每半年就要住院治疗。利百加终于大四了，可是最后一个学期很吃力，她得了肺炎。23岁的时候，她比以前更虚弱。我总是害怕会失去她。那个医师说得对，患慢性病的孩子压力很大。但是，当诺兰和我一起祈祷的时候，上天帮我们战胜了恐惧。

住院10天后，利百加的身体恢复过来了，肺炎也好了，正好回家过圣诞节。令人惊讶的是，她继续上大学去了。奇迹发生了！利百加从北得克萨斯大学顺利毕业了，取得了教育学学位。

那一天，诺兰和我不住地流泪，我为女儿取得的成绩赞叹。利百加抱着我们说："你们相信我一定能拿到大学学位，谢谢你们的支持和信任！"

年复一年，我们"在一起更坚强"的理论被一次次证明是正确的！我们赞扬上天的力量，征服了我女儿的疾病，帮我战胜了一切压力、恐惧、经济负担，甚至是医疗保险上的挫折。我们在一起能应对一切。现在，一个患有囊肿性纤维症的成年人的平均寿命是 30 岁左右。但是我们见过活到 50 岁以上的患者，研究声称治疗此病的方法就是活在当下。我们相信女儿会继续实现她的梦想。

现在我们的婚姻比我们第一次宣誓的时候更加牢固。原因很简单：我们深爱彼此，坚持祷告，经常沟通，相信上天。多么美妙的一个团体！结婚 37 年了，我们的誓词——"我发誓，无论环境是好是坏，是富贵是贫贱，是健康是疾病，我都会爱你，尊敬你并且珍惜你，直到死亡将我们分开"愈久弥坚。我们能坚定地说："无论环境好坏，我们的婚姻都会跟我们的生命一样长久。"

——玛里琳·菲利普斯

Anything for a Buck
一切为了钱

It's so easy to fall in love but hard to find someone who will catch you.

~Author Unknown

If "Living without a Primary Source of Income" were a place, I would be the Queen of the Land. I don't accept this title willingly, but I have repeatedly been given the opportunity to learn how to manage our household on an irregular, minimal budget. In the ten short years that I've been married to my King, he has been out of work four times. Three times were for a period of almost a year. When he lost his job this time, the first words out of my mouth were "You'll get a new job immediately! You'll be back to work in a month!" I half-heartedly believed my words, uttered through a pasted-on smile, over a year ago.

This time we were victims of the economy, like so many others. My husband was replaced by a young chickadee taking home a paycheck half the size of his. However, knowing that fact didn't make it any easier to digest that all of our financial dreams were going to be put aside. We were going to slip out of thriving mode into surviving mode—again.

The next few days were a blur. Not just because I had difficulty seeing through my tears, but I was blinded with anger. I couldn't make eye contact with him, let alone body contact. I was physically unable to provide what my hurting man needed the most: an ego-building, estrogen-driven boost of confidence from his loving wife. How could he allow himself to be in a position that could jeopardize his loving family—again? Would he ever be a consistent provider? When would I have the security that I longed for? And the hardest question of all: Did I marry a loser?

I knew my most important wifely priority was to be my husband's number-one cheerleader in order to prevent him from becoming engulfed in both depression and our deep, comfy couch. Some couples quote their timelines by new babies or houses. Our timeline is based on "Oh, yeah, that was after you were laid off from the ice cream manufacturer but before you sold nuts and bolts." At least we had a freezer full of Ben and Jerry's to get us over that hump.

Terry has never simply been fired, or at least never fired simply. When I get into the details of his employment history, I begin to doubt the truth myself, and I was there. If another man's wife told me this dramatic tale, I know I wouldn't believe her. How can one man have such a long string of unfair treatment? I began to convince myself that not only had he deserved it, but he brought it on himself. But then I stepped back and took a look at the big picture. I realized that was logically impossible. If it wasn't Terry's fault, maybe it was God's. If even God wasn't going to help Terry with his career, who would be willing to hire a man who has never held a job for more than a few years? On top of my fear that I had possibly chosen the wrong man to marry, I had begun to develop a mistrust of employers. Any company that would hire him wouldn't be worth working for, and any job he was offered wouldn't be worth accepting.

Wow—some cheerleader I was turning out to be. But, I have to admit I was both surprised and proud at how Terry reacted to the situation. He got himself back into his job-hunting groups, signed up at the workforce center, and wasted no time in updating his résumé. He got a haircut, sent his suits to the cleaners, and registered for unemployment. He knew the drill, the steps that had to be followed, and he did them. He even skipped some of his usual self-deprecating detours like anti-depressants and getting sucked into watching infomercials in the wee hours of the morning. If he could deal with this like a mature adult, why couldn't I?

As word began to spread of Terry's new employment status, calls of condolence and curiosity began to come in from across the country. Most were kind and supportive. Some just dripped with pity. But one anger-driven, venomous call came from a relative who loves me dearly. She spewed indictments and grilled me with accusatory questions. How dare she label my husband as selfish, accusing him of not making his family the top priority? It was okay for me to think it, but for her to say it out loud? The nerve. In hindsight, I am grateful for her inappropriate behavior because it provoked me to fight back. It was in the act of defending my husband that I began to see the return of the respect I once had for him.

Each time a new call came in, it became easier to brag about the positive steps that Terry was taking to move forward. Each time I hung up the phone, I found it a little easier to feel the respect for him that he deserved. Eventually, I became the cheerleader that he longed for and requires for success. I support and encourage him in all his job-hunting efforts from application to interview. Participating every step of the way has made it "our" job search, "our" career goal.

If our past year were a game show, I imagine it would go something like this: "I'm Bob Womack, your host of *Anything For A Buck*! The game show that challenges your humility by asking 'Just what will YOU do for a buck?' Our first contestant is a happily-married father of two from Colorful Colorado! Welcome Terry!"

"Thanks Bob, glad to be here."

"As you know, Terry, our game is all about just how you are willing to humble yourself to earn money. So, contestant number one, just what will you do for a buck?"

"Anything, Bob. I am willing to do anything to care for my family. I will get up hours before the sun in the dead of winter and drive to the state line to set up cardboard cutouts of the Seinfeld cast on a college campus in order to put food on the table. I will carry two cases of beer, three dozen licorice ropes and a duffle bag filled with peanuts up and down the steep steps of a football arena, a baseball stadium, the rodeo show grounds, and two concert pavilions if it means I can pay the mortgage. I will do market research studies on consumer products and political opinions. I will mystery-shop hamburger chains and barbershops. Bob, I will even dress up as a six-foot gecko, ride around a racecar track in a golf cart and shoot T-shirts into the screaming crowd to keep the lights turned on. I will do anything for a buck!"

The real winner of this show is me. I won the grand prize: a husband I am proud of. One who is willing to do anything not just for a buck, but for our love and for our family. How could I not respect that?

~Karen O'Keeffe

坠入爱河很容易，但要找到一个能征服你的人却很难。

——逸名

如果有一个"没有主要收入来源也可以生活"的地方，那我肯定是这块土地的女王。我并不很喜欢这个题目，但是我已经有很多次机会去学习如何用不稳定的、最小的预算来维持生活。我嫁给丈夫的短短十年，他已经失业四次了。其中三次失业都长达近一年。所以这次知道他失业后，我说的第一句话是："你马上去找个新工作，一个月内就会再就业的！"一年前我勉强地笑着对他说，连自己都半信半疑。

这次我们和其他人一样，经济上深受其害。我的丈夫被一个菜鸟取代了，因为他的工资是我丈夫的一半。但是，知道真相对事情并没有什么好处，很难接受我们的发财梦再一次搁浅，我们只得把大手大脚的花钱方式改为精打细算。

接下来的几天感觉迷迷糊糊的。不仅仅是因为我哭得眼睛肿了看不清东西，而是气得什么都看不清楚了。我们没有了眼神交流，更别说是身体接触了。我根本做不到给受伤的他最需要的东西——他爱妻给他的信心，让他重拾自信，激发他的雄心斗志。他怎么能够允许自己陷入这样的境地，并且再一次危及他的家庭呢？他是个能养家糊口的人吗？我什么时候才能拥有我期待已久的安全感？最难的问题是：我是不是嫁错人了？

我知道作为一个妻子，优先考虑的是要在第一时间为丈夫加油鼓劲，以防他变得沮丧，沉浸在舒适的沙发里一蹶不振。一些夫妻觉得生小孩和买新房是婚姻生活的里程碑，而我们的里程碑是"哦，那是你被冰激凌工厂辞去但还没有开始卖螺帽和螺栓的时候"，至少我们还有本和杰里的冰箱来跨过这个坎。

特里并不是简简单单地被解雇，我了解了他的职业生涯后，开始怀疑这是不是真的，可我就在他身边亲眼目睹了这些事情啊。如果另一个男人的妻子告诉我这个颇有戏剧性的故事，我知道我不会相信。一个人怎么会遭受这么不公平的待遇呢？我开始说服自己不是他活该倒霉，但这也是他自己造成的。然而我又转念一想，明白了这个逻辑上是可能的。如果不是特里的错误，那可能是上天的错误。如果上天不打算在职业生涯上帮助特里，那谁会雇用一个每份工作都干不长的人？恐惧感袭上心头，我觉得我可能嫁错人了。我也开始对用人单位不信任，任何一家会雇用他的公司都不值得去，那这些公司提供的工作也就不值得接受了。

哇，我要变成拉拉队队长了。但是我不得不承认特里对待这些事情的态度让我既惊讶又自豪。他又开始找工作了，在就业中心签字报名，并花了很多时间修改简历。他还剪了头发，把工作服送到干洗店，在失业人数统计中心挂名。

他知道这是他必须经历的磨难，他做到了。甚至还少走了自甘堕落的弯路，如服用抗抑郁药，在凌晨一两点钟还沉浸在电视节目中。如果他都能成熟地应对这件事，那我为什么不能？

随着特里再次失业的消息的传开，我每天都会接到很多慰问和好奇的电话。大部分是出于关心和支持，尽管有些只是同情和怜悯。但是也接到了一个特别爱我的亲戚打来的电话，她特别生气，说话也很尖刻。她生气地痛诉，并责问了我几个问题。她怎么敢说我丈夫自私，责怪他不把家庭放在第一位？我这样想还行，但是她凭什么这样说出来？神经病！但是事后，我很感激她这样的行为，因为她激发我去反抗。在为丈夫辩护的时候，我发现我以前对他的尊重又回来了。

每次接到一个新电话，我都能很容易地说出积极的理由，说到特里在不断进步。每次我挂断电话的时候，我觉得我更尊重他了，而且他本来就应该被尊重。最后，我真的成为他期待已久的拉拉队长了，不断鼓励他成功。我支持和鼓励他求职过程中所作的一切努力，不管是求职申请还是面试。每一步我都积极参与，这已经成了"我们俩"在求职，"我们共同"的职业规划了。

如果过去是一场游戏节目，我觉得它会是这个样子："我是鲍勃·沃马克，《一切为了钱》节目的主持人！这个节目问你'为了钱你愿意做什么？'从而挑战你的自尊底线。我们第一个参赛选手来自美丽多彩的科罗拉多州，是一个有着幸福家庭的父亲，欢迎特里！""谢谢你鲍勃，很高兴来到这里。"

"你知道的，特里，我们的游戏是，为了赚钱你愿意付出多少？所以一号选手，你会怎么做？"

"我愿意做任何事，鲍勃。为了我的家庭我愿意付出一切。寒冷的冬天，我愿意在日出前起床，开车去州界线，去为校园里的塞恩菲尔德剧组挖剪硬纸板，以便让他们把食物放在桌子上。如果能帮我还贷款，我愿意拎着两箱啤酒，三打草绳和一个装满花生的行李袋在足球场、棒球场、马术表演场，以及两个演唱会场馆爬上爬下，到处奔波。我愿意作各种市场调研，无论是消费品还是政治观点。我愿意开一家汉堡包连锁店或理发店。鲍勃，我甚至还愿意装扮成六英尺长的壁虎，愿意在高尔夫球场的赛道上骑车帮忙捡球，把自己的 T 恤扔向尖叫着的人群，保持活跃的气氛。为了赚钱我什么都愿意做！"

这个游戏的真正胜利者是我。我赢得了大奖：一个令我自豪的丈夫。一个不仅仅为了钱愿意付出一切，更是为了我们的爱、我们的家庭愿意付出一切的丈夫。我有什么理由不尊重他呢？

——凯伦·奥基夫

Twice in a Lifetime
一生拥有两次真爱

The past is behind us, love is in front and all around us.
~Emine Woodhull-Bäche

"All our efforts to save him failed." A faceless doctor's words echoed in my head, as I sank to the emergency room floor in total disbelief. My fifty-six-year-old husband, Sid—my soulmate for almost thirty-eight years, was dead from a sudden heart attack.

After the shock of his death wore off, I struggled with the many stages of grief, including depression, anger and confusion. Grief counseling helped tremendously, particularly with issues that were so unexpected, like happiness guilt.

When I then met and fell in love with Tom, I was elated and confused at the same time. How could I love someone other than Sid? I felt like a cheating wife. My head told me that Sid would want me to be happy again, but getting my heart to accept that fact took a lot of time and work on my part.

One of the things that helped me deal with those guilty feelings was the realization that I was really a lucky woman. Many people never find true love once in a lifetime, yet I loved and was loved by two wonderful, very different men. Sid was perfect for the young, naive, teenage bride, and Tom was right for the sixty-year-old more confident, independent woman I had become since my husband's untimely death.

Almost two years after Sid died, Tom and I visited his grave. I was in the arms of one man I loved, sobbing over another man I also loved. But oddly enough, it did not feel strange. And as we sat there, total peace began to surround me. I was comforted by Tom's loving embrace, but it was more than that.

That chilly November day, the wind was as cold as the large concrete bench that stately guarded the family plot. Suddenly a gentle warm breeze kissed my face and caressed my hair. I knew it was Sid telling me he was happy for me, and that he was with me—just a smile away. My heart would always hold those wonderful memories of love from the past. But also I had enough love in my heart to give to someone new. I felt the last remnants of happiness guilt float away, and I imagined those feelings assimilating into the fluffy clouds above us.

I sighed and rested my head on Tom's shoulder. "How blessed I am," I said. "I found true love twice in a lifetime."

~Melinda Richarz Lyons

过去在我们身后，而真爱会永远在我们身边。

——埃姆·伍德哈尔·巴彻

"我们已经尽力了，抢救失败。"一个医生的话语不断地在我脑海中回响。我跌倒在急救室的地上，完全不敢相信这个事实。我56岁的丈夫希德，我38年的灵魂伴侣，因心脏病突发而去世了。

我渐渐地从震惊中回过神来，在各种痛苦中挣扎、沮丧、生气、困惑。悲伤辅导课极大地帮助了我，尤其是对那些意料之外的问题，比如它消除了我重获幸福的罪恶感。

然后，我认识并爱上了汤姆，我感到既兴奋又困惑。我怎么会爱上除希德以外的其他男人呢？我感觉自己就像出轨了。我的头脑告诉我希德是希望我再次获得幸福，但是让我由衷地接受这个事实却很难。

当我意识到我有多么幸运的时候，这种感觉帮我战胜了罪恶感。很多人一生都得不到一次真爱，而我却与两个都很完美但又完全不同的男人深深地相爱。希德非常适合那个年轻的、天真的少女新娘，而汤姆却特别适合这个60岁的、因丈夫早逝而变得自信独立的我。

希德去世近两年后，我和汤姆拜访了他的墓碑。我挽着我爱的男人，缅怀另一个我深爱的男人。但是很怪异的是，我们一点都不觉得奇怪。我们坐在那里，感到无比的平静。汤姆深情地拥抱我、安慰我，但是我知道，这个拥抱不止是出于安慰。

在 11 月寒冷的一天，风像保卫房屋的混凝土长凳一样冷，突然一阵温暖的微风亲吻我的脸，轻拂我的头发。我知道这是希德告诉我他很为我高兴，他与我同在——然后一笑而过。我的心总是保留着过去对爱美好的回忆。我心中也有足够的爱去给别人。我感到最后残留的一丝罪恶感像头顶松软的云彩一样，渐渐消散了。

我叹了一口气，头靠在汤姆的肩膀上，说："我好幸运，一生拥有两次真爱。"

——梅林达·里夏茨·里昂

What You Don't Know
你永远无法预知

Love one another and you will be happy. It's as simple and as difficult as that.

~Michael Leunig

When you are young and uneducated in the game of life and picking a spouse—particularly if you are a young, stupid Christian and trying to obey God—your reasons for getting married probably don't go much further than the fact that you are "In Love" and your hormones are raging. A year seems like a long time to have been together, thirteen years is rather obscure, and a lifetime is unfathomable.

You don't know that thirteen years will pass in the blink of an eye.

When you put on the white dress and vow "for better or for worse," you don't know how bad the worse can really be. You don't know how hard it is to suffer three years of infertility, defend your decision to adopt to people who think you should put your resources into fertility treatments, or how another three years of postpartum depression when you do have a baby can tear you apart. You don't know when you vow "for richer or poorer" how poor that really means. You don't know that the $100 a month you lived on in college will look like a windfall after thirteen months of no income with small children.

When you pack up your things and move into your new home together, you don't realize that that pair of pants that he wads up on the floor will always be there, and the dishes she leaves in the sink will, too. Even though you didn't intend to marry your father or mother, you don't know that you will pull them into an argument in order to make your point that dishes shouldn't be left in the sink and pants don't belong on the floor if you intended to wear them again.

You don't know that those deals you made in the first week, on the honeymoon, won't be kept and that no matter how much you hate it, no matter how many times you remind them, the dirty dishes will still be out and the toilet will still have a ring (until the mother-in-law comes to visit).

You have no idea that he will still want you with baby flab and saggy breasts. You don't know how special it will be to look into little blue eyes and see your spouse. You don't know that when you look into the brown face of your son, you will also see your husband because nurture makes a fool of nature. You don't know that when you do finally get pregnant after adopting that your husband will tell you that when a white baby comes out, he'll know you've cheated because his babies are brown.

You don't know that when you get a wild idea to become a writer or start your own company that your spouse will be your biggest cheerleader. You don't know that when even your family thinks your spouse is crazy, you'll cling even tighter to him. You don't know the good that will come.

Face it, when you're young and stupid, you don't know what you are getting into.

You don't.

But I'm glad I got into it.

~Jamie Driggers

彼此相爱就是幸福。如此简单，又如此困难。

——迈克·洛伊尼希

　　没有多少社会经验的年轻人，尤其是那些仅仅试图从上天那里获得指示的年轻而幼稚的基督教徒，选择伴侣结婚的原因可能只是因为"彼此相爱"，以及那日益增长的荷尔蒙作祟。一起相处一年都感觉悠远漫长，到了 13 年就相当不可思议，而一生更是深不可测了。

　　其实你不知道，13 年转瞬即逝。

　　当你披上白纱宣誓"无论境况好坏，一生在一起"时，你不知道情况到底会变得多坏：你不知道不孕不育的痛苦，你不知道拒绝做亢进治疗而坚持领养孩子是多么艰难；你不知道在你最终有了孩子却得了产后抑郁症时，是多么让你崩溃。你也不知道在你发誓"无论贫穷还是富有，一生在一起"时，你会变得多么穷困；你更不知道在生了孩子后连续 13 个月没有收入时，获得大学时代 100 块钱份额大小的生活费都会让你觉得是天降奇财。

当你们收拾好家当一起搬进新家时，你不知道他会把裤子揉成一团扔在地板上不再理会，而她也会把饭后的餐具永远放在水槽里不管不顾。尽管你不想与你父母那样的人结婚，但是你从未想到过你们也会像你的父母一样，仅仅为了告诉对方饭后的餐具不应该永远放在水槽里或者再穿的裤子不应该扔在地上这样的琐事而跟对方一遍遍争吵。

你不知道，你跟他在度蜜月时订的条约不会持久，不管你多么厌恶，不管你曾多少次提醒对方，那些用完的餐具还是会被扔在外面，结婚戒指还是被忘在厕所里，直到岳母来的时候才被发现。

其实你更不知道，即使你肌肉松弛、胸部下垂，他还是会和你在一起。你不知道深情地看着他那双蓝色的眼睛对他来说有多么特别的意义。你不知道看着儿子棕色的脸，也有丈夫的影子，发觉遗传对于孩子的作用还不如亲手养育。你不知道在你领养了一个孩子却又怀孕了之后，丈夫会开玩笑地说，如果你生出一个白色婴儿，就说明你出轨了，因为他的孩子应该是棕色皮肤。

你不知道，当你有成为一个作家或者创业的想法时，他会是你最积极的拉拉队员为你鼓舞喝彩。你不知道，即使你的家人都觉得他在发疯时，你会更紧密地黏着他。你不知道，好事就要来了。

勇敢面对吧，年轻的时候很幼稚，你无法预知自己会走进怎样的生活。

虽然你无法预知，但我很庆幸我进入了。

——杰米·德里杰斯

He Turned Me into a Queen
他给了我女王般的幸福

Love is not love which alters when it alteration finds.
~William Shakespeare

Gene, my fiancé, held me close as we exited the doctor's office. "Nothing will happen to your eyes." He lifted my chin with his fingertips and wiped a tear from my cheek. "We have a wedding to plan."

I relished his tenderness, but my thoughts still echoed the doctor's words just minutes prior. He had shined a bright light into my dilated pupils. "Hmm… your retina is deteriorating."

My hands got moist and my heart drummed.

"You need to prepare," he said. "No one knows how long you'll have your sight."

I leaned on Gene, his body strong and loving as I dismissed the bleak prognosis. Besides, for the moment, my eyesight was fine, I was in love, and my dream wedding was about to come true.

Months passed, and my wedding day finally arrived! Dressed in pure white, I prepared to walk down the aisle and meet my prince.

"Are you ready?" Dad whispered.

I nodded and put my trembling arm through his. Our steps were slow as we made our way down the aisle to the sound of royal and elegant trumpets. The colorful arrangements of fresh flowers along the sides made an invisible canopy of soft fragrances. The sun beaming through the huge stained-glass windows painted reflections of a variety of hues on the marble floor, adding to the magic of our day.

"For better or for worse…"

Those words referred to a distant concept back then, and my heart lit up with dreams of the "better." But nine years later, my world darkened with the reality of the "worse" as the words from the ophthalmologist way back then echoed with a sobering truth. My peripheral vision had begun to close in, and it was closing in way too quickly. I sat beside Gene on the couch. "I need to tell you something."

He pressed the remote, silenced the TV, and turned to me. "What's the matter?"

"I don't think I can drive anymore. Something's wrong with my eyes."

The explanation for my frequent bumping into the children and open cabinet doors, and even missing steps, didn't surprise him. He knew and so did I. But talking about made it painfully real.

With each month that passed, my field vision decreased. Desperate searches for treatments, and visits to specialists increased, but all of the answers gave us no hope. Our anguish intensified.

A few short months swept by. All I saw was what one sees through a keyhole. Then the day came—I woke up and my narrow field vision had closed in completely. Bitterness and anger filled my days. And the unfair misfortune touched us both. What we dreaded became an unwelcomed intruder into our marriage.

Each of us faced it differently. He withdrew, and I fought my own desperation at losing my ability to be a wife, a mom, and the woman Gene married. I felt worthless, unlovable, and ugly. But our three small sons gave me a reason to keep on trying, keep on adjusting, and continue to live a normal life in spite of my blindness.

Gene and I began to pray together—an uncomfortable thing for us—but we persisted anyway. "We'll be okay," he assured me.

The household tasks I performed easily before now took twice as long. But the outcome revealed Gene's patience. Separating the laundry—white from color—was an impossibility for me. One day, in a hurry, I emptied the clothes hamper into the washing machine. That's when Gene's understanding radiated as he softly suggested a bit of bleach was needed for his pink T-shirts.

The dishes I prepared didn't follow written recipes. Instead, I added ingredients according to my tastes. To my delight, the results pleased Gene and our small sons.

Years swept by, turning the pages of our lives together. Some of the pages were stained with the pain of losing our youngest son, while others wrinkled with adjustments to unexpected financial setbacks. But each page was carefully taped together, framed with the commitment reflecting God's power in the midst of adversity.

Although unable to see my own reflection in the mirror, I saw God's image in the mirror of our marriage. The faint, but sweet aroma of Gene's cologne surrounded me with reassurance as he held my hand and prayed for my day before leaving for work.

When I commented, "It sure is chilly in this restaurant, isn't it?" moments later, I felt a light sweater around me. Gene had quickly slipped away and retrieved it from the car. He draped it around me and deposited a kiss on my cheek. "Can I fix you another plate from the salad bar?" he asked at the precise moment I finished what he'd brought me the first time. Far from an isolated incidence, this thoughtfulness continues to this day.

My thoughts often wander. How I wish I could return what he has given me—his unconditional love. How I long to have one opportunity to say, "Don't worry, honey, stay home and rest. I'll take care of those errands." Or maybe, "How about if I read something to you for a change." But these thoughts never come to fruition.

On one occasion, he paused after reading a book to me for a long while. I asked, "Do you sometimes wish you were married to someone who could see?" I'd never asked this before, but I continued, "Then you wouldn't need to do so much. Tell me the truth." I held my breath waiting for his answer.

After a few moments of silence, I heard him place his eyeglasses on the table. "The truth is, you probably do much more for me than I ever do for you. We make a good team just the way we are, and we'll make it to the end."

Lying next to my sleeping husband, I stretch my hand to find his strong arm. In the stillness of the night, my thoughts race. Tears stream down my cheeks as the well of gratitude within me overflows. Listening to the sound of Gene's rhythmic breathing, I sigh with admiration for the man who saw beyond the ugliness of my blindness. With his love and understanding, he turned me into a queen.

~Janet Perez Eckles

如若因变生变，爱便不再是爱。

从医生办公室出来的时候，我的未婚夫吉恩紧紧地抱着我。他用指尖轻轻抬起我的下巴，拭去我脸颊的泪珠，说："你的眼睛不会有事的，我们还要一起策划婚礼呢。"

他的温柔让我沉醉，但是我脑海中还是回响着医生几分钟前所说的话。他用强烈的灯光照进我放大的瞳孔里，说："嗯，你的视网膜受损了。"

我手心里全是冷汗，心也扑通扑通地跳个不停。

他说："你要作好心理准备，现在还不能预料到你什么时候就会失明。"

我推开这令人绝望的诊断书，靠在吉恩强壮而充满怜爱的身上。

现在，我还能看见，我们彼此相爱，而且我就要举行婚礼了。

几个月后，终于到我的婚礼了！我穿着洁白的婚纱，准备走下红地毯去跟我的白马王子相见。

"你准备好了吗？"父亲低语道。

我点了点头，颤抖地挽着父亲的臂膀。在庄严典雅的婚礼进行曲下，我们缓缓地走上通道。

四周五颜六色的鲜花，无形的天棚散发着淡淡的芳香。阳光穿过硕大的彩色玻璃窗照了进来，地板都被映射得色彩斑斓，为我们这特殊的一天增添了更多神奇。

"无论境况好坏，一生在一起。"

那时，感觉那些词语所指很遥远，我的心全被"美好"点亮了。但是九年后，眼科医生的话让我清醒地认识到这"残酷"的现实，我的世界灰暗了。我的外围视力变得越来越差，而且恶化得非常快。我坐在吉恩身边，说："我得告诉你一些事情。"

他拿起遥控，把电视静音，转过身来回答："怎么了？"

"我觉得我不能开车了，我的眼睛有问题。"

他对这解释一点都不惊讶。因为我最近经常撞到孩子和开着的橱门，甚至还下错楼梯。我和他都知道原因。但是现在要开诚布公地谈论这些却着实让人痛苦不堪。

短短几个月过去了，我只能看到类似别人从钥匙孔中看到的东西。

紧接着，那天到来了。我醒来后发现自己完全失明了。我的生活充满了痛苦和愤怒。命运对我们如此不公。我们担忧的事情最终还是无情地侵入了我们的生活。

我们对待这件事的态度不同。他像往常一样，而我顽强地与这绝望的命运抗争着。我就要失去做一个妻子、一个母亲、一个女人的能力。我觉得自己毫无价值，不讨人喜欢，甚至很丑陋。但是我的三个儿子让我有了继续尝试、不断适应的理由，继续过着跟过去一样的生活，就像没失明一样。

吉恩开始和我一起祈祷，这让我们觉得很不舒服，但是我们还是坚持下来了。"我们会好的。"他安慰我道。

以前驾轻就熟的家务活现在要花费两倍的时间。但是这也能看出吉恩多么有耐心。可洗衣服时区分衣服的颜色对我来说几乎不可能了。一天，我匆匆忙忙地把一篮子的衣服扔进洗衣机里，然后吉恩轻轻地建议给他粉色的 T 恤上放点漂白剂。他是多么善解人意啊。

我没有根据菜谱做菜，而是根据我自己的味觉加了一些别的作料。可喜的是，吉恩和儿子们都很喜欢。

几年过去了，回顾我们这几年一起生活的日子，有失去小儿子的痛彻心肺，还有为经济上突如其来的挫折而一筹莫展。生活的每一页我们都妥善保存着，我们用上帝赐予的强大力量和对彼此坚贞不渝的承诺，应对着这些不幸。

在镜子里，我看不到自己的影子，但是在婚姻的镜子中我能看见上帝。在出去工作前，吉恩总是拉着我的手祈祷，身上淡淡的古龙香水味围绕着我，让我安心。当我说："这饭店好冷，不是吗？"一会儿，我感到身上披了件薄毛衣，是吉恩快速溜回车上拿来给我的，他给我披上，轻吻了一下我的脸颊。他总是在我吃完他给我拿来的东西后，第一时间问我："我从沙拉台上再给你拿一盘吧？"这不是一次性的，他至今都对我体贴入微。

我总是胡思乱想。我该怎么回报他无条件的爱呢？我多么渴望我也有机会说："亲爱的，别着急，你在家里休息就好，这些事我会处理。"或者说："换我给你读点东西吧，怎么样？"但是这些想法从未实现过。

有一次，他给我读了很长时间的书，突然停了下来，我便问道："有时候，你会希望你娶的是一个未失明的人吗？"我从来没问过他这个问题，但我还是继续了，"这样你就不用付出这么多了。告诉我实话好吗？"我屏气凝息地等着他的回答。

　　沉默了一会儿后，我听见他把眼镜放在桌子上，他说："实话就是，如果失明的人是我，你为我做的可能比现在我为你做的还要多。我们是一支团结的团队，我们要坚持到最后。"

　　躺在熟睡的丈夫身边，我拽出他的手，挽着他强壮的胳膊。在寂静的深夜里，我思绪万千，感动地流下泪来。听着吉恩有节奏的呼吸声，我为这个男人发出钦佩的叹息，他无视我的失明与丑陋，而是用全部的爱和理解，让我像女王般幸福。

——珍妮特·法勒斯·埃克尔斯

Shaken and Stirred
地震来袭

Love is like an earthquake—unpredictable, a little scary, but when the hard part is over you realize how lucky you truly are.

~Source Unknown

My husband and I needed this vacation on the Big Island of Hawaii. Work back home in Southern California had been hectic for both of us and the hours we'd been putting in meant we had no time for each other. Dinners were fast and on the go, weekends we caught up on paperwork or yard work, and forget about sleeping in late or just cuddling. I couldn't remember the last time we actually held each other longer than a quick kiss on the cheek.

The second morning we were there, we were finally getting into the groove of being on vacation. We looked forward to a drive around the island, stopping at little stores along the way and having lunch at a local restaurant.

"I'm going to shave, then you can have the bathroom," Roger said.

I stood near the floor-to-ceiling windows at the front of our fifth-floor room. "Okay," I replied.

Suddenly, the room started to shake. The windows rattled, the mirror above the dresser banged against its mount, the floor quivered.

"Earthquake!" Roger yelled.

"Oh, my God!" I shouted.

"Come over here, quick."

I ran into his arms and he held me close. So close I almost couldn't breathe. The hotel shook so hard there was no way to get out; the floor and the walls were moving so much we couldn't have walked anywhere. I kept repeating the same thing over and over, "Oh, my God," and surprised myself with how many times I said it. It seemed to go on forever. I was terrified that something would fall on top of us, or the floor would split or the walls would crack. The whole building shook so violently that I thought it would crumble into pieces.

My husband used one arm to hold me tightly to him and the other to shelter my head. I was petrified, but his strength felt comforting. Finally, the violent shaking stopped.

"That was a big one," Roger said. "Let's get outside—there might be aftershocks."

We threw on some shoes, I grabbed my purse, and Roger took the car keys. We ran down the stairs and were barely twenty-five feet from the building when everything started shaking again. We ran as fast as we could to the parking lot.

"What happened?" a woman from Minnesota said.

"An earthquake," a man replied. "The first one was probably more than a 6. The second was an aftershock."

"We're on an island; won't the water rise and drown us?" said another.

"Yeah, what about a tsunami?"

Panic rippled through the crowd. The hotel manager gathered everyone. "We're glad you are all out and safe. Stay here until the hotel is checked for structural damage. We'll let you know when you can go back inside."

Roger and I went to our car and turned on the radio. The news announcer said it was a 6.5 earthquake and a 2.9 aftershock. The epicenter was just six miles away.

"No wonder it was so bad," Roger said. "We were almost on top of it."

The news also said we were not in danger of a tsunami, but that didn't quell the panic rising in the people around us.

"You guys are from California, right?" a man asked with his wife and two children at his side. "We're from Boston. Was this a bad one, or what?"

"Yeah, it was pretty bad. The worst we've ever been in," we replied.

"Would you leave? Will you get out of here?"

"No, we'll stay. If they say it's safe, we'll stay."

We waited in the parking lot, and turned our car on periodically to get updates. Airports were closed and power was out. Two hours later, a ripple of terror filled the air. People started running away from the hotel, up toward the hillside. "Tsunami warning! Get to higher ground!"

We hadn't heard any news of danger, but still it made me nervous. "Should we go higher?" I asked Roger.

"They said no danger of a tsunami." He grabbed my hand and held it tight. "We'll be fine," he reassured me.

Later, they allowed us all back inside. A young girl, walking just behind her parents, commented. "My mom thought we were all going to die." I put my arm around her. She cried quietly.

That afternoon the sun came out. The trade winds caused the palm trees to sway. The hotel put out a free barbecue for all the guests. We sat outside with others, grateful that we had escaped an act of nature that often included a high toll in deaths.

"I'm so glad to be alive," I said.

"Me, too," Roger said. "Do you want to leave when we can get off the island?"

"I don't think so, do you?"

"We have these at home sometimes too, except we're not usually right on top of them. I'm okay here if you're okay."

"As long as we're together, I'm fine."

He reached out his hand for mine and pulled me out of my lounge chair. "Come here," he said. I sat beside him and he put his arms around me.

"I love you," I told him.

"I love you, too."

We stayed, even after the airports re-opened and flights resumed. Many places were boarded up and closed for good, but the only thing that happened to us personally from the shaking was a stirring in our souls. Life is sometimes short. An earthquake can open your eyes to that fact. We came home from our trip with a renewed sense of what is really important in life, and it isn't long hours on the job, though we have to work to pay bills. What's important is taking time out for each other. Now we spend more time hugging, cuddling, and enjoying the quiet, still moments. I wouldn't wish for another earth-shaking experience, but that one did stir a little passion in our souls and re-ignited our love for each other.

~B.J. Taylor

爱就像一场地震——不可预测，稍有惊恐，但是当最艰难的部分
过去之后，你才会真正明白你有多么幸运。

——逸名

我和丈夫十分需要这次在夏威夷大岛上的休假。一回到在南加利福尼亚的家里，我们的工作都会十分繁忙，我们投入工作中过多的时间导致我们没有空闲留给对方。晚餐都是快速而忙碌的，周末的时候我们又会赶着做一些文书或是照看花园，对熬夜毫不介意，有时仅仅是相互抱一下。我都记不起来我们上一次真正拥抱对方是什么时候了，一般都仅仅是快速地亲吻下彼此的脸颊。

我们到这来的第二天，才终于习惯了度假的节奏。我们希望能在岛上开车转一转，途中在某个小店前面停下，在一家当地的饭馆里吃个午饭。

罗杰叫我说："我去刮胡子，你去洗个澡吧。"

我们住在五层，我站在和整面墙一样高的窗户前说："好的。"

突然，房间开始摇晃。窗户咯咯作响，化妆台上面的镜子撞到了底座，砰的一声响，地板也开始颤抖。

罗杰大叫："地震了！"

我惊呼道:"天啊!"

"快到这边来!"

我跑到了他的怀里,罗杰紧紧地拥着我,我几乎都无法呼吸了。旅馆猛烈地摇晃着,想跑出去是不可能了;地板和墙也都剧烈地抖动着,我们一动都不能动。我不停地说:"天啊,天啊。"我自己都惊讶于我怎么一直在重复着这句话。这一切好像不会停止一样。我十分害怕什么东西会从头上砸下来,或者是地板将会裂开,墙壁会倒塌。整幢大楼都在猛烈地摇晃,我以为它会崩毁成碎片。

我的丈夫一手紧紧地拥着我,另一只手盖在我的头上。我吓呆了,但是他的力量使我得到安慰。最终,剧烈的摇晃停止了。

罗杰说:"这次地震不小。我们出去吧,可能还会有余震。"

我们匆忙穿上鞋,我抓起我的钱包,罗杰拿了车钥匙。我们跑下楼梯,在离楼只有 25 英尺的时候,周围又开始摇晃起来。我们拼命地向停车场跑去。

一位来自明尼苏达州的妇女问道:"到底怎么了?"

一个人回答说:"地震了。第一次可能在 6 级以上,第二次是余震。"

另一个人说道:"我们这是在岛上啊,潮水会不会涌起来把我们给淹了?"

"是呀,会不会引发海啸啊?"

恐慌在人群中开始蔓延。旅馆经理把大家召集起来,说:"我们很高兴大家都逃出来了,还很安全。我们正在检查旅馆有没有受到结构性的损坏,在这之前,大家最好待在这里。如果可以回去了,我们会通知大家的。"

我和罗杰走到我们的车里,打开收音机。新闻说刚才发生了 6.5 级的地震和 2.9 级的余震。震中就在 9.6 公里以外。

罗杰说："难怪这么剧烈，我们几乎就在震中的头顶上。"

新闻还说这里没有海啸的危险，但是这并不能缓解人群的恐慌。

那边一个男的带着妻子和两个孩子，他问："你们是从加利福尼亚来的吧？我们是波士顿的。这次地震挺糟糕的吧？"

我们回答道："是呀，相当糟糕，是我们见过的最严重的了。"

"你们想要离开吗？离开这儿？"

"不，我们要待在这儿。如果报告说这里安全的话，我们就留下来。"

我们在停车场等着，不时地把汽车的收音机打开，听听新信息。机场关闭了，电也停了。两小时过去了，周围的气氛更加的恐慌。人们从旅馆跑开，爬上小山丘。"海啸要来了！爬到高的地方去！"

我们没有收听到任何危险警告，但是这仍然让我很害怕。我问罗杰："我们要去高一点的地方吗？"

他抓住我的手，用力握了握，安慰我说："新闻说没有海啸，我们没事的。"

后来，他们让我们都回到旅馆里了。一个小女孩在她父母后面走着，说："我妈妈觉得我们都要死了。"我拥抱着她，她无声地抽泣着。

那天下午太阳出来了。信风吹拂，棕榈树摇曳着。旅馆为所有的旅客准备了一场免费的烤肉。我们和其他人一起坐在露天里，我们十分庆幸我们逃过了一场大自然的灾难，这种灾难通常会造成大量的伤亡。

我说："真庆幸我还活着。"

罗杰说："我也是。如果我们能离开这个岛了，你想走吗？"

"不想，你呢？"

"我们在家里也会遇到这些，只是我们通常不会正好处在震中上方罢了。如果你没问题，我待在这儿也没问题。"

"只要我们在一起，我就可以。"

他向我伸出双臂，把我拉出了躺椅，说："过来。"我坐在他身边，让他的双臂紧紧地拥着我。

我说："我爱你。"

"我也爱你。"

当机场重新开放、航班恢复后，我们仍然待在这儿。很多地方为了保险起见都被封闭了，但是地震带给我们唯一的变化就是，我们的心灵受到了触动。生命有时很短暂。一次地震能让你认清现实。我们旅行归来，意念重生一般，认识到了什么才是生命中真正重要的东西，它不是工作了多长时间，虽然我们不得不工作赚钱。真正重要的是为彼此付出的时间。现在我们会用更多的时间来拥抱、依偎，享受宁静、静止的时刻。我并不希望再来一次地震的体验，但是那一次确实触动了我们的灵魂，重燃了我们对彼此的爱。

——B.J. 泰勒

On the Way to Forever
通向永远的路上

> Soulmates are people who bring out the best in you. They are not perfect but are always perfect for you.
> ~Author Unknown

I once thought that love meant flowers and chocolates from a handsome man in a dashing tuxedo, singing love songs. I was sure that love meant being swept off my feet by someone who thought that I was the most beautiful girl in the world. I was blessed to find exactly that.

My wonderful soulmate appeared in my life when I was not sure what to do with him. I could feel that something was missing—something that school, work, and friends were not providing. When God sent Layne into my life, as clichéd as it sounds, something clicked and I felt whole.

Our courtship was short, but sweet. He took me to fancy restaurants and on carriage rides around the city. He made me lasagna and played "Moonlight Sonata" on the piano. We talked for hours about everything and nothing. I was excited to hear his voice on the phone and counted the hours until I could see him again.

We were married on a cold day in February, surrounded by family and friends. The idea of forever didn't seem like long enough to spend with someone I loved so much, and I can honestly say that on that day, I loved Layne with my whole heart and soul. I couldn't imagine loving him more.

Our first two years of marriage were fun. Sure, we had the usual adjustments, but our lives fit together very well and the time passed quickly. Soon, however, the two of us felt like something was missing.

That something turned out to be three beautiful children who came over the next five years. Our lives had been fun without them, but now they were hectic and crazy, and rich and full at the same time.

Gradually, I began to see how very little I really had loved him on that cold day in February. Granted, I had loved Layne with my whole heart, but something happened on the way to forever—my heart grew by leaps and bounds.

You see, we've experienced our share of trials. We've seen deaths in our families, children in hospitals, and financial struggles. We've faced the everyday battles of too much to do in too little time. Life has happened to us, just as it happens to every family.

Each and every challenge we've overcome—every sickness, every mistake and every tragedy—broke my heart. The funny thing about broken hearts though, is that when they are mended by love, the process of repairing them makes them larger.

Love looks different to me now. Instead of flowers and chocolates, I am swept off my feet when my wonderful husband offers to clean up vomit. I am flattered (and grateful) when he tells me that I'm beautiful even though I'm wearing my cut-off sweats with my hair in a crooked ponytail. And, I've found that he's even more handsome singing lullabies to our babies in his bathrobe than when he used to wear tuxedos and sing love songs to me.

Just like on our wedding day, I can't imagine loving him more than I do today. However, I am wiser now, and I know that growing old together will give me countless opportunities to increase my capacity to love him. I look forward to all of the blessings and even the sorrows inherent in intertwining my life so completely with that of another person.

Suddenly, forever seems like the perfect amount of time to spend with someone I couldn't imagine living without.

~Kimberlee B. Garrett

心心相印的人们能够激发出彼此生命中最好的一面。他们并不完美，但是对彼此来说就是最合适的。

——逸名

我曾经以为爱情就是一个英俊的男人带着鲜花和巧克力、穿着潇洒的燕尾服、唱着爱情歌曲。我确信，爱情意味着一个人认为我是世界上最美丽的女孩，对我佩服得五体投地。上天注定，我会找到那么一个人的。

我那最好的心心相印的人出现在我生命里的时候，我都不知道怎么和他相处。我以前总感觉到缺少了些什么——那些东西是学校、工作和朋友所不能给你的。当老天把莱恩带到我生命中的时候，就像最俗套的那样，什么东西叩响了我的心门，我觉得生命完整了。

我们的恋爱过程很短但是很甜蜜。他带我去高档餐厅，坐着马车环游这个城市。他为我做意大利面，用钢琴弹奏《月光奏鸣曲》。我们一聊几小时，好像什么都聊，又好像什么都没说一样。我在电话里一听到他的声音就兴奋，计算着离我下次见他还有多长时间。

我们在 2 月的一天结婚了，那天天很冷，家人朋友们欢聚一堂。让我与一个我如此爱的人相处，永远这个概念似乎都不够长，我可以坦荡地说，在那天，我爱莱恩，全心全意的爱，用我所有的感情和灵魂爱着他。我觉得自己已经爱他到极致了。

我们结婚的前两年十分有趣。诚然，我们需要一些日常的适应，但是我们的生活十分默契，时间过得很快。然而，不久之后，我们两人都觉得生活中少了点什么。

少了孩子。在接下来的五年里，我们添了三个漂亮的孩子。没有他们，我们的生活也曾经很快乐，但是现在他们的到来使得生活繁忙而疯狂，同时也充实和多彩。

逐渐地我认识到，在那个 2 月寒冷的一天，我对他的爱其实是那么的少。确实，我曾经全身心地爱着莱恩呢，但是在我们走向永远的路上，一些事情发生了——我心的容量也急速地变大了。

要知道，我们共同经历磨难。我们目睹了家人的死亡，经历了孩子生病住院，克服财政危机。我们每天都像在打仗一样，有太多的事情需要做，而时间实在太少。就像每一个家庭一样，生活展现在我们眼前。

每当我们克服一个挑战——每一次生病，每一次错误，每一次灾难——我都会心碎。然而，关于心碎的有趣的事情是，当它被爱修补好之后，修补的过程都会把心的容量变大一些。

现在对我来说，爱不同了。爱不再是鲜花和巧克力了，当我亲爱的丈夫把脏东西清洁干净的时候，我才会对他佩服得五体投地。甚至当我穿着裤腿剪短的运动套装，梳着马尾辫子，他若夸我很美丽，我也会飘飘然，当然还会心存感激。而且，我还发现，当他穿着睡衣，对着我们的孩子唱摇篮曲的时候，是那么帅，比当初他穿着燕尾服对我唱情歌时还要迷人。

　　就像我们结婚那天一样，我觉得今天的我已经爱他到极致了。然而，现在的我更理智了，我知道，在一起变老的时光中，将要给我无数的机会增强我爱他的能力。我期望所有的幸福，甚至生命中固有的悲伤，它们在我的生活中交织，成为完整的生命，让我与另一个人一同分享。

　　突然间，我发现，当我无法想象与另一个人分开时，永远似乎是一个最完美的时间量度，来度量与他在一起的时光。

——金伯里·B.加勒特

第三部分 欢乐篇

Chapter 3
Happily Ever Laughter

Laughter is the shortest distance between two people.
~Victor Borge

欢笑是两个人之间最短的距离。

——维克多·伯奇

Husband Instruction Manual
丈夫使用说明书

Why does a woman work ten years to change a man's habits and then complain that he's not the man she married?

~Barbra Streisand

Congratulations on the acquisition of your brand new 2010 husband. You have chosen the best that modern biology has to offer in the way of life partners. While your 2010 husband is built to last a lifetime, these care and handling instructions will help you get the most out of your man.

Laundry instructions: Although we have implemented many improvements in this year's model (e.g.—automatic toilet seat replacement, limited childcare abilities, expectoration and flatulence control), we have not yet perfected an automatic self-laundering option. Thus, you must repeatedly remind your husband to pick up his dirty clothes, sort his laundry by color, and wash appropriate-sized loads. Some owners have found it easier to simply perform these functions themselves.

Dressing instructions: Most husbands come with only two wardrobe options—work and casual. Therefore please ensure that you assist your husband in any clothing purchases in order to avoid nasty fashion surprises. As in past years, the 2010 husband has pre-set fashion preferences which may clash with your taste. To date, we have yet to perfect an acceptable "color sense" module although the deluxe accessory package does include a formalwear option for occasional use. WARNING: Constant wardrobe monitoring is strongly recommended especially on weekends. Repeated exposure to baggy sweatpants and hole-filled T-shirts may void the warranty.

Cooking instructions: If you chose the deluxe accessory package, you can count on your husband to successfully cook meals on his own for many years to come. The standard model, on the other hand, has few kitchen skills and a limited cuisine. Unless you're willing to invest the time necessary to train your husband in the culinary arts, don't expect much beyond making toast and boiling water. However, all models do come equipped with the outdoor barbecue function.

Listening instructions: Despite years of research, we have not yet been able to produce a husband who really listens. Wives are free to urge their spouses to listen and "express their feelings" but we can offer no guarantees that you will achieve any meaningful results. Through persistent effort, some customers have trained their husbands to adopt a semi-satisfying simulated listening posture.

Fitness instructions: Your 2010 husband is properly proportioned and in good shape. However, in order to retain that shape and those proportions, you must insist on a strict regimen of daily exercise and a healthy diet. Failure to keep your husband active and eating properly will often result in a sluggish spouse with a widening waistline and a sagging seat. WARNING: Do not rely on in-home exercise equipment and always ration beer, pizza, and chips carefully.

Romance instructions: Although the listening capabilities of the 2010 husband are limited, he does possess excellent eyesight. Thus, in order to activate the romance function, emphasize visual stimuli. Sophisticated conversational and emotional skills are still not available on the 2010 husband although our genetic engineers hope to have an improved product ready by the next millennium.

LIMITED WARRANTY: Our 2010 husband is guaranteed against defects in workmanship for ninety (90) days. If, for any reason, you wish to return your husband during the warranty period, we will issue a full refund but only if he is returned in his original packaging. After that, you're on your own.

~David Martin

为什么一个女人会用十年的时间来改变一个男人的习惯，到头来还在抱怨这个男人变了？

——芭芭拉·史翠珊

恭喜你把 2010 新好丈夫收入囊中！在现代生物学所能提供的生活伴侣的方式中，你已经选择了最好的一种。如果你想要你的 2010 好丈夫能持久好用一辈子的话，就要注意下面的注意事项和使用说明了，它们能帮你最大限度地挖掘你丈夫的好处。

洗衣功能使用说明：虽然在今年的丈夫版本中，我们已经做了很多的改进（比如已经可以自动更换马桶座圈、有限的育儿能力，吐痰和肠胃气胀也得到了控制），但我们尚未完善自动洗衣的选项。于是，你必须反复提醒你的丈夫捡起他的脏衣服，然后按照颜色分门别类地放在洗衣房，再选择合适的洗衣机负载量开始洗衣。一些使用者发现，她们自己做这些要容易得多。

穿衣功能使用说明：大部分丈夫的衣柜里只有两种衣服——正式装和休闲装。因此，在你的丈夫添置任何衣物时，请确保都要帮助他，以避免出现可怕的风格混搭。在过去几年中，2010 丈夫已经预先设置了风格偏向，这可能与您的品位相冲突。至今，我们还没能完善一个可以普遍接受的"色彩感觉"模块，虽然豪华套装的附件包中包含了偶尔可以使用的正装选项。警告：要经常监测他的衣柜，特别是在周末的时候！让他经常穿松松垮垮的运动裤和都是洞洞的 T 恤可能会导致保修失效。

厨艺功能使用说明：如果你选择了豪华套装的附件包，在几年之后，你可以指望你的丈夫自己成功地做出一顿饭来。另一方面，至于标准模式，几乎没有包括厨房技能，烹饪知识也十分有限。除非你愿意花费必要的时间，来训练你丈夫的厨艺，否则除了烤个面包烧个水外，不要指望太多。然而，所有的版本都装配了户外烤肉的功能。

倾听功能使用说明：尽管经年累月地研究，但是我们仍不能开发出能够真正倾听的丈夫。妻子大可以督促她的丈夫来听她说话，并且"表达他们的感受"，但是我们不能保证你能得到任何有意义的结果。通过不懈地努力，部分客户已经训练她们的丈夫采用了一种半满意的模拟聆听状态。

健康状态使用说明：你的 2010 丈夫是完全体态匀称、身形健美的。然而，为了让他们保持体形，你必须坚持严格的日常锻炼的生活规律，并且饮食健康。如果不能让你的丈夫坚持运动和适当饮食，通常将会导致他变得懒惰、腰围变大、臀部下垂。警告：不要指望室内运动器械，对于啤酒、比萨、薯条等一定要严格地限量供应。

浪漫模式使用说明：虽然 2010 丈夫的倾听功能有限，但是他的视力良好。所以，为了激活浪漫功能，要强调视觉刺激。2010 丈夫仍然不具备复杂的对话和情感技能，我们的基因工程师希望在下一个千年，能够推出改良的新产品。

有限质量保证：在工艺上，我们的 2010 丈夫 90 天内保证无瑕疵。无论何种原因，您若要求在保质期内退货，只要包装尚未拆毁，我们将全额退款。保质期过后，概不负责。

——大卫·马丁

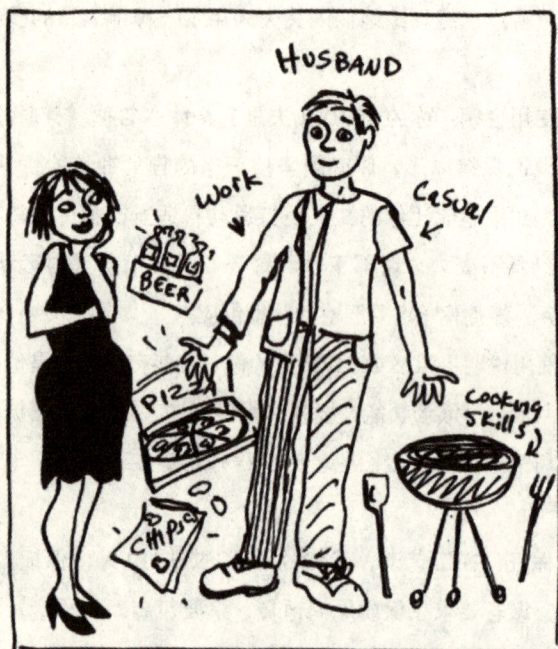

"新版丈夫的好处在于：他可能并不完美，但他是我的！"

Married to a Metrosexual
嫁给都市中性男

We cannot really love anybody with whom we never laugh.
~Agnes Repplier

I still remember vividly my first date with my husband. He showed up on my doorstep wearing a black silk suit with elegant lace-up shoes and took me to see a jazz pianist. Before that, I'd mostly dated sloppy, preppy types clad in faded Izod shirts, whose musical tastes ran to Dire Straits and Warren Zevon. So it was a bit of an adjustment to be seen with a man who openly sported a thumb ring and was known to purchase the odd facial product.

Over time, however (fifteen years to be precise), I've come to terms with the fact that I'm married to a metrosexual. But it hasn't been easy.

Take a recent incident in a sporting goods store. We were on a trip back to New Jersey from our current home in London when my husband decided to buy himself a new outfit for power yoga.

"What do you think?" he asked the proprietor,

emerging from the dressing room in a pair of form-fitting yoga pants.

The small, muscular man looked away awkwardly. "I... um... I think those are meant for... the, uh... ladies."

Even my otherwise soigné husband felt sufficiently chagrined that he opted for the less well-fitting Men's Medium over said Women's Large. But not without second-guessing himself the entire next week.

"They did fit better," he kept insisting.

"Was it the panty-liner that got you?" I wanted to ask.

According to Wikipedia, "metrosexual" is "...a neologism generally applied to heterosexual men with a strong concern for their appearance, or whose lifestyle displays attributes stereotypically seen among gay men." In the self-editing spirit of Wikipedia, allow me to offer some empirical data to flesh this definition out.

First: "a strong concern for their appearance." Absolutely. At one point, back when we lived in Chicago, my husband even had a personal shopper. This man—I think his name was Oscar—would leave messages for my husband inviting him to "Men's Night" at the local Marshall Field's. He'd invariably come home with all these tight-fitting ribbed sweaters à la Will of Will and Grace (prompting me to question whether Oscar's interest in my husband's look was entirely commercial). And, yes, in case you're wondering, my husband has experimented with cologne (he didn't inhale).

The second defining element of the metrosexual is a taste for the finer things in life. The first time they met, my husband described the wine as "grassy" to my father (who grew up in Newark and was thus more familiar with Pabst than Pinot Noir). More recently, when we were trying to remember the name of a certain *chocolatier* in Paris, my husband told me to go into his Outlook folder and search for the "Dark Chocolate" entry. It goes without saying that we only drink espresso in our home. Indeed, we've been together so long that it didn't strike me as odd when he recently e-mailed me a video about the optimal way to froth milk. And did I mention the yoga?

Finally, the metrosexual has an avowed fondness for gadgets. The $1,200 espresso machine and matching grinder are perhaps the most visible expression of this trait in our home. But my husband is forever reading catalogs from places like Levenger's, rendering us the proud owners of (to list a few): that magical thing that holds your bagel in place while you slice it in half… that essential stand that props your newspaper up so you can read one column at a time... and that miniature razor blade that cuts newspaper clippings without having to use scissors. While emptying our suitcases after our recent forage through Target, I was not at all surprised to discover a device that doubled as an avocado scooper and slicer. Because you never know when you'll need one of those….

To be sure, there are some advantages to having a husband who isn't—in the vernacular of my adopted country—terribly "bloke-ish." For starters, I have my very own live-in fashion consultant. My husband's well-honed Euro-sensibilities mean that whatever I'm wearing is also subject to his critical eye: "You really shouldn't do high-waisted," he'll observe as I come downstairs in a pair of shorts that extends a centimeter above my navel. Or "Oh no! Eggplant is definitely not your color." And though I'm often loathe to admit it, he's invariably right. I think I'm the only woman I know who's shopped for bras with her husband. (The owner of the bra shop thought he was a pervert, but no matter...)

Second, I've also picked up some really useful skills along the way. Formerly a Mr. Coffee kind of gal, I can now tamp an espresso with the best of them. In a city like London, where a cappuccino can easily set you back five bucks, it's highly cost-effective to be able to rival the best brews on High Street. And how many people do you know who can scoop and slice an avocado in one seamless gesture?

Finally, what other guy would be willing to watch all those Merchant and Ivory films with me?

Mostly, however, I revel in the nuances that my husband's unabashed metrosexuality affords. Jung famously suggested that all men harbor an inner feminine figure in their unconscious. I like to think that my children benefit from having a dad who's more in touch than the average Joe with his inner Josephine. My son, in particular, knows that it's okay to play the violin and enjoy museums, and that you don't have to give up those interests just because you also like soccer. And in a world where we make all sorts of gender-based stereotypes—some with profound consequences for public policy—I'm proud to have a husband who defies easy labeling. Finally, how cool is it that more than a decade into our marriage—yoga pants notwithstanding—I still find myself agreeing with the gay office intern who once confided to me that my husband was "hot"?

Would you care for an espresso?

~Delia Lloyd

若那个人都不能逗我一笑，那我肯定不爱他。
——艾格尼丝·雷普利尔

　　我和丈夫第一次约会时的情景至今仍历历在目。他穿着一件黑色的丝绸西装，优雅地踩着系带的鞋子，出现在我家门口，带我去看了一场爵士钢琴演奏。在那之前，我的约会对象大多是懒散的、穿得像大学预科生似的类型，他们穿着退色的艾佐德（"IZOD"，艾佐德是一个著名的美国男士休闲服装品牌。其消费群体主要是 25~45 岁的喜欢运动的上班族）衬衫，音乐品位停留在恐怖海峡（一支英国摇滚乐队，于 1976 年组建于伦敦西南部的代特福德，活跃于 1977 至 1995 年期间。他们是自 20 世纪 70 年代以来最成功的摇滚组合之一，在全世界销售了近 2000 万张唱片）和沃伦·泽方（出生于 1947 年 1 月 24 日，因癌症卒于 2003 年 9 月 7 日，是一名民谣歌手。沃伦的歌曲以辛辣的讽刺和嘲弄出名）的水平。有些男人会大方炫耀戴着的拇指环，还去买奇奇怪怪的面部护理产品，若别人看见你和这样一个男人约会，你还真需要一点适应的过程。

然而，时间久了（准确地说是 15 年之后），我承认了这个事实，那就是我嫁给了一个都市中性男。但是，这真不容易。

比如，最近在运动用品店里就发生了一件事。我们现在住在伦敦（是位于加拿大安大略省西南部的一座城市，离安大略省首府多伦多不远。加拿大著名的西安大略大学就位于这座城市。注意：不是英国的伦敦），在我们回新泽西（美国东部的一个州，是美国第四小以及人口密度最高的州）的路上，我丈夫决定给自己买一套练习力量瑜伽的新装备。

他从试衣间出来，穿着一条紧身的瑜伽裤，问老板道："你觉得怎么样？"

这个矮小健壮的老板尴尬地把目光移开，说："我觉得……嗯……这是……女式的衣服。"

他后来选择了不是那么合适的男式中号，而不是想要的女式大号，对此，我那一向优雅的丈夫感到十分失望。但是在接下来的整整一周里，他不止一次地事后评论。

他坚持说："那款更适合我。"

我真想问他："你是说那款女式底裤吗？"

根据维基百科的说法，"都市中性男"是"一个新名词，用于形容特别关注自己外表的异性恋男人，或者说这类人的生活方式在典型的同性恋男人中更为常见"。基于维基百科的自我编辑的精神，我可以提供一些由经验而来的资料，使这条定义更加丰满。

第一，"特别关注自己的外表"。绝对是这样。当我们居住在芝加哥的时候，曾经一度我丈夫有一名私人代购师。我记得这个人叫奥斯卡——会给我丈夫留言，邀请他去参加当地的马歇尔·菲尔德（2010年世界十大富翁第七名，内战期间创立马歇尔百货商店，"顾客就是上帝"即为他的名言）的商店举办的"男人之夜"。他总是会带着一大堆紧身带棱纹的毛衣回家，就像《威尔和格雷斯》（是美国首部由有线电视播出的引入"同志"题材的情景喜剧，也是非常成功的一部剧集，其中两位主角都是"同志"）里的威尔（主角之一，男同性恋）一样（这使我怀疑是否全都是由于商业利益的驱使，才使得奥斯卡对于打扮我丈夫这么兴致盎然）。而且，你肯定想知道，是的，我丈夫使用古龙水（但他从不吸入）。

都市中性男定义的第二个因素是：对生活中美好事物的品位。我丈夫第一次和我爸爸见面时，他形容喝的酒味道"就像草一样"。我爸爸在纽瓦克长大，他对帕布斯特（美国著名啤酒品牌）要比对黑皮诺葡萄酒（法国勃艮地产区红葡萄酒的唯一品种，全世界没有其他品种像黑皮诺这样难侍候，是名贵红酒用葡萄的皇后。其酒体温柔清雅，其特点是年轻时清雅芳香，成熟时温柔雅致，果味充盈而复合，并带有较明显的草莓和樱桃的香气。是公认难以栽植的葡萄品种）熟悉得多。就在最近，当我们试图记住巴黎的一种巧克力的名字的时候，我丈夫让我进入他的Outlook文件夹，搜索"黑巧克力"，然后进入文件夹。不用说，在我家只喝意式咖啡。实际上，由于我们在一起这么久了，当他最近用邮件发给我一个视频，教我们做牛奶泡沫的最佳方法，我也就见怪不怪了。对了，我提到瑜伽了吗？

最后，都市中性男都会有一个小玩意儿来宣告他的嗜好。在我们家里，这一特征最明显的表现可能就是他那1200美元的意式咖啡机和与之相配的研磨器。但是我的丈夫永远都会阅读从路上收到的产品目录，比如Levenger（美国家具、办公用品品牌）的目录，它会使我们这些购买者骄傲地觉得（以下仅列几项为例）：在你想把百吉饼切成两半的时候，那个神奇的工具可以把它固定在合适的位置……那个支架真的很有必要，因为它可以把你的报纸支撑起来，那样你就能每次读一栏了……那个微型刀片可以用来切割剪报，这样就不用剪刀了。所以，当最近有一次，我们野外活动，完成了一次搜索粮草的任务之后，我清空行李包时，发现了一个既可以做挖鳄梨的勺子也可以做切片器用的工具时，我就一点也不惊奇了。因为你永远也不会知道，也许什么时候你就需要这么个工具了……

的确，有一个不是那么特别——用我所寄居的国家的方言来说——"浑蛋"的丈夫，也是有些好处的。对于一个初学者来说，我在家里就有一个自己的时尚顾问。我丈夫有着精心磨炼出来的欧洲式的审美观，那就是说无论我穿什么，都要屈服于他挑剔的眼光。若我穿了一条腰部高出肚脐一厘米的短裤走下楼来，他会评论说："你真不应该穿高腰的衣服。"或者会说："哦！不！你绝对不适合黑紫色。"虽然，我通常不愿意承认，但他总是对的。我想在我所认识的人里面，我是唯一一个会和丈夫一起去买文胸的女人。（文胸店的老板觉得他是个色狼，但是无所谓啦……）

第二，在这一过程中，我确实也学到了一些有用的技能。我以前是一个只喝"咖啡先生"（美国一个咖啡联营店）的女孩，我现在能够压榨制作出最好的意式咖啡。在像伦敦这样的城市里，一杯卡布奇诺都能轻易卖到 5 美元，如果你做的咖啡能和商业街中最好的饮料一较高下，这是相当划算的。又有多少人可以用一种不变的姿势挖空一个鳄梨，再把它切片呢？

最后，其他人谁会愿意陪我看完所有的那些商人象牙生产（1961 年创办的影片公司，该公司影片的最初目标是："在印度拍英文电影，瞄准国际市场"，但是后来在英国和美国拍摄了很多电影。该公司的影片有一种特殊的风格，其全盛时期是 20 世纪 80 年代和 90 年代，以豪华的背景刻画悲剧中人物的纠结和觉醒，多采用高级英国演员）的电影呢？

然而，在大部分的时间里，对于我丈夫不加掩饰的都市中性男所带来的微妙之处，我都陶醉其中。荣格有一段著名的论断，即所有男人在无意识中，都藏匿着一个内在的女性形象。我很高兴地认为，我的孩子与他们父亲的接触比其他人得到的更多，孩子们从中受益良多，在他们的心中藏着一颗约瑟芬的心。尤其是我的儿子，他知道他可以去玩小提琴，也可以去欣赏博物馆，他完全没有必要仅仅因为也喜欢足球而放弃这些兴趣。在这个世界上，我们有各种基于性别的刻板形象——一些来自于社会政策带来的深刻影响——我很骄傲我的丈夫公然藐视这样的标签。最后，曾经有一个办公室的同性恋实习生偷偷地告诉我，我的丈夫很"热辣"，在我们结婚超过 10 年之后，我仍然同意他的话——尽管还是存在瑜伽裤的问题——但是，这样多酷啊！

你会在乎一杯意式咖啡吗？

——迪莉娅·劳埃德

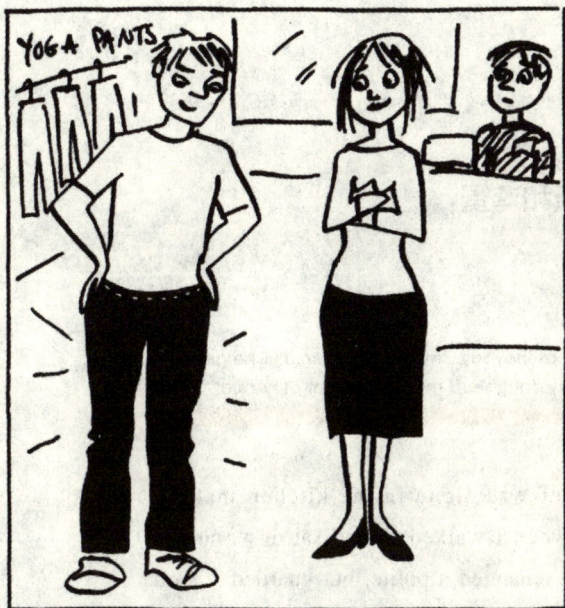

"They may be meant for the ladies, but I think I'm man enough to carry them off!"

"这可能是女款的，但我想我完全有勇气穿！"

Dolores and the Eggs
德洛里斯和鸡蛋

You know what they say: "My son's my son until he gets him a wife, but my daughter's my daughter all of her life."

~Stanley Banks in Father of the Bride

Dolores was alone in the kitchen making breakfast when I walked in and sat down at the table. We exchanged a polite, but guarded "Good morning," and I watched her as she huddled over the stove. She was frying the eggs, so I concluded the tears I saw suddenly welling in her eyes were not from chopping onions for an omelet.

My future mother-in-law had met me for the first time the night before. I had recently arrived back in the States following two and a half years vagabonding throughout Europe after graduating college in 1971. It was the thing to do back then, and I arrived at her home sporting the typical regalia of those wandering times: shoulder-length hair, a full beard and absolutely no prospects for the future, other than a decision to marry Dolores' only daughter Denise, whom I had met while traveling.

That news had preceded my arrival, and I could immediately discern that my overall appearance had done nothing to soften the cold shock of that original announcement.

I watched her focusing in on that frying pan like it was an air traffic controller's screen. She was attempting to conceal her tears, but wasn't doing a very good job of it.

"Are those tears about me?" I asked. She nodded affirmatively.

"Is it because I'm marrying your daughter?" Her affirmation was again quickly forthcoming.

"And you're afraid I won't be committed to the marriage?" Her less-than-reluctant nod confirmed I was three-for-three. I admired her honesty, and I'd like to think she admired me for diving right into those eggs of hers without having her daughter taste them first.

Over the years my commitment to my marriage took on less significance in my mother-in-law's eyes than some of my decision-making within its confines. Like the time I had quit my first job as a bank teller, without another job waiting in the wings. That my decision had been driven by a third armed robbery in less than a year at the bank seemed little justification compared to suddenly exposing her daughter to a husband without means. Or my hesitancy over having children. Or the time I had decided to buy our first house in a section of South Philadelphia that had not as yet shown any signs of "coming back" demographically speaking. Or the time I decided to take a job in far upstate New York, thus banishing her only daughter and now beloved twin grandchildren to the American Siberia. By then I am sure my continued commitment to the marriage had become a lot less important from her perspective. That the house I bought there was "old, run down and ugly" according to my father-in-law probably was more than enough to convince Dolores that I would provide only the bad things enumerated in the marriage vows (i.e., poorer, sickness, death).

But while Dolores could not hide her feelings about me (there was a certain wordless gaze she could cast my way as if she were looking toward a distant hill, one containing perhaps a silhouette of a hanging tree) she always kept her own counsel. In every way, she comported herself as the ideal mother-in-law, never meddling or intruding in her daughter's marriage—except perhaps the occasional early nudge about children, which I ultimately and manfully assisted in providing. After becoming a parent to adult daughters myself, I could look back and understand better the train wreck she thought I'd turn out to be. I have the highest admiration for her. And she was the absolute best grandmother you could ever hope to have for your children.

Some years later, I accepted a transfer to more hospitable climes in Atlanta. On what turned out to be our last destination Dolores would be alive to see, she visited us in our new home. It was a bright, modern colonial with aluminum siding and a patio deck that looked out to a private golf course. South Philly and northern New York State it was not. I admitted to Dolores one afternoon that I had finally bought a house her daughter considered a dream home. Dolores fixed what had become that recognizable gaze of judgment and execution, but this time that familiar gaze came with words.

"And it's about time!" she exclaimed with a special emphasis that seemed to echo back through all the previous years to that initial meeting in her kitchen.

Dolores passed away in that dream home of her daughter's during one of those Atlanta visits. Maybe she felt her work of protectress had been completed at long last, and she could trust me to do the right thing from there on in. From many perspectives, Dolores had died too soon, but from the point of view of trusting me to do the right thing, it may have been the most untimely of those perspectives. There followed two questionable and unfulfilling moves out to the Midwest, before the sensible one of returning her daughter to the Philadelphia area finally took place. But even with that, there was one more twist of fate that I'm certain would have made her rue her decision not to put something in those eggs back when she had had the chance.

A friend once described my decision to leave the relative security of the corporate world to become a fulltime writer as "courageous and foolish." The decision still bounces back and forth between those two poles. After ten years, there are still many afternoons when I am pacing the floors of my home, anxiously awaiting the arrival of a freelance check in the day's mail needed to pay bills that are due. I swear at those times I can sense a stirring in my mother-in-law's grave. It makes me think she is somehow maintaining a presence that prevents even more foolish decisions.

As a precaution, though, I insist on making my own eggs to this day. For there are times when Dolores's daughter, who over the years has transformed her mother's distant gaze into something that can only be described as The Look, suggests that it is probably a wise course of action to take.

~Reid Champagne

你一定知道一句话：“当我的儿子结婚了，他就不是我的儿子了，但是我的女儿永远都是我的女儿。”

——斯坦利·班克斯，《新岳父大人》

　　当我进来在桌边坐下的时候，德洛里斯正一个人在厨房里做早餐。我们相视一笑，礼貌而又拘谨，互相问候道：“早上好。”她在炉子前忙活的时候，我看着她，她突然间热泪盈眶。她正在煎鸡蛋，那么我肯定这眼泪不是因为切要放在煎

Chapter 3 Happily Ever Laughter
第三部分 欢乐篇

蛋卷里的洋葱而流的。

那是我初次见到我的岳母的第二天早上。在1971年大学毕业之后，我在欧洲漂泊了两年半的时间，那时才回到美国。这都是当年的事情了，那时，当我到她家门口的时候，我像一个典型的流浪汉那样打扮夸张：披肩长发、络腮胡子，对未来完全没有期望，只有一个愿望，那就是娶她唯一的女儿丹妮丝。我和丹妮丝是在一次旅行中认识的。我要和她结婚的消息已经先一步传来了，本来消息传来时已经使众人震惊了。现在，我立即察觉到我出现时的打扮完全没能缓解这份震惊。

我发现她盯着煎锅发呆，就好像那是一个空中飞行器的操作屏幕一样。她试着不让我发现她哭了，但是毫无作用。

我问她："你是因为我哭的吗？"她点点头。

"是因为我要娶你女儿了吗？"她再次表示肯定。

"你怕我对这份婚姻不负责任？"她不太情愿地又一次承认了。我三次都猜对了。我欣赏她的坦诚，我也愿意相信，当她先把煎鸡蛋盛给我吃，而不是先让她的女儿尝一尝，那是因为她喜欢我。

很多年过去了，在我岳母的眼里，我对婚姻的承诺远比不上我的几次决定带来的影响大。就像那次，我辞去了银行出纳的工作，但又没有下一份工作可做。那是由于不到一年的时间里，我所在的银行遭到了三次武装抢劫。但这与我的岳母突然间要把她的女儿嫁给一个一无所有的丈夫相比，就显得毫无道理了。或者是那次，我决定在费城南部买我们的首套房子，并且没有任何迹象表明我们还会回来住。又或者是那一次，我决定到遥远的纽约北部去工作，那就意味着会把她唯一的女儿和两个宝贝外孙也带到"美国的西伯利亚"去。从那时起，我就知道，在她的眼里，我对婚姻持久的承诺变得不那么重要了。按我岳父的说法，我买的那套房子是"很旧，快要拆了，又难看"，似乎用来向德洛里斯证明：我只能绰绰有余地提供婚姻誓词中不好的方面（比如贫穷、疾病和死亡）。

但是，现在德洛里斯似乎不能再隐藏她对我的想法了（她向我的方向投来了无声的凝视，就好像她在凝望远山，远山上可能有一株摇摇欲坠的大树的剪影），虽然她一直都掩饰得很好。在各个方面，她都表现得像一个完美的岳母那样，从来不介入或侵扰她女儿的婚姻生活。在我自己的女儿长大成人之后，回想起来，我可以更好地理解她了，她把她女儿当初和我在火车上的相遇看似一场灾难。我非常地尊敬她。她可以说是我所遇见过的孩子们最好的外祖母了。

一些年之后，我们移居到了亚特兰大，那里有更适宜的环境。她来这儿看我们的新家，后来证明，这是德洛里斯生前看到的最后一处我们的住所。那是一所明亮现代的房子，有铝制的墙板和一个大平台，从平台上可以看到一个私人的高尔夫球场。费城南部和纽约北部都没有这样的条件。一天下午，我向德洛里斯承认，我终于买了一所她女儿认为是梦幻般的房子。德洛里斯用那种我熟悉的评判和苛责的眼神看着我，但是这次，她说话了。

"这都多少年了！"她强调说，就好像是为了和很多年前，我和她在她家厨房里的初次见面时所说的话相对应一样。

德洛里斯在一次来亚特兰大拜访时，在她女儿所认为的梦幻般的房子里去世了。也许她认为保护女儿的职责终于完成了，从那时起，她可以信任我会做正确的事情了。从很多方面看来，德洛里斯去世得太早了，但是从她选择信任我这一点来看，上面的观点就显得不合时宜了。在她想实施她认为理智的决定，即把她的女儿带回费城之前，我已经作了两次让人质疑的和显得不那么可靠的决定，即迁移到中西部地区去。但是即使这样，命运还是发生了不止一次的转变。在她有机会把女儿带回去的时候，我就表明如果她那么做的话，她会后悔的。

对于我离开相对安稳的公司，而去选择当一名职业作家的时候，我的一个朋友曾经形容我是"勇气可嘉，行为愚蠢"。我的决定也一直在这两种极端之间犹豫不决。十年之后，仍然有很多个下午我在家里走来走去，焦急地等待着作为一名自由作家的稿费寄来，好让我及时付了账单。我发誓，在那种时候，我甚至能感受得到我的岳母在天堂仍对我愤愤不满。这使我认为，她仍然存在在我们周围，防止我作一些更加愚蠢的决定。

然而，为了以备万一，我坚持自己煎鸡蛋吃。有好几次，德洛里斯的女儿都建议现在采取些行动是一个明智之举，这么多年来，她已经继承了她妈妈向远方凝望的神情，这种神情只能被形容为"在凝望"。

——里德·尚帕涅

More than Words
言语之外

> Are we not like two volumes of one book?
> ~Marceline Desbordes-Valmore

Last week, my husband Bob and I celebrated our twenty-fifth wedding anniversary. I think one of the reasons our marriage works is because we speak so well in silence.

Recently we were at a brunch where an obnoxious fellow was spouting about politics. Bob and I sat across the table from each other. With just a glance, we communicated, "Yuck, yuck and... did I say yuck?" We continued this conversation, neither of us saying one word out loud.

"Can we go now?" Bob asked with a look I know so well.

I poured him some wine. "Not yet," that signaled.

"Get us out of here," he pleaded with his eyes.

I sat next to him. "I'm thinking! I'm thinking!" I said silently.

He coughed. I took his hand, which meant,

"Don't do the flu thing. Everybody always knows you're faking."

He squeezed my hand. "Say you have a female problem. No one will ask you about it," I could tell he was saying.

I squeezed back. "I had that last month. If I say it again, people will begin to think I'm icky."

He touched his upper lip, which told me, "There's a white glop of clam dip stuck to your face." I wiped it off and nodded silently, "Thanks."

I get nervous at parties. Okay, I get nervous everywhere. But at one holiday gathering of writers, I forced myself to talk to a woman who intimidated me. Fortunately Bob was behind me. And our silent communication really mattered. "I loved your story," I said to her. From behind, Bob could see that I had my velvet blouse tucked—not into my velvet slacks—but into the panty hose which were much higher on my waist than the slacks. It wasn't pretty.

He sidled up next to me and made darting motions with his eyes, in the direction of my panty hose. "Not here," I said without words. "Are you perverted or what?"

He put his arm around me, looked down at my questioning face and quickly untucked my blouse from my hose. I smiled gratefully up at him. "Could you check my hair for toilet paper?" he heard me think. "Last year there was that piece on my head. I still can't figure out how it got there."

He looked down at me. "You are so unsophisticated. I love that part of you," he was thinking.

"I am sophisticated," I wordlessly replied while spreading a chunk of Brie on a cracker with my fingers.

And so, for our twenty-fifth anniversary, I had a pal from Indiana overnight a dozen Krispy Kreme donuts for Bob. They're not for sale where we live.

That floored him. But get this. He handmade a sampler for me. On it, he embroidered the words to our favorite song, "I'll be loving you… always." It's the most beautiful cross-stitch sampler you could imagine.

But I'll tell you. If the sampler had no words on it, I would have known what he meant to say. And when it comes to what makes a relationship work, I think that's it. A compassionate awareness of how the other feels. Bob's warm touch when I'm scared, for seemingly no reason, in the night. A leap into his arms when a story I've written gets accepted by a publication. A "keep trying" hug when my next ten stories get rejected. An "it doesn't matter" shrug when I am terribly embarrassed because of something I should or shouldn't have said at a party.

Silent communication. I bet we all do this a dozen times a day. But with someone we love, I think that moments like these are what matter the most. Because they mean more than words can ever say.

~Saralee Perel

我们不正像是一本书的上下册吗？

——玛瑟琳·德博尔德·瓦尔莫

上个星期，我和丈夫鲍勃庆祝我们的 25 周年结婚纪念日。我觉得我们的婚姻如此和谐的一个原因就是我们不用说话也可以沟通得很好。

我们最近有一次去吃早午餐，那儿有一个可恶的家伙在滔滔不绝地评论时政。我和鲍勃坐在桌子的对面。我们只需对视一眼，就交流了意见：

"呸，呸……我说呸了吗？"我们继续这种对话，两个人都没有大声说一个字。

鲍勃给我个眼神，我非常了解，他想说："我们可以走了吧？"

我给他倒了一杯酒，那是一个信号，意思是："再待会儿。"

他用眼神恳求说："我们出去吧。"

我坐在他的旁边，无声地说："我考虑一下，考虑一下啊。"

他大声咳嗽，我握了握他的手，意味着："别在那儿装感冒，谁都看得出来你是装的。"

他捏了一下我的手，我能感觉得到他在说："就说你不舒服，女人的那点事儿，没人会细问你的。"

我捏了回去，意思是："我上个月已经说过一次了。如果我再这么说的话，大家就会觉得我讨厌了。"

他摸了摸他的上嘴唇，这是告诉我："这儿有一个白色的黏糊糊的蛤蜊酱汁沾在你脸上。"我擦了擦，默默地点点头，那是说："谢了。"

在聚会上我会很紧张。好吧，我在哪儿都会紧张。但是在一次作家的假日聚会上，我强迫自己和一个对我很亲热的女作家谈话。幸运的是，鲍勃在我身后。我们无声的沟通真的很管用。我对她说："我真喜欢你的小说。"在我身后，鲍勃看见我的天鹅绒衬衫打褶了——没有塞到我的外面的宽松裤里，而是塞到了我的长筒裤袜里，那条裤袜提到了我的腰部，比宽松裤要高很多。这样很不得体。

他悄悄地走到我的旁边，目光飞了过来，看向我的裤袜。我悄悄地说："别看那儿，你是色狼吗？"

他用胳膊搂起我，看着我一脸的疑问，迅速地把我的衬衫从裤袜里拉了出来。我对他感激地一笑。他仿佛能听见我说："你给我检查检查头发吧，看看上面有没有厕纸啊？去年就有一片粘到了我的头上。我至今都不知道到底是怎么粘上去的。"

他俯视着我，在想着："你怎么这么单纯呢，我就喜欢你这一面。"

我一边把一大块乳酪抹在我的饼干上，一边无声地抗议："我才不单纯呢。"

在我们 25 周年纪念日的时候，我一个朋友突然从印第安纳州寄来了一大堆饼干和甜甜圈给鲍勃。在我们住的地方这些没有卖。

这使鲍勃很吃惊。但是为了以示报答。他亲手给我做了一个刺绣的花样。他在上面镶嵌了我们最喜欢的歌词："我将永远爱你。"这是你所能想象的最精美的十字绣了。

但是我告诉你，如果这幅十字绣上什么也没写，我也知道他就是这个意思。若要我说是什么让我们如此相爱，我觉得就是这个：总是为对方着想，知道对方的感受。当我在晚上害怕时，似乎毫无理由的，鲍勃就会温柔地抚摸我。在我连续十篇小说被拒绝了之后，他会给我一个"继续加油"的拥抱。若在一个派对上，我说了什么不该说的话，或者是在该说什么的时候没有说，在我特别尴尬的时候，他会对我耸耸肩，这代表"没事的"。

无声的交流，我打赌我们每天都会有十几次。但是和我爱的人在一起，我觉得这些时刻就是最重要的时刻。因为它所代表的不是言语所能表达的。

——莎莉·佩雷尔

"Sometimes we don't need words to get our point across... because love is the perfect communicator!"

"有些时候，我们并不需要语言来表达……因为爱是最好的交流！"

One of Those Mornings
那些天早上

Flowers grow out of dark moments.
~Corita Kent

The irritating buzz of the alarm dragged me from my dreams. I stretched my arm from beneath the covers to silence it. My fumbling fingers found the snooze button, pressed and then recoiled in shock at the feel of the frigid plastic. "Oh no," I groaned, "not again!"

Rolling on to my side I hauled the covers higher on my shoulder, pressed up against my wife, Carol, and kissed her awake. The radio clicked on and the local station's morning man confirmed my fear. Overnight, the temperature in Orillia had plummeted to a record thirty degrees below zero. This would be, "one of those mornings."

As newlyweds, Carol and I had overcome many challenges, not the least of them learning to work together to cope with rural life in Canada's mid-north. One of the toughest tests of our love was surviving our first winter in the wilds. It was mid-February 1970 and I was teaching in a nearby town. Although we were eager to move to the heart of Ontario's "cottage country," like most young couples Carol and I were long on ambition and short on cash. However, we had managed to scrape together a down payment and over Christmas break we abandoned our comfortable city apartment and took up residence in a very old cottage on the shore of Lake Couchiching.

Although idyllic in the summer, our new home was isolated and ill-suited to winter occupancy. We had managed to install an indoor toilet and a bathtub, but the conditions were still spartan. A tiny acorn fireplace and temperamental old oil stove were our only sources of heat and there was no insulation, so frozen pipes and drains were a common and frustrating occurrence in our frigid abode. We prided ourselves on our ability to cope. Outfitted in arctic boots and one-piece snowsuits, we spent that first winter shoveling tons of snow, splitting forests of wood, and on really cold mornings using a hair dryer to thaw our frozen plumbing. Our love was tested and grew stronger as we battled the elements together, coming to grips daily with the rigors of rural living. However, it seemed that this morning would provide us with our toughest test yet.

We had awakened in a freezer! The minus-thirty degree temperature had jellied the stove oil, cutting the flow of fuel to the space heater, and I knew our water lines would be frozen. It would have been a perfect day to stay in bed; however, as a probationary teacher, I just had to get to school.

I tested the temperature with a puff of breath over the edge of the bedspread, and watched in horror as a vapourous cloud rose toward the ceiling. Bracing myself, I flipped the covers off and leaped to the floor. The icy cold of the linoleum seared my naked feet as, like a novice firewalker, I danced my way down the hallway to the oil heater. I opened the reserve tank, struck a match and thankfully the flame caught.

Fortunately the pipes in the bathroom had not split and after some carefully applied heat from the blow dryer, hot water steamed from the bathtub spout. As I settled thankfully into the wonderful warmth of the water, I heard some thumping from the front room. Carol must have risen to begin her chores. After thawing the kitchen taps, she would leave them running to flush the system and she would use her trusty hatchet to split kindling for the fireplace.

"What a team!" I thought, as I lay in the bath, unaware of the drama unfolding in the kitchen.

Although the kitchen taps had thawed, the sink's drain was still frozen. The water running in was not running out. The sink soon overflowed and water began splashing onto the super-cooled surface of the linoleum floor. Distracted, Carol turned her attention away from her task, just as the hatchet was descending. Her shriek of pain split the arctic air.

Galvanized, I leaped from the tub, water streaming from my body as I rushed to her rescue. When I reached the front room, I was confronted by a grisly scene.

My mate was seated in front of the fireplace, left hand clutched in her right, blood seeping from between her fingers and dripping on to the hearth.

She was crying, "I cut my finger off! I cut my finger off!"

With my attention focused on Carol, I failed to spot the danger awaiting me and stepped, naked and unprepared, firmly onto the slick icy floor of the kitchen. My feet flew out from underneath me; I crashed down butt first in the slush, slid wildly across the room, and slammed into the wall. By the time my head cleared, Carol was alternating between sobbing in pain and laughing at me.

Still, it was obvious that swift medical attention was needed. Carol was already dressed, so I wrapped her hand in a makeshift tea-towel bandage and hastily donned my own snowsuit for the trip to town. Thankfully, the block heater had kept our faithful Chevy warm enough to start. However the rest of the vehicle, including the heater, was frozen solid. No problem! With me driving and Carol wielding a window scraper in her uninjured hand, we pounded on flat-spotted tires along miles of rural road to the town hospital.

The nurse in Emergency escorted Carol directly in for treatment, leaving me to handle the paperwork. Needing my wallet, I reached up and grabbed the zipper on my one-piece snowsuit and pulled, opening it to my navel. "Oops!" I was nude underneath.

While the receptionist and I turned matching shades of red, I hastily re-zipped and provided from memory what information I could.

A nurse appeared and invited me into the treatment room. Carol had been very lucky! The doctor explained that although she would suffer a permanent loss of feeling in the tip of her finger, the bone was undamaged. Her nail and much of the severed flesh would grow back! After some stitches, a bandage and sling, and a call to my very understanding school principal, we headed home.

Once there I carefully rekindled the fireplace and made coffee. As Carol and I sat quietly in the glow of the fire, looking at each other over the rims of our steaming mugs, subtle smiles spread slowly across our faces. Although bruised and bloodied; we toasted each other and sipped, silently congratulating ourselves on surviving another trial.

Our young love would face more challenges before we reached our first anniversary and overcome many others as the years passed. But early adversity builds strong relationships and now forty years later, when winter's winds wail and the temperature plummets in Ontario, we toast each other over our morning coffee in Arizona, thankful that we no longer have to face "one of those mornings."

~John Forrest

花朵开放于最黑暗的时候。

——考瑞塔·肯特

　　烦人的闹钟嗡嗡直响，把我从睡梦中惊醒。我把胳膊从被子里伸出来，把它按停了。我手指哆哆嗦嗦地摸到了暂停按钮，按下去之后，塑料冰冷的触感让我一下子把手缩了回来。我呻吟道："这样什么时候是个头啊！"

　　翻回到我的那一边，我把被子拉到肩膀以上，把我妻子卡罗包裹严实，亲吻她，把她叫醒。打开电台，当地电台晨间播音男主持的声音响起，播报的内容让我更加畏缩了。昨天夜里，奥里利亚的气温急剧下降到了破纪录的零下30度。这意味着，这是"那些早上"中的一个了。

　　作为一对新婚夫妻，我和卡罗克服了很多困难，我们学着如何在加拿大中北地区的乡间一起生活和工作，但这不是最难的。对我们的爱最艰难的考验之一是在荒郊野地里怎么度过我们的第一个冬天。那是 1970 年的 2 月中旬，我在附近的一个小镇教书。虽然我们急于想要搬到奥里利亚中心地带的"乡村别墅"里去，就像很多年轻夫妻一样，我和卡罗目标远大但现金短缺。然而，我们已经成功地凑齐了首付，圣诞节假期过后，我们就搬出了城市里舒适的公寓，在库契钦湖畔的一间破旧的农舍中安居下来。

虽然我们的新家在夏天如田园诗般美丽，但是它孤立于外界，冬天实在不适合居住。我们已经成功地安装了一个室内卫生间和一个浴缸，但这仍然很简陋。一个很小的橡木的壁炉和一个时好时坏的有些年头的油灶是我们唯一的热源。房子没有保温层，所以，在我们寒冷的小窝里，水管和下水道经常被冻住，这是最令人沮丧的事情。很令人骄傲，我们应付过来了。穿着北极靴和一件套的防雪服，我们度过了我们在这里的第一个冬天。那年冬天我们铲了好几吨雪，砍伐林子里的树木，在那些特别寒冷的早上用吹风机融化被冻住的水管。我们的爱经受住了考验，并在我们和各种困难的战斗中变得越来越牢固，我们克服了乡村生活中每天都要面对的艰难。然而，这个早上似乎给我们带来了从没遇见过的最艰难的考验。

我们早上被冻醒了！零下30度的气温已经把炉灶里的油冻住了，加热器的燃料供给被切断，我知道我们的水管肯定也被冻住了。今天只适合待在被窝里；但是，作为一名实习老师，我不得不去学校。

我测试一下温度，在床单边缘吹了一口气，惊恐地看见一团雾状的云向天花板升起。我挣扎着起来，掀开被子，跳到了地板上。冰冷的油毡把我赤裸的双脚灼得生疼，我像一个蹩脚的火灾警戒员，在走廊里蹦跳着走向油灶。我打开备用油箱，划着了一根火柴，谢天谢地，我点燃了火焰。

幸运的是，浴室的水管没有被冻裂，用吹风机仔细地加热了一番，热水从浴缸的喷头中流了出来。当我高兴地正想跳进温暖的热水中时，我听见前屋传来了一声重响。肯定是卡罗起来收拾家务了。在把厨房龙头解冻之后，她会让水一直流，让整个管道通畅，她还会用她好用的短柄小斧子劈柴，点燃壁炉的柴火。

我躺在浴缸里想："合作得多好啊！"完全没有意识到厨房里正在发生什么。

虽然水龙头通畅了，但是水池的下水道仍然被冻着。流出来的水没法流出去。水池很快就盛满了水，水开始流到油毡地板极冷的表面。卡罗在小斧子落下时一走神，马上她痛苦的尖叫声就划破了北极寒冷的空气。

像被电击了一样，我一下子就从浴缸里跳出来，我身上的水汽还在蒸发，就冲到卡罗那里去救她。当我冲到前屋的时候，我面前是一个可怕的场景。

我的妻子坐在壁炉前面，右手抓着左手，血从她的指尖流出来，滴在壁炉边。

她哭喊着："我把手指切掉了！把手指切掉了！"

我的注意力都集中在卡罗身上，我没能看见眼前的危险，我一迈步，没穿衣服也毫无防备，就重重地跌在了厨房湿滑结冰的地板上。我的脚身不由己地飞了出去；我极力想在应声而倒时屁股先着地，在屋子里一通乱滑，砰的一声撞到了墙上。在我头脑清醒之后，我发现卡罗一会儿疼得抽泣，一会儿在嘲笑我。

不过，很显然，我们需要马上就医。卡罗已经穿好衣服了，于是我临时用一个擦杯子用的毛巾当做绷带，包上了她的手，急速地穿上我的防雪服，就向镇上冲去。谢天谢地，加热器部件让我们忠实的雪佛兰仍然足够温暖得以启动。然而，车的其他部分，包括加热器都被冻得结结实实的。没问题！我来开车，卡罗用她没受伤的那只手挥舞着窗擦，我们的轮胎没气了，在乡村的路上砰砰直响，开往镇上的医院。

急诊室的护士护送着卡罗直接去治疗，留下我办一堆手续。需要拿出钱包来，我抬起手，抓到了我的一件套的防雪服的拉链，一直拉到肚脐才想起来，"哦！"我里面什么也没穿。

接待员和我一下子都脸红了，我赶快把拉链拉上，回想一下我刚才干了什么。

一个护士出来了，请我去治疗室。卡罗真的很幸运。医生说虽然她的指尖会永远地失去知觉，但是没伤到骨头。她的指甲和新肉会再长出来的！她经过了一番缝针、绑绷带和吊带，我给我那善解人意的校长打了一个电话，我们回家了。

回到家，我重新点燃了壁炉，煮上咖啡。我和卡罗在壁炉火光的映照下，手里捧着热气腾腾的杯子，彼此对视着，会心的笑容满满地浮上我们的脸庞。虽然又是流血又是撞伤；我们还是举杯相碰，轻抿一口，默默地庆祝我们又从一次劫难中生存了下来。

在我们第一次结婚周年纪念之前，我们年轻的爱还经受了很多磨难，在后来的岁月里，我们还克服了很多很多。但是，早年间，在逆境中，我们建立了稳固的关系。现在，40年过去了，每当冬天来临、寒风呼啸、安大略省的气温又骤降的时候，在亚利桑那州的我们都会在喝晨间咖啡时举杯相碰，感激上天，我们不用再面对"那样的早上"了。

——约翰·弗里斯特

One Damaged Headlight
一盏受损的车前灯

Three years into my marriage, I was diagnosed with Advanced Stage III breast cancer. From the beginning, my husband was there for me. He called for referrals, scheduled my appointments, and gave me extra tender, loving care. His gentle, quiet force wasn't just a nice guy act. He was my unsung hero, and I loved him deeply.

He drove me from one doctor's visit to another without complaining. He laughed and cried with me and was more faithful than Lassie. I don't know what I would have done without him.

After my second chemotherapy treatment, tiny little hairs began shedding all over, so he offered to shave my head. He buzzed the sides, and then stopped long enough to take a picture of my Mohawk before finishing the task.

He handed me a mirror and said, "Smile, Mr. T."

"Very funny."

Our song when we first started dating was Randy Travis's "Forever and Ever." The words couldn't have been more fitting: He sings about how he is not in love with her hair and if it fell out he'd love her anyway. And he did.

After six months of chemotherapy to shrink the tumor, the surgeon performed a partial mastectomy. Due to the huge bandage, I had no idea what my incision looked like.

On the way to the doctor to have the sutures removed, my husband read the troubled expression in my eyes. He'd assured me from the beginning that all that mattered was that I win the battle against cancer so we could grow old together. But now would he still feel the same way?

"Honey, don't worry," he said. "It's going to be fine."

When my name was called, he offered to go in with me. Not sure of my own reaction, I promised I'd be okay. The doctor unwound the last of the gauze, and I was shocked to see the damage to my breast.

But he seemed pleased with his handiwork and said, "It looks great."

Easy for him to say.

My husband jumped up when I walked in the waiting room and asked "Is everything alright?"

I nodded, but deep down, I worried about how he'd feel when he saw my body. We tried conversation, but silence worked best.

Back home, I ran for the privacy of our bedroom and took a good long look in the mirror. Quietly, my husband joined me and gave me a gentle hug. But when he looked down and started laughing, I was not amused.

"Honey, you remind me of my '55 Chevy."

"What's that supposed to mean?" I asked.

"You've got one headlight pointing in the wrong direction."

Glancing down, I discovered he was right. Removing over a fourth of my breast had the effect of an upward lift—one was pointing due north, and thanks to gravity, the other was headed south. His belly laugh filled the room. He explained that he and his brother had taken their old wrecked jalopy raccoon hunting. The damaged headlight shined up into the trees and assured a successful hunt.

He tried to keep a straight face, but a huge grin spread to the corners of his mouth. When I broke out in fits of giggles, he supported me in his arms and we laughed till it hurt.

When we finally stopped cackling, he said, "The hides are probably worth a lot more today."

Without skipping a beat, I said, "When are we going hunting?"

I was ready to move on with my life with my partner at my side.

~Alice E. Muschany

笑声就像阳光，能驱走人脸上的寒冬。

——维克多·雨果

　　我结婚三年的时候，被诊断出患有乳腺癌晚期。从一开始，我的丈夫就一直支持着我。他带我到处治病，为我预约医生，给我特别温柔的爱护。他温柔平静的力量不仅仅是一个好男人就能做到的。他是我默默无闻的英雄，我深深地爱着他。

　　他带我看了一个又一个医生，毫无抱怨。他陪我哭陪我笑，比莱西更为可靠。如果没有了他，我真不知道该怎么办。

在我第二次化疗结束之后，我本来就稀疏的头发开始完全脱落了，于是他帮我剃头发。他剃完了一边之后，停下来好久，在全部完成之前，要把我的莫霍克发型（该发型需要剔掉所有的头发，只在头顶中间留下一窄条头发，再把这些头发向上竖起）给照下来。

他递给我一面镜子，说："笑一笑，T 先生。"

"好搞笑啊。"

我们第一次约会时的歌曲是朗地·特维斯（是新传统主义的代表人物，格莱美最佳乡村男歌手。他凭借优美的旋律和精致的声线把传统主义带到了乡村音乐的前端）的《永永远远》。这些歌词用在这里是再合适不过了：他唱到他不喜欢那个女孩的头发，如果她的头发全没了的话，他怎么样都会爱她的。确实如此。

在 6 个月的化疗手术之后，肿瘤变小了一些，将要进行一次乳房的部分切除手术。由于手术的创伤很大，我不知道伤口看起来会怎么样。

在去医院拆缝合线的路上，我的丈夫发现了我担忧的表情。他曾经安慰我说，从一开始就注定了，你一定会赢得这场对抗癌症的战争，我们一定会一起变老。但是他现在仍然这么想吗？

他说："亲爱的，别担心，一切都会好的。"

当我的名字被叫到的时候，他要陪我进去。我不知道情况会怎样，我说我自己可以的。当医生展开了最后一层纱布的时候，我被胸口的伤疤震惊了。

但是医生对着他的作品还很满意，说："恢复得很好。"

对他来说当然没问题。

当我走进等候室的时候，我丈夫从椅子上跳了起来，问我："怎么样了？"

我点点头，但是在心底里，我十分担心若他看到我的伤疤之后会是什么反应。我们试图交谈，但是什么都没说。

回到家之后，我一个人跑到卧室里，对着镜子看着我的伤疤，看了很久很久。我的丈夫过来了，轻轻地拥抱了我。当他低下头之后，就开始笑。我不知道为什么，我又没逗他。

"亲爱的，你让我想起了我1955年的雪佛兰车。"

我问他："那是什么意思？"

"你的一只车前灯指错了方向。"

低头看看，我发现他说对了。切掉了四分之一的乳房，影响了它向上的托力——一边指向它本来应该朝向的北边，另一边由于重力作用，指向了南边。他的捧腹大笑在屋子里久久回响。他和他的弟弟开着他们破旧的小破车去猎浣熊。受损了的车前灯在林子里照亮，动物就会误判车的方向，他们打猎大获成功。

他试图恢复正常的表情，但是嘴角还是止不住地咧起来。当我也开始忍不住大笑的时候，他拥抱着我，我们一直笑到伤口痛了才不得不停下来。

我们最后不笑了，他说："我们什么时候去打猎呀？"

我已经准备好，要和我身边的人一起度过一生。

——爱丽丝·E.穆斯查尼

Laurel Rosenberg Schwartz Rosenberg Schwartz
Rosenberg

萝瑞尔·罗森伯格·施瓦兹·罗森伯格·施瓦兹·罗森伯格

What's in a name? That which we call a rose by any other
name would smell as sweet.

~William Shakespeare

For the moment, I am Laurel Rosenberg. I
used to be Laurel Schwartz. Before that, I was
Laurel Rosenberg, and would you believe before
that, Laurel Schwartz… and before that my birth or
commonly called "maiden" name Laurel Rosenberg.
Each change distinguished by a different husband.
Perhaps you could say I have gone full circle or
certainly squared.

When I was a young girl, listening to Johnny
Mathis, I dreamt of finding Prince Charming and
marrying him. Names like Frankie Avalon, Ricky
Nelson, Steve McQueen, Bobby Darin, Neil
Diamond, Paul McCartney and even Elvis Presley
danced through my imagination. I would write
my name… Mrs. "Any of the above" on tablets of

drawing paper and decorate the edges with hearts and butterflies. It was all very romantic. Never in any of my fantasies did I imagine my future to be an extended hyphenation.

I truly believe a "love chip" must have been implanted in me before birth... a magnet programmed to attract Rosenbergs and Schwartzes. It must be in the back of my neck because I never see them coming... until they capture my heart and I marry them.

And lo and behold I sail away on a sea of matrimonial bliss without concern, over and over and over again. It's good I don't get seasick.

Some women would rather have their husband's last name because they don't like their own. Not me. For me it's all the same, except there is no DNA or family relationship tie. However there is an inherent confusion cast upon me and many who cross my path.

Let's start with my legal identity. Do you have any idea how many documents there are to fill out when you change your name? Lord knows how many times I have had to call, write, and further communicate to make changes. I am careful to speak clearly. It's like playing "Who's on First." The conversations go like this: "What is your maiden name? Then what is your married name? No, you said that's your maiden name," and the more times I repeat the correct name, the more it goes on and on and on till I am not sure who I am. I have had forms returned because "they" think I have made an error with my own name. Across desks and counters, I have received stares of disbelief, and everything from winks and grins to robust laughter. Beginning with my social security, driver's license, credit cards of which I have many, passport, insurance and real estate licenses, forms, forms, and more forms. Then there's my vehicle registration, and the post office, bank, the IRS... and my utility bills and my house, etc. So all in all, approximately fifty documents changed four times equal at least 200 documents over my lifetime... and it's not over yet…. I have the intention to marry again "someday."

And with that, I raise the issue of the monograms on my towels and linens. The luxuriously soft Egyptian cotton bath wraps, and the slinky silver satin and the white lace elegantly stitched sheets. If I had any idea of what was in store, I would have kept them to match the appropriate last name. My sterling silver, Old Maryland Engraved, has remained with me longer than any relationship. Luckily it was never engraved or the handles would have worn away.

Regarding personalized jewelry, I am careful when I wear it and pay close attention to my rings. Although on one occasion, an elegant dinner party, that current spouse brought to my attention the fact that I was not wearing "our" wedding ring. I quickly asked for another glass of champagne.

Mail creates another problem. Even with alerting the post office of my name change, some acquaintances, friends, and business associates cannot always keep up, while some mail carriers have given up even trying to figure it out. They get rewarded at Christmas.

Not to mention my embarrassment when, on any given day, I answer to either Rosenberg or Schwartz only to realize I am currently the other. In this day and age, it is common for a lady to be confused and forget her age, but her name? People get worried.

Since there are new options for changing last names, and I have already hyphenated mine, I understand that it is acceptable to combine both last names. Please, Schwartzberg-Rosewartz, or a variation thereof?

Now, let's talk about the in-between times during my states of single status which is called "Divorced," yet another label or name. So besides that stigma and not to confuse you further, please consider my confusion as to what last name to use.

Not wishing to date myself, but do you remember at baggage claim when they still verified your identity? I was stopped at the airport and created quite a scene, with some fellow passengers snarling at the delay while others were giggling at the reason. Somehow the claim ticket had been pulled off my luggage during transit and the leather nametag, on my suitcase was Schwartz, while the name on my ticket was guess who? Rosenberg! So I had to show my identification and explain my "legacy" once again, very slowly and to several attendants.

I am not a gambler by nature. The odds of mating with someone of the same last name are high… marrying them very high… my odds are off the chart. Want to place a bet?

Since my last marriage there have been four more Schwartzes, a Schwartzstein and a Rosenberg who gallantly attempted to win my affection. Oh and there was another gentleman from Rosenberg, Texas.

Even with the help of professionals, my "love chip" seems impenetrable, so I fervently request all Smith, Jones, Kennedy, etc… PLEASE line up and step to the FRONT!!!!

Or perhaps husband # 4 will take my last name.

In the meantime, "Let the Rosenberg-Schwartz be with you," It's already been with me!

~Laurel Rosenberg

名字包含着什么？我们无论把一株玫瑰冠以任何名字，它都芬芳依旧。

——威廉·莎士比亚

此刻，我是萝瑞尔·罗森伯格。我曾经是萝瑞尔·施瓦兹。在那之前，我是萝瑞尔·罗森伯格，而且，你也许不相信，在那之前，我是萝瑞尔·施瓦兹……而且，在那些之前，我出生时的名字或者说是未婚时的名字是萝瑞尔·罗森伯格。每一任丈夫就会带来一次改变。你也许会说，我已经绕了一个大圆圈或者说是一个正方形。

当我是个年轻女孩的时候，我听约翰尼·马西斯的歌，梦想着找到我的白马王子，并且嫁给他。比如说叫弗兰基·艾瓦隆 、瑞奇·尼尔森、史蒂芬·麦奎因、鲍比·达林、尼尔·戴蒙德、保罗·麦卡特尼，甚至猫王的名字也曾进入过我的脑海。我会在绘图纸的不同的纸条上，把我的名字分别写成某某夫人（某某可以是上面任何一个名字），再在旁边装饰上心形图案和蝴蝶。这一切都是那么浪漫。我从来没有想象过，我未来的名字会是一连串不断扩展的断字。

我真的相信，在我出生之前，就被植入了一个"爱的芯片"，那个芯片载有吸引罗森伯格和施瓦兹的程序。它肯定被安装在我的脖子后面，因为我从来也看不到它是怎么运行的，直到姓罗森伯格或施瓦兹的人会突然间抓住我的心，然后我就会嫁给他们。

你瞧！我在幸福婚姻的大海上航行，毫无担心，一次又一次，一次又一次地航行。很庆幸我还不晕船。

一些妇女因为不喜欢自己的姓氏，就用她们丈夫的姓氏，而不用自己的。我不是这种人。除了没有 DNA 或是家庭关系的纽带，否则姓什么对我来说都一样。然而，我自己和很多遇见我的人都会产生根深蒂固的迷惑。

让我从我的合法身份开始说起。如果你想改个名字的话，你知道你有多少文件要填吗？每改一次名字，天知道我要打多少次电话，写多少次材料，要做多少后续沟通。我总是仔细地说清楚，就好像在玩"谁先来”的游戏一样。对话一般是这样的：“你未婚时的名字是什么？你结婚后的名字是什么？不，你说成了你未婚时的名字”，我越重复我正确的名字，这样的情况就越是一遍一遍地重复，直到最后我都弄不清我到底是谁了。我曾经被退回过一些表格，因为“他们”认为我把自己的名字写错了。每次去办什么业务，隔着柜台，我早已惯了怀疑的眼神，还有挤眉弄眼和忍不住的哈哈大笑。从我的社保、驾照、各种信用卡、护照、保险单、房产证到各种表格，都是这样。还有我的车辆登记、邮局、银行、国税局……乃至我的公用事业账单和我的房子等也是同样。所以，所有加起来几乎有 50 份文件，每份变更 4 次，等于我一生至少变更了 200 份文件……而且这还没有结束……我现在仍有意愿在“某一天”再次结婚。

而且，我想说说下面这个问题，我会在毛巾和亚麻床单上绣上交织字母。我绣过豪华柔软的埃及纯棉浴袍，优美的银色缎子，还有镶着白色蕾丝的优雅的刺绣床单。如果当时我知道将来会发生什么，我一定会在上面绣上相匹配的姓氏。我有一尊纯银的古老的马里兰雕刻，它时刻提醒我，它陪伴我的时间比任何一段感情都要长。幸运的是，我从来没有在上面刻过姓与名的相关字母，或者说曾经刻过也被磨掉了。

至于私人珠宝，每当戴的时候我都会非常小心，特别是戒指。曾经有一次，在一个高级晚宴上，当时的丈夫提醒我说我戴的结婚戒指不是“我们的”。我迅速地要了一杯香槟来掩饰。

邮件是另一个问题。即使通知了邮局说我的名字改了，一些熟人、朋友和生意伙伴并不能总是跟得上变化，于是一些送信人甚至都不想再去试着弄明白了（因为有很多无法投递的礼物），他们在圣诞节的时候总能得到不少好处。

更别提那些尴尬事了，在很多时候，别人叫罗森伯格或是施瓦兹，我都会答应，应声过后才想起来我已经不是应下的那一个了。在这个时代，人们搞混一位女士的年龄，哪怕她自己都忘了，这都不足为奇。但是她忘了自己的名字？人们就搞不明白怎么回事了。

由于现在对于改姓有了新的选择，我已经把我的两个姓用连字符连起来，改成复姓了。我知道把两个姓结合起来是可以被接受的。请叫我：罗森伯格·施瓦兹，抑或我把这两个单词弄个变体？

现在，让我们来讨论一下我在两段婚姻之间的单身状态吧，就是人们所谓的"离婚"。这个时间我用什么标签或者说用什么名字呢？我不去想那段耻辱的时光，也为了不让读者更加混淆，请想一想我那时是多么迷惑我该用什么姓吧。

这不是为了希望自己能再有个约会，但是你还记得在机场认领行李时，他们仍然会核实身份吗？我在机场就被拦下过，造成了不小的麻烦，一些同机的乘客因被耽搁而冲我咆哮，而一些人知道缘由后在旁边取笑。不知怎么的，在运输过程中，我行李上的行李索取票被扯掉了，我的小提箱上的皮质名签上写着施瓦兹，你猜猜我手里的提取票上写的是谁？罗森伯格！于是，我不得不出示我的身份证，对好几个服务员再一次解释我的"过去"，非常麻烦。

我本性上并不是一个赌徒。但约会的几个对象是同姓的概率很高……和同姓的人结婚的概率也很高……而发生在我身上的概率是极其高！谁敢跟我赌这个？

自从我的上段婚姻结束之后，已经有另外 4 个姓施瓦兹的、一个姓施瓦兹斯汀的、一个姓罗森伯格的殷勤地想要追我了。哦，还有一个得克萨斯的绅士也姓罗森伯格。

我甚至寻求过专业帮助，但是我身上的"爱的芯片"似乎是坚不可摧的。所以，我热切地请求所有的史密斯、琼斯 、肯尼迪……请你们排好队，走到前面来！

或者我可以让我的 4 号丈夫跟我姓？

在这段时间里，"你就姓罗森伯格·施瓦兹吧。"我已经姓罗森伯格·施瓦兹了！

——萝瑞尔·罗森伯格

Domestic Romance
家庭浪漫

Only two things are necessary to keep one's wife happy. One is to let her think she is having her own way, the other, to let her have it.

~Lyndon B. Johnson

In my ongoing attempts to bridge the linguistic chasm between the sexes, I thought I had the meaning of one word down pat: "romantic." After all, how hard is it to define that word?

"Romantic" is a moonlit walk hand-in-hand along the beach. Or a quiet candlelit dinner for two at a quaint out-of-the-way country inn. Or a late night torch-lit champagne dip in a backyard whirlpool.

Whatever "romantic" meant, I knew it had to be at night, involve my wife and include a word ending with the suffix "lit." Even a flashlight-lit night camping in a tent should qualify by my reckoning.

But apparently "romantic" has a far more flexible and mysterious meaning if my wife's lexicon is any indication.

On more than one occasion, Cheryl has suggested some work-related endeavor that the two of us could pursue together. Something like digging up the garden or assembling a piece of IKEA furniture. When proposing such a project, she invariably closes by saying, "It would be romantic."

At first, I always thought she was kidding. After all, sweating, grunting, and groaning while holding a hammer, saw, or shovel does not seem romantic to me in the least unless, of course, it involves some slightly kinky sexual role-playing.

But I'm now convinced that my wife really means it when she says that performing household chores together will be romantic.

Recently Cheryl mentioned that the apple tree in our backyard desperately needed some major trimming. Notwithstanding it was the first day of my holidays, I foolishly suggested we rent a chainsaw and cut the offending branches. "Yes," said Cheryl, jumping at my offer. "That would be romantic."

So we headed off to the hardware store where we picked up a chainsaw and some chainsaw oil. Since the rental was for four hours, the only thing I had in mind was getting home and getting the job done as quickly as possible. Cheryl, on the other hand, seemed to be enjoying the romance of the moment.

For our romantic encounter, I donned work boots, old pants, a red flannel work shirt, and a pair of work gloves. In my mind, this was undoubtedly the least sexy outfit I had ever worn, except perhaps for my gardening ensemble which features rubber boots and a silly hat. But for Cheryl, it was apparently akin to a knight in shining armor.

Four hours later, we had removed and trimmed two large branches from our apple tree and a couple of smaller ones from the neighboring birch. Tied-up bundles of branches and two bags of leaves, twigs and apples ended up at the curb for pickup and some prime firewood was delivered to a neighbor for his fireplace.

At the end of our afternoon of torture, I found myself sweaty and exhausted. Years ago, I might have considered that an apt description of a romantic encounter. But since this one involved a chainsaw and a ladder, it was hard for me to find the romance in the now-completed task.

Yet Cheryl persisted in her belief that our afternoon chore had been romantic. Since it took place before sunset and there was no extra light involved (apart from the sunlight reflecting off my sweat-soaked brow), I failed to see how it qualified. To me, the only common denominators seemed to be that I had to wear protection and I needed to take a shower after it was over. But I sure didn't have that satisfied feeling I usually associate with romance.

After our latest romantic afternoon, however, I think I have a better handle on the meaning of the word "romantic." It doesn't necessarily have to occur at night with soft lighting. Apparently it can happen any time so long as it involves the two of us and some measure of extended physical exertion.

As I now see it, romance simply involves togetherness. So to husbands everywhere, the next time you want to sweep your wife off her feet, forget about candies, flowers, dining and dancing. All you have to do is say: "Honey, let's clean out the septic tank." It may sound like work to you, but trust me, it will be sweet music to her ears.

~David Martin

只要两件事情就能让你的妻子高兴。一件事情就是让她认为一切
在按她的方式进行着，另一件事情就是，让这变成事实。

——林登·约翰逊

我不断地试图弄清男人和女人之间对一些语
言上理解的分歧，我自认为弄明白了这个词——
浪漫。给这个词下定义终究有多难呢？

"浪漫"就是在月光下在海滩上手牵着手散步；

或者是两个人在一个偏远的古色古香的乡村小屋里安静地吃着烛光晚餐；又或者是在一个深夜，在后院里共享"香槟浴"。

无论浪漫是什么意思，我只知道那必须是一个夜晚，我和妻子在一起，还要"点燃"些什么。哪怕是两个人露营，在帐篷里点个手电筒，我认为这也是浪漫。

但是，显然，如果我妻子的字典里有过表述的话，浪漫有一个要灵活得多也神秘得多的含义。

谢莉尔已经不止一次地提议，要做一些需要我们两个人一同努力的事情。比如说一起收拾一下花园，或者是拼装一件宜家的家具。每当这么建议的时候，她一般都会加一句："这一定很浪漫。"

起初，我总是觉得她太孩子气了。毕竟，拿着锤子、锯子、铲子，在那大汗淋漓地喘息着呻吟着，在我看来一点都不浪漫。除非，当然了，如果是一场略微变态的色情角色扮演，那就另当别论了。

但是，现在我知道了，我的妻子真的觉得我们一起做那些家务琐事会很浪漫。

最近，谢莉尔提到，我家后院的苹果树十分需要大规模地修剪一下了。虽然这是我休假的第一天，但是我还是愚蠢地建议去借一把电锯来，以便把旁枝修剪掉。谢莉尔因我同意而欢欣鼓舞，说："好呀。这一定很浪漫。"

于是，我们赶往五金商店，租了一把电锯，买了一些电锯油。由于租期只有 4 小时，我一心只想赶快回家，尽快把活干完。然而，谢莉尔似乎沉浸在享受这样的浪漫时光里。

为了这场浪漫，我穿上了干活用的靴子、旧裤子、一件红色法兰绒的工作衫，还戴了一副工作手套。我觉得，除了我那套园艺全套服装，就是有一双橡胶靴子和一顶傻透顶的帽子的那套，这毫无疑问是我穿过的最不性感的套装了。但是，谢莉尔觉得，我现在完全可以和穿着闪亮盔甲的骑士相媲美。

四小时之后，我们剪掉了苹果树上的两段大枝丫，还有旁边桦树上的一些小树枝。捆了好几捆树枝，装了两大袋树叶。嫩枝和苹果被收拾好放在路边，以便于拾取，一些适合做柴火的树枝被送给隔壁有壁炉的邻居了。

在一下午的折磨之后，我发现自己大汗淋漓、筋疲力尽了。几年前，我可能还会思考一个自以为聪明的对浪漫的解释。但是由于这个解释涉及电锯和梯子，对我来说，已经经历过这种工作了，很难在其中发现什么浪漫。

但是，谢莉尔坚持她的想法，认为我们一起做家务的那个下午十分浪漫。鉴于这一切发生在太阳落山之前，还没有什么额外的光线被点燃（除了阳光反射着我那被汗水浸透的脸庞），我真不知道这哪一点符合浪漫的标准。对我来说，唯一的共同点是，我不得不穿上一层防护服，并且在结束之后冲个澡。但是与我通常认为的浪漫相比，我没有任何满足的感觉。

然而，在我们最近的一次浪漫的下午，我觉得我能更好地理解"浪漫"这个词了。浪漫没必要发生在夜晚，也没必要一定要有柔和的光线。只要我们两个人都在，并且发生了一些体力上的消耗，诚然，在任何时候都可能很浪漫。

我现在看来，浪漫仅仅在于两个人在一起。所以，男人们啊，无论你在哪里，下一次，如果你想让你的妻子对你佩服得五体投地的话，别再弄什么蜡烛啊，花啊，晚餐啊，跳舞啊之类的了。你唯一要做的就是，说："亲爱的，来把化粪池清理一下吧。"这对你来说是一项苦工，但是，相信我，对她来说，这就是最甜蜜的音乐。

——大卫·马丁

The Detective
侦探

Anyone can be passionate, but it takes real lovers to be silly.

~Rose Franken

There really is truth to the statement that those who are in love literally know each other's thoughts and can see into one another's... uh... ice cream bowl. This truth became extraordinarily real to me just days before our twenty-second wedding anniversary.

At about 11:00 A.M., the phone rang at our home. It was my husband Gary—just calling to see what was up:

"Hello," I answered.

"Hi. What are you up to today?"

"Oh nothing," I said, "just having a little early lunch while I work on the computer."

"So... how's the coffee ice cream I bought?" he asked. I could almost "hear" him smiling.

"What?" I asked innocently.

"I asked how you like the ice cream you are

eating."

I was stunned—absolutely stunned. I swung my head around and looked behind me at the window to see if somehow he could see me. The shade was down. How in the world did he know I was eating ice cream? I NEVER get into the ice cream… especially in the morning. Plus, he knows that I had been trying to diet… again.

Nonetheless, I could barely hide the laughter in my voice as I calmly asked, "Why would you think I'm eating coffee ice cream?"

Gary chuckled. "Uh… several things. One being the fact that you said, 'Just having a little early lunch' in a guilty, high-pitched voice." He then imitated it before going on. "Two… your tongue must be a little frozen because your words were a bit sluggish." (I'm laughing out loud now.)

Spurred on by my laughter, he kept going… "The other thing is, I figured that when I cracked the seal on that carton of coffee ice cream last night and you didn't eat any, that it was sort of like leaving a line of cocaine on the counter for an addict to find."

We laughed long and hard together before he asked me, "What happened?"

"What do you mean?" I said, still laughing.

"Something must have happened to make you eat ice cream before lunch," he answered sympathetically.

Suddenly, I felt a rush of love for the man on the other end of the line. He knew me well—cared enough to find out what was bothering me, and trusted me enough to help me laugh at myself. What a satisfying and beautiful testament to twenty-two years.

I was reminded at that very moment, that whether I was blessed with one more year, or fifty more years, I would always and forever love my husband.

~Elizabeth Schmeidler

任何人都可能激情冲动，但这使得真正相爱的人显得傻傻的。

——罗斯·弗兰肯

下面这条理论一定是真的，那就是相爱着的人们简直可以知道彼此的思想，甚至可以看到对方的……嗯……冰激凌碗。这条真理几天前在我身上应验了，那是我们22周年结婚纪念日的前几天。

在上午11点左右，家里的电话响了，是我的丈夫加里打来的，就是为了看看我在干什么。

我说："喂？"

"喂。今天在家干什么呢？"

我说："没干什么呀。刚提前吃了午饭，在电脑前忙活呢。"

他问道："那……我买的咖啡冰激凌怎么样啊？"我几乎都能想象得到他在那头坏笑。

我故作无辜地问了一句："什么？"

"我是在问你正在吃着的冰激凌怎么样？"

我呆住了——完全呆住了。我四处看看，想看看我后面的窗子那儿，是否有什么地方他能看得见我。一切如常。他到底是怎么知道我吃了冰激凌的？我从来对冰激凌不怎么感兴趣……特别是在早上。而且，他知道我正在又一次地节食。

然而，我隐藏住我声音中的笑意，装作平静地问道："你凭什么认为我吃了冰激凌啊？"

加里咯咯笑了。"嗯……一些迹象吧。第一，你用紧张的、充满罪恶感的语气说：'提前吃了午饭。'"他在那头模仿着我刚才的声音，"第二，你的舌头肯定有点凉着了，因为你说话有点迟钝。"（我哈哈大笑起来。）

为我的笑声所鼓舞，他继续说："另一件事就是，我就知道，昨晚我打开了咖啡冰激凌的包装盒，而你一点也没吃，那就相当于给一个瘾君子留了一包可卡因在桌子上。"

我们一直笑得很厉害，直到他问我："发生了什么？"

我仍然在大笑，说："你说什么？"

他用略带怜惜的语气回答说："能让你在午饭前吃冰激凌，一定发生了什么事情。"

突然间，我感到电话线那头传来了一阵爱意。他知我甚深——那么关心我，发现了我被什么事情烦扰着，信任我，逗我开怀大笑。这是对我们之间 22 年的时光最令人满意和美好的证明。

我记起那个美好的时刻，今后无论上天赐予我和他在一起的时光是一年还是 50 年，我都会永远永远地爱他。

——伊丽莎白·施迈德勒

第四部分 心灵礼物篇

Chapter 4
Gifts from the Heart

May no gift be too small to give, nor too simple to receive, which is wrapped in thoughtfulness and tied with love.

~L.O. Baird

一份用心准备、用爱凝聚的礼物，永远不会显得太小而拿不出手，收到的人也不会觉得无足轻重。

——L．O. 贝尔德

22 and Counting

22 and Counting
22 周年结婚纪念

At the touch of love, everyone becomes a poet.

~Plato

For my 22nd wedding anniversary, I got a wild idea. I decided that I would write my wife Sheila twenty-two poems to describe my love to her. Not being a poet, I had no idea what I was about to embark on. I also decided that I would have a surprise party to catch her off guard; after all, who has ever heard of a surprise 22nd wedding anniversary party?

I started out months in advance, writing poems and coordinating with a couple of my wife's friends. One of them ran a small printing business and another does crafts and drawings. So, I enlisted their help in making custom cards for each of the twenty-two poems.

Had I known how much effort it was going to be to make twenty-two custom cards for twenty-two poems about my love for my wife, I might have come up with a different idea. However, by the time I was beginning to run out of ideas for poems, I was within reach, so I kept on task.

I also decided that I was going to have twenty-one of her friends at the party to each give her a card and a rose. Then, I would recite the twenty-second poem from heart in front of her friends.

Some good friends volunteered to host the party at their house. The question then was how to get my wife to the party without raising her suspicions. I told my wife that for our anniversary I would make reservations at a suitably nice restaurant, so she didn't have to plan anything.

There was one other crucial decision: Which poem would I recite to my wife in front of all of her friends? Being a guy, one of the shorter ones seemed like the logical choice, but in the end my heart was drawn to a particular poem that describes how we met. I've always believed that there was divine intervention at work to bring us together, and I had written a poem about that. I couldn't shake the thought that this was the poem I needed to memorize. The problem was that this particular poem had nineteen verses. I had to get busy memorizing—and fast!

Finally, on the day of the party, I had pre-arranged with the party host to call me at home early in the afternoon to set the trap. He called right on cue to say that he really needed to get back a book that I had borrowed. In my wife's presence, I told him that we were heading out to dinner and could drop the book off on our way. Now, we could drive right to the party house without arousing suspicion.

When we pulled up to the house, I suggested that perhaps Sheila should accompany me to the door and say a quick hello—we wouldn't want to be rude to our friends.

We made our way up the steps and inside the house where the surprise was sprung. We had a terrific dinner surrounded by friends. One at a time, twenty-one of Sheila's friends presented her with a card and a rose. Then, I got up and recited all nineteen verses of a poem titled "Pure Luck." I wanted desperately to get it right—and I did!

That was five years ago, and I can still recite all nineteen verses by heart.

~Dan DeVries

一遇到爱情，每个人都会变成诗人。

——柏拉图

在我第 22 个结婚纪念日的时候，我有了一个疯狂的想法。我决定给我的妻子希拉写 22 首诗来表达我对她的爱。我不是一个诗人，我不知道我可以从哪里着手。我也决定我要为她办一个惊喜派对，给她一个意外的惊喜；毕竟，谁听说过有人办过结婚 22 周年的惊喜派对？

我提前几个月就开始写诗，并且和我妻子的一些朋友们联系。他们中的一个人开一个小印刷店，另一个人制作工艺品和绘画。所以，我得到了他们的支持，来帮我制作 22 张自己设计的卡片，一张卡片上有一首诗。

如果我事先知道，想要为 22 首诗制作 22 张自定义的卡片，每张卡片上都书写了我对我妻子的爱，做这些要花费那么多精力，我可能就会换一个主意了。然而，这时，我已经开始写诗了，似乎我就快要成功了，于是我坚持了下来。

　　我还决定，在派对上，要找 21 个她的朋友，每人给她一张卡片和一枝玫瑰。然后，我将要在她的朋友面前深情地朗诵第 22 首诗。

　　一些好朋友主动要在他们的家里举办派对。问题在于，如何把我的妻子带到派对上去，并且不引起她的怀疑。我告诉我的妻子，为了庆祝我们的结婚纪念日，我在一家高档餐厅定了位子，所以，她什么都不用准备了。

　　这里还有一个关键的决定：在她的朋友们面前，我将为我的妻子背诵哪首诗呢？对一般人来说，合理的选择是选一首短诗，但是在最后，我心中中意的是一首描述我们如何相遇的诗。我一直相信，我们的相遇一定是上帝的安排，于是我为此写了一首诗。我坚信不疑，这就是我要背的诗。问题是，这首诗有 19 行。我不得不背很多内容——还要背得快！

　　最终，在派对举办的那天，我事先安排举办派对的那家主人，在下午给我家里打了个电话，设下了个圈套。根据设计好的情节，他打电话说他急需我把从他那借的一本书还给他。我的妻子也在场，我对他说，我们将要去吃晚饭，路上可以顺便把书递给他。现在，我可以名正言顺地驾车去举办派对那家，而且不被引起怀疑了。

　　在我们快要到的时候，我向希拉建议说她陪我应个门，打个招呼——别让人家觉得我们不礼貌。

　　我们走进了屋子，惊喜突然间涌现出来。我们和朋友们度过了一个美妙的夜晚。席间，希拉的 21 位朋友送给她卡片和玫瑰。然后，我站起来，背诵了那首叫做《纯粹的幸运》的 19 行诗。我要一字不落地背下来——我做到了！

　　那是五年前的事了，如今，我还可以在心里背诵那首 19 行的诗。

——丹·德弗里斯

A Dying Gift
临终礼物

There is a land of the living and a land of the dead, and the bridge is love.

~Thornton Wilder

Out of the blue he said, "I think it's time we get that puppy you've been wanting for so long." He was wrapped in a furry lap robe, sitting in the glider I had moved into the kitchen so he could be near me while I prepared meals. His black hair had turned to silver, his voice had lost its clarity, and the sparkle had faded from the dark brown eyes that had shown his love for me through forty-eight years. I knew that he knew it wouldn't be many more months before the cancer won and the chemo treatments would become ineffective.

For several years I had been begging to have a puppy, but his response had always been, "Not until you retire, because I don't want to be the one getting up in the night with a whining pup!" Now I had given up my job, not because I was of retirement age, but because I needed to be home to care for him while he battled the monster lurking in his bone marrow.

We went the next day to West Rock Kennels and picked out an adorable Shih-Tzu puppy, the healthiest-looking one of the litter. For several days I concentrated on choosing the perfect name for this adorable little distraction. Precious? Fritz? Piddles? At the suggestion of my sister, I finally settled on Skoshi, the Japanese word for small. While part of me wasted away along with my dying husband, Skoshi provided a silly kernel of delight that kept me going.

The diagnosis had come as a complete shock in the summer of 2002. During a routine checkup at our local clinic, his primary physician noted an unusual spike in a blood protein and referred us to a specialist for further follow-up, never mentioning the dreaded "C" word. As we drove up to the professional building in Robbinsdale, Minnesota, our hearts skipped a beat as we read the words "Humphrey Cancer Center" in bold design above the door. After further tests and consultation with an oncologist, it was confirmed. He had multiple myeloma, the technical term for bone marrow cancer, considered to be one of the more difficult cancers to treat.

As the months went by, we had many conversations about his impending departure, and he made lists of the important things I should know how to do when he was no longer around. To put his mind at ease, I assured him that I would be fine and that he needn't worry about me.

One day, in October 2005, a clinic appointment for a blood draw indicated that his chest cavity was filling up with fluid, and he had to be hospitalized. The doctors planned to remove the fluid the following morning and advised me to go home and get some rest. Sleep did not come. I prayed and committed the man who had been my best friend and lover for so many years to the Lord's care, asking that he be spared further suffering.

The next morning I rushed back to the hospital and found him somewhat confused. I reminded him who his visitors had been the previous day—grandson William, son Bruce, daughter-in-law Jeri, Pastor Tim. Then a strange look came across his face, as he said, "Oh, Marg, I feel so dizzy, so dizzy!" He lost consciousness, as I frantically ran into the hallway, calling for the nurse. Within minutes the once vibrant man I had loved since our teenage years lay still and silent, as I lay my head upon his chest and wept. The inevitable day had arrived.

I was strong and resolute throughout the week of making plans for his memorial service. Our grown children came to be with me. Together we chose music that he had loved, flowers to grace his casket, and special friends to take part. The last time I looked on his dear, familiar face, I wanted to climb into his burial bed and go to eternal rest along with him. But I greeted friends and relatives with a smile. I watched proudly as his children eulogized him, his granddaughters read his favorite Scriptures, and his seven grandsons carried him to the family plot to take his place alongside his mother, father, and grandparents, where one day I will finally lie beside him again.

Kicking aside the dead oak leaves as I walked the circle of my driveway in the late afternoons, I called out to the sky, "Where are you? Do you see me? Do you know my heart is broken?" My husband was finally free from the cancer's pain and suffering, but I never dreamed being left behind would hurt so much. As I walked, Skoshi faithfully watched and waited from the kitchen window. Day after day, spent from crying, I went inside to the joyful, wiggling, tail-wagging welcome from Skoshi, who needed my attention.

Friends called me from time to time to ask how I was doing. I always replied with a lie, "Oh, I'm fine. It's hard, but I'm doing fine." Funny how we want everyone to think we can handle situations that have rendered us immobile, unable to cope. I continued attending church, my one refuge, but as I sang the beautiful praise songs, the tears would not be denied and would soon stream down my cheeks. I felt a compulsion to destroy things that once held meaning to me, but no longer did. I stood in my living area and contemplated ripping all the books off the shelves and slamming them around the room.

When I went to my closet to dress in the morning, I wanted to pull the clothes off the hangers and stomp on them.

I could sense that my children were becoming concerned, especially my daughter who began calling every night just to chat and make suggestions.

"Mom, maybe you should make an appointment with your physician and ask about taking an anti-depressant?"

"Mom, I'm worried about you."

"Mom, have you thought about seeing a counselor? Take down this number; he's a good one."

Most days I wanted to stay in bed, turn my face to the wall and never get up. As I lay there on a dark December day in 2005, Skoshi, curled in sleep behind my back, began to stir. He stretched, stood up and found his way to my pillow. As he licked my chin, I finally realized I needed help. I gathered that precious little dog into my arms, the last gift of love my life partner had given me, and murmured, "Thank you, my beloved Gordon," into Skoshi's furry little body. Once again, even in death, he had come through for me. Skoshi smiled at me, as Shih Tzu are known to do. Then with all the courage I could muster, I picked up the phone and dialed.

~Margaret M. Marty

有一个生的世界和一个死亡的世界，爱就是其间的桥梁。

——桑顿·王尔德

他突然对我说："我觉得我们应该买一只小狗了，你都想要很久了。"他裹着大毛及膝的睡袍，坐在我移进厨房的轮椅上，这样在我做饭的时候，他可以离我近一点。他的黑发已经发白，声音也含混不清了，深棕色的眼睛里也已经失去了神采，那双眼睛在过去的48年中无时无刻不充满着对我的爱。我知道，他肯定清楚在癌症最终夺去自己的生命之前，他只有几个月的时间了，化疗也没有用了。

很多年来，我一直求他允许我养一只小狗，但是他的回答永远都是："你退休了再养吧。我可不想在半夜被小狗的呜呜叫声给吵醒！"现在，我辞去了我的工作，并不是因为我到了退休的年纪，而是因为我要在家照顾他，他正在和潜伏在他骨髓中的病魔作斗争。

第二天，我们就去了西岩狗舍，挑选了一只可爱的狮子狗，那是一窝幼崽中看起来最健康的一只。接下来的几天里，我一直在想着给这只可爱的小家伙取一个合适的名字。叫宝贝？弗里茨？小混混？在我妹妹的建议下，最终，我给这个小家伙取名叫斯考西，这是一个日本名字。在我花费了一部分时间陪伴我那病危的丈夫时，斯考西成了一个快乐的源泉，支撑我走下去。

在2002年夏天，诊断结果对我们来说，完全就是晴天霹雳。在一次当地诊所的例行检查中，他的主治医生指出在他的血液蛋白中有长钉状的异物，让我们到专科做一个跟进检查，从来没有提到"癌"这个字。当我们驱车赶到明尼苏达州的罗宾斯戴尔的时候，我们发现了我们要去的那个大楼的门上用粗体写着"汉弗里癌症中心"，我们的心脏就好像漏跳了一拍似的。在进一步检查之后，又咨询了肿瘤专家，他的病确诊了。他患有多发性骨髓瘤，这是骨髓癌的专业术语，这种癌症一直被认为是很难治愈的一种。

几个月过去了，对于他即将来临的离开，我们之间谈了很多。他列了一个重要事项的清单，让我知道，如果他不在我身边了，我应该怎么做。为了让他放心，我许诺说我会一切都好的，他不用担心我。

2005 年 10 月的一天，一次在诊所预约的抽血结果显示：他的胸腔中已经充满了液体，必须入院治疗。医生计划在第二天早上清除液体，劝我回家休息一晚。我当然睡不着。我祈祷，把他交给上天来关照，希望他可以免除接下来的苦难。这个男人这么多年来一直在我身边，他是我最好的朋友，也是我的爱人。

第二天一早，我匆匆赶回医院，发现他有点神志不清。我提醒他昨天有谁来看过他——孙子威廉姆、儿子布鲁斯、媳妇杰莉、牧师吉姆。然后，他的脸上出现了一种奇怪的表情，他说："哦，玛格，我觉得头晕，太晕了！"他失去了意识，我疯狂地跑向走廊，叫护士过来。在几分钟之内，这个曾经生龙活虎、和我青梅竹马的男人就那样静静地躺着，我把头贴在他的胸前抽泣着，这一天还是不可避免地到来了。

在为他的追悼会筹备的整整一周里，我都表现得勇敢而坚强。我们已经成年的孩子们回来陪伴我。我们一起挑选他最喜欢的音乐，挑选美丽的鲜花围绕在他的灵柩旁边，并且确定参加葬礼的朋友名单。当我最后一次看着他那亲爱的熟悉的脸时，我是多么想爬上他的棺床，和他一起长眠。但是我微笑招呼我们的朋友和亲戚。我一直骄傲地看着这一切：他的孩子们祭奠他，他的孙女们朗读他最喜爱的经文，他的七个孙子扶灵，把他送到家族墓地中去，那里埋葬着他的父亲母亲、祖父祖母，有一天最终我也会到那里去，再次陪在他身边。

有多少个傍晚，我在院子里的车道上来回走动，踢开枯落的橡树叶子，向天空高喊："你在哪里？你能看见我吗？你知道我为你心碎了吗？"我的丈夫最终从癌症的痛苦和折磨中解脱了，但是我从没想到一个人留下是如此心痛。每当我散步的时候，斯考西都会忠实地从厨房窗户里看着我，等着我。日复一日，我哭泣过后，一走进屋子，都会看见斯考西快乐地、摇头摆尾地欢迎我，它是多么想得到我的关注啊。

朋友们不时地会问我过得怎么样。我总是撒谎说："哦，我很好。虽然这很难，但是我做得还不错。"我们总是想要别人认为自己能把那些棘手的难以处理的事情做得很好，这是多么可笑啊。我继续参加教堂活动，这是我的一个避难所。但是每当我唱着那些动人的颂歌，我的眼泪就再也不可抑止，直到泪流满面。我感到有必要强迫自己销毁那些曾经对我十分有意义的事物，这些东西如今什么用也没有了。我站在起居室里，想着要把所有的书从书架上扯下来，把它们狠狠地摔在屋里。当我早上打开衣橱，打扮我自己的时候，我想要把所有的衣服都从架子上拽下来，在上面踩几脚。

我能感觉得到，我的孩子们注意到了我的想法，特别是我的女儿，她开始每天晚上都给我打电话，仅仅就是聊天和提点建议。

"妈妈，你是不是可以和医生预约一下，让他给你开点兴奋剂？"

"妈妈，我很担心你。"

"妈妈，你想过去找个咨询师看看吗？记下这个号码，这位还不错。"

大部分的时候，我都躺在床上，面朝墙壁，从不起床。在 2005 年 12 月的一天晚上，斯考西蜷缩在我背后睡觉，开始颤抖。它舒展了身体，站起来，往我枕头走过来。当它舔我的下巴时，我突然意识到，我需要帮助。我把这珍贵的小狗抱在我的怀里，这是我今生的另一半留给我最后的礼物。我对着毛茸茸的小斯考西轻声说："谢谢你，我的至爱，戈登。"他再一次地来到了我身边，甚至死亡也阻止不了他。斯考西对我微笑，这是狮子犬有名的招牌动作。然后，我鼓起勇气，拿起电话，拨下了号码。

——玛格丽特·M.马蒂

Best Friends

最好的朋友

A friend loves at all times...

~Proverbs 17:17

I'm a hopeless romantic. But my husband, Mike, is probably the most unromantic guy I know. When I was growing up I pictured myself being married to someone who would take my hand when we went for walks, shower me with affection, and enjoy long, heartfelt conversations about special feelings and philosophies.

I think Mike reached for my hand once since we've been married. He was lying in a hospital bed waiting for surgery and fearing he might die. That doesn't count!

Hugs I get—when he wants a new car, a $300 Precision Graphite Classic OS tennis racquet, or a golf trip with his buddies.

As for philosophical talks, forget it. I don't even try.

And when it comes to romantic lingo—after I say "I love you" Mike's typical response is, "Right back at ya, kid," or "Me, too, you, Babe." Hardly heartwarming.

I think Mike was the inspiration for the story about the woman who said to her husband on their anniversary: "Honey, we've been married forty years and since our wedding you have never said I love you." The husband replied, "I said it once and if anything changes I'll let you know."

But there is chemistry between us and a joyful oneness of spirit—like when he says or does goofy things to make me laugh so hard my sides ache and I can't catch my breath and I have to beg him to stop; or when something happens that reminds us of the past and we say the same thing at the same time and others haven't a clue what we're talking about; or when he looks at me during a concert of beautiful music with tears in his eyes and wipes my wet cheek knowing our hearts are one at that moment.

Mike says I am his best friend. I guess that's more important than a lot of romantic jargon, public display of affection, and all those other fantasies of mine.

And I do know that he loves me. After back surgery, the doctor said I shouldn't use a vacuum cleaner for at least a year. Now, twenty-nine years later, Mike still does all of the vacuuming. "It might hurt your back," he says. He has never voiced a complaint or even accused me of bribing the doctor. Now if that's not love, I don't know what is!

~Kay Conner Pliszka

一个在任何时候都会爱你的朋友……

——谚语 17:17

　　我是一个无可救药的渴望浪漫的人。但是，我的丈夫迈克可能是我所知道的人中最不浪漫的一个了。在我成长的过程中，我幻想我将来嫁的人会在散步的时候牵着我的手，会用他的爱把我包围，我们可以享受长长的、心与心的对话，谈谈我们特殊的情感和哲理。

　　我认为自从我们结婚以来，迈克只拉过我的手一次。那一次他躺在医院病床上，就要上手术台，他害怕自己会死掉。那次不算！

　　我们拥抱的几次——一次是他想要买一台新车，一次是他想要买一副 300 美元的精密石墨制作的经典绝版网球拍，还有一次是他和哥们儿一起去打一场高尔夫球。

　　至于富有哲理的对话，算了吧，我都不指望了。

　　每次一说到浪漫的关键词——在我说"我爱你"之后，迈克的典型回答是"乖，我会很早回来"，或者是："我也一样，宝贝"。这一点都不感人。

　　我觉得迈克是从这个故事得到的启发的：一个女人在结婚纪念日上对她的丈夫说："亲爱的，我们已经结婚40年了，从我们结婚以后，你就从来没有说过我爱你。"丈夫回答说："我说过一次，如果发生了什么改变，我会让你知道的。"

　　但是我们之间相当"来电"，在一起也很欢乐。比如当他说了什么或做了什么搞笑的事情的时候，我会笑到肚子疼，都快喘不过气了，我就不得不求他停下来；或者是有时候发生了一些事情，让我们想起了以前的事，我们就会同时说相同的话，而其他人则一头雾水；又或者我们在看一场精彩的音乐会的时候，他会感动得泪眼蒙眬，扭头一看，我也是泪流满面，他会为我擦去泪水，那时我们知道，我们的心灵是相通的。

　　迈克说我是他最好的朋友。我觉得这句话比很多浪漫的话语、比在公开场合示爱、比我生活中所有其他的幻想都要重要。

　　我真真切切地知道——他爱我。背部手术过后，医生说我有至少一年的时间不能用真空吸尘器。现在，手术过去已经29年了，迈克仍然负责家里所有的打扫工作。他说："这可能对你的背不好。"他从来没有埋怨过我，甚至没有说过我这是在滥用医嘱。如果这都不是爱的话，我真不知道什么是爱了。

——凯·康纳·普里斯卡

A Bottle of Cologne
一瓶古龙水

Grow old with me! The best is yet to be.

~Robert Browning

The bottle sits on my bathroom counter next to my comb and brush. It is three-quarters empty now. "Casaque by Jean d'Albret" proclaims the label, its blue color faded over forty years.

I use my special cologne sparingly now and only on very important occasions, because there will be none to replace it when these last few precious drops are gone.

It is the second bottle of this particular scent that I have owned. Jack gave me the first bottle... a very small one... on our first anniversary.

I'd heard the sound of the noisy muffler on our old maroon Ford and the crunch of its worn tires on the gravel of our driveway. He'd come home from his medical school classes early that Wednesday afternoon many years ago. After pausing for a moment to sniff his appreciation for the pie I had cooling on the kitchen windowsill, he handed me a small paper sack.

"Happy anniversary, honey! I brought you something special."

"Special and expensive, I think! The bag says Suzanne's. You know we can't afford anything from there."

"I can't afford NOT to give something special to the world's most beautiful bride. Especially for one who baked such a wonderful-smelling dessert for our anniversary dinner."

His arms circled my waist and he untied the strings on my apron.

"Now come in here and sit down and open my present."

He led me into the only other room in our tiny apartment and sat beside me on the worn old sofa.

My hands trembled as I took a small package from the bag. I hesitated to disturb the artistry of the elegant gold foil wrapping paper and black velvet ribbon.

"Open it, honey. Open it."

"But I thought we agreed to save the money for your tuition and not get each other anything," I protested somewhat half-heartedly.

"Open it, honey," Jack persisted.

The lovely wrappings fell away to reveal a bottle of French cologne. I knew it must be very expensive. I held it to my nose and smelled the most delicate odor I could ever imagine.

"Oh, Jack! It's heavenly! I'll never wear any other cologne as long as I live."

Looking down at my faded blue jeans and ugly, ragged tennis shoes, I wondered if I would ever be worthy of this marvelous scent. I would certainly try.

I used my precious Casaque carefully and sparingly over those early years of our marriage. Even after Jack's medical school and postgraduate training were completed and our life was easier financially, still, I was frugal. Even when we had a new sofa in a big, new house and five children to fill that house, I continued to jealously guard my fragrant treasure, a symbol of the foolishly extravagant love of a young husband.

And then one day three-year-old Jim drank my precious Casaque!

The day had been depressing because of the gloom and the rain. The new puppy had kept me awake half the night with his whining and barking. And I had just looked in the refrigerator to find we were out of milk. I went into my bedroom to get my purse and car keys only to discover that Jim had drunk my Casaque! The evidence was clear. He was sitting on the floor holding the empty bottle, his lips were wet, and he was making an awful face.

"Jack, come quick," I wailed. "Can cologne hurt the baby? Jim just drank the rest of the bottle of my Casaque!"

"It's mostly just alcohol, honey," Jack reassured me. "But we'll take him to the ER just to be sure."

Little Jim was fine, and my concern for my child assuaged, I now mourned my empty cologne bottle.

"Don't worry, hon. We can afford another bottle."

A few weeks later Jack came home, again with an elegantly wrapped package… this time a much larger bottle of my beloved scent.

"Sorry it took me a while to replace it. The lady at Suzanne's had to order it from Kansas City. They don't sell a whole lot of it anymore."

Though life was good and worries about tuition payments and cars with noisy mufflers were long past, I prized my new bottle of Casaque as much as I had the earlier one and used it with care bordering on parsimony. Still, one day it reached the half-empty mark, and I thought it best to get another bottle. It might have gotten even harder to obtain than it had been years ago.

The young lady at the counter at Suzanne's smiled what I'm sure she considered a charitable smile as she said, "Casaque? We haven't had any of that for years now. In fact, I don't think there is even a Jean d'Albret maker any more. We have some other lovely scents for a woman of your age, though."

"Is Miss Suzanne here? Maybe she knows how to order it. She got some for me a few years ago... from Kansas City, I think."

"It must have been quite a few years ago. Miss Suzanne has been dead for five years. The shop is now owned by her son George."

Time goes so quickly. One day I look at the cologne bottle and there isn't much left. I've been so careful of it over the years. Jim and his four siblings are all grown now. He is a successful lawyer and doesn't drink cologne anymore. He has moved on to more sophisticated drinks. Jack's hair has grown gray. He goes fishing and spends time surfing the Internet and would still buy large bottles of Casaque for me if Jean d'Albret still existed. I think he is perhaps even foolish enough to think I'm still a beautiful bride.

My bottle of Casaque is not three-quarters empty. It is still one-quarter full. Perhaps at over seventy years of age... if I'm very careful... I can count on using it for the rest of my life.

~Toni Somers

与子偕老。这是我听过的最好的事。

——罗伯特·布朗宁

那个瓶子放在浴室的柜子上，就放在我的梳子和牙刷的旁边。里面已经用完四分之三了。瓶子标签上的蓝色在 40 多年的时光中已经退了色，标签显示它的牌子是珍·德·阿尔布雷（香水品牌）的“卡萨克”。

这瓶特别的古龙香水我现在用得非常省，只在特别重要的场合才会用，因为如果最后这一点用完了，就再也没有能代替它的了。

这种特殊香味的古龙水，我一共有过两瓶，这是第二瓶。杰克给了我第一瓶……非常小的一瓶……在我们第一次结婚纪念日的时候。

我还能听到栗色老“福特”的消声器发出的噪声，还有车子破旧的轮胎在车道的砂砾上吱吱咯咯的声音。很多年前的那个周三下午，他从他的医学院上课早早回来了。在厨房的窗沿下，他停了一会儿，深吸了一口我做的派的香气，然后他递给我一个小纸包。

“亲爱的，周年纪念日快乐！我给你买了些特别的礼物。”

“我想不仅特别，还很贵吧。这个是苏珊娜（著名商店品牌）的袋子。你知道我们可买不起里面的东西。”

“如果不给这个世界上最美丽的新娘子买点特别的东西，我可受不了。特别是那个新娘子还会在我们的周年纪念日晚餐上烤出这么美味的甜点。”

他搂着我的腰，解开了我围裙上的带子。

“过来坐下，打开看看。”

他把我拉到了隔壁，那是我们狭小的公寓里除了厨房外唯一的屋子，我们坐在旁边破旧的沙发上。

当我从袋子里拿出一个小包裹的时候，我的手都在抖。我犹豫着要不要打开这像艺术品一样的包装，优雅的金色锡箔包装纸和黑色的天鹅绒丝带。

“打开它，亲爱的，打开吧。”

“但是我们说过要为你攒学费，两个人都不用买什么礼物的。”我违心地抗议道。

杰克坚持说："打开它，亲爱的。"

这可爱的包装拆开之后，里面是一瓶法国古龙水。我知道这一定很贵。我把它举到我的鼻子跟前，闻着这我所能想象到的最精妙的香味。

"啊！杰克！这太棒了！我还从来没用过古龙水呢。"

低头望了望我掉了色的牛仔裤和难看破旧的网球鞋，我想找到一点地方证明我配得上这完美的香味。我确实努力试了。

在我们结婚的早些年，我用这珍贵的"卡萨克"异常节省。甚至到杰克医学院毕业和研究生也都毕业了，我们的生活也不那么拮据了，我仍然用它很节省。甚至当我们住进了一所新的大房子，有了新的沙发，还有了5个孩子之后，我仍然斤斤计较地保护着我那芬芳的财产，那标志着一个年轻的丈夫对爱情的一次傻傻的奢侈的浪漫。

然而，有一天，我们3岁的儿子吉米喝掉了我珍贵的"卡萨克"！

我那天心情郁闷，天色阴沉，淫雨霏霏。新领回来的小狗一直又闹又叫，我到半夜都没有睡着。我打开冰箱，发现没有牛奶了。我去拿钱包和钥匙，竟然发现吉米把我的"卡萨克"给喝了！证据确凿。他坐在地板上，举着空瓶子，嘴角还是湿的，脸色惊恐。

我尖叫着："杰克，快过来！古龙水对孩子有毒没？吉米刚才把我剩下的'卡萨克'都喝了！"

他安慰我说："亲爱的，里面顶多有些酒精。但保险起见，我们还是把他带到急诊室去看看吧。"

小吉米没事，我对孩子的担心减轻了，现在我开始哀悼我那空空的古龙水瓶子了。

"别伤心了，亲爱的，我们可以再买一瓶的。"

几周之后的一天，杰克回到家，又一次带了一个包装优雅的小包裹……这次盛着我最爱的香味的瓶子大了很多。

"对不起，我花了一些时间才找到一样的。苏珊娜的营业员是从堪萨斯城才订购来的。这种卖的可不多了。"

虽然生活很顺利，学费的烦恼和汽车消声器烦人的噪音这些都过去很久了，我拿着我新的"卡萨克"仍然很骄傲，就像我第一次得到它时那样，节省地使用它，都可以说是吝啬了。但仍然有一天，发现已经用掉了半瓶，我觉得最好再买一瓶。那时可能比几年前更加难买了。

苏珊娜柜台里的营业员笑了笑，我确定她认为这对我是一种安慰，她说："'卡萨克'？我们已经好多年都不卖了。实际上，我觉得珍·德·阿尔布雷已经不再生产了。但是，我们有一些其他的适合您这个年纪的香水。"

"苏珊娜女士在吗？也许她知道怎么能订到它。我想她几年前为我从堪萨斯城订了一瓶。"

"那肯定是很多年前了。苏珊娜女士五年前就已经过世了。这个商店现在属于她的儿子乔治了。"

时光如梭。一天，我看着这瓶古龙水，它已经所剩无几了。这么多年来我一直用得很小心。吉米和他的四个兄弟姐妹也已经长大了。他是一名成功的律师，再也不会喝古龙水了。他开始喝那些更高档的饮料。杰克的头发也已花白了。他喜欢去钓钓鱼、上上网，如果珍·德·阿尔布雷仍然存在的话，他还会继续为我买"卡萨克"的。我觉得他肯定傻傻地觉得我还是当初那个美丽的新娘。

我的古龙水并不是用完了四分之三，而是还有四分之一。可能在 70 岁以后……如果我节省点用的话……我能够指望在我的余生一直用下去。

——托尼·萨默斯

Nutty as a Fruitcake
有坚果的水果蛋糕

...love knows not its own depth until the hour of separation.

~Kahlil Gibran

The marriage of my maternal grandparents was pretty out of the ordinary for an older couple. They often yelled at each other or snapped an insult over simple everyday tasks. I remember as a child wondering why they were even a couple. At times they were like oil and water, not a retired couple enjoying their golden years.

It seemed as though they had to have each other though. She didn't drive and he couldn't cook. He ran errands daily for her. She always sent him looking for just the perfect pepper or a certain cut of steak. If he came in with anything slightly different than she had requested, he was on the receiving end of a tongue lashing. She could cook anything. The minute you walked in the house, you smelled something cooking. She made fresh biscuits and gravy, mashed potatoes from scratch, and any kind of cake or pie you could ask for. You had to eat something at each visit. People came by daily for leftovers and conversation.

He was happy to be the chauffeur and gofer. He went out four or five times per day. He said he enjoyed the peace and quiet.

They worked together at Christmas to make her signature cakes as gifts. Each year everyone had an orange slice cake, a spice cake, and a fruitcake from my grandparents. The fruitcakes were fodder for many arguments and insults during the baking. They spit insults at each other during the entire process. Of course, they were funny to everyone.

"Are you blind? This is NOT the brand of cinnamon that I sent for!"

"Of course I'm blind—I married you!"

Several days and many arguments later, many cakes were delivered. I don't really remember eating the fruitcakes, but they were my grandfather's favorite. They made several extra and he ate them long after Christmas was over. It was his afternoon snack with his coffee or late night treat with a glass of milk. She would tell him he was going to have indigestion for eating so late and he would eat another slice.

My grandmother passed away in the spring of their fifty-third year together. My grandfather was completely lost without her. Everything he saw or heard reminded him of her. Nothing he ate tasted like her cooking and he was unable to eat much at all. Her birthday came soon after, the family reunion, Mother's Day… all days that she loved. Getting through each of the firsts was almost unbearable for him.

As Christmas approached my cousin and I dreaded the thought of him alone in the house, knowing it was time to make their special cakes. We decided to bring a new tradition to him. We would bake cakes and have him help decorate and deliver them. He finally acquiesced but really wasn't in the mood. The house was certainly lacking her presence and it was evident that he was missing her.

Even though he and my grandmother really did nothing special on Christmas morning, I couldn't stand the thought of him being alone. I made it a point to be there as early as I could. As I came in the back door to the kitchen, I saw him eating a slice of fruitcake for breakfast. I asked him where he got that one, secretly hoping he wouldn't offer me any.

He looked at me with a tear in his eyes and said, "This is the last fruitcake that your grandmother made. She put it in the freezer last year and I never did eat it. I'm so glad I didn't because now I can still have her with me at Christmas."

The years that my grandfather lived after that opened my eyes to the love that they really shared. He was dedicated to her memory and then I saw that their marriage was more than a dependence on each other. They were together because they wanted to be. They were in love.

~Dena May

只有在分别时，你才知道爱得有多深。

——纪伯伦

我的外祖母和祖父的婚姻和大多数老年人的不太一样。在每天的生活中，他们经常对对方吼叫，还会辱骂对方。我记得当我是个孩子的时候，我就想为什么他们会是一对夫妻呢？有时，他们就像油和水，互不相容，而不是一对退休了之后，享受黄金晚年的老夫妇。

这似乎是因为他们相互离不开对方。她不会

开车，而他不会做饭。他每天为她跑腿。她总是派他去买最好的胡椒粉或者是某种牛排之类的。如果他买回来的东西和她要求的有一点点不同，他就会被唠叨个没完。她做饭特别棒。一走进屋子里，就会闻见她在做什么好吃的。她会做新鲜的饼干、肉汁土豆泥，以及你能想到的各种饼干和派。你每次来都不得不吃点东西。人们每天来聊聊天，走的时候再带点什么回去。

他乐呵呵地做着司机和杂役。每天跑出去四五次。他说他享受着这份安宁和平静。

圣诞节时，他们会合力工作，做她标志性的蛋糕作为礼物。每一年，每个人都会收到他们做的甜橙切片蛋糕、香草蛋糕，还有一个水果蛋糕。这个水果蛋糕是在争吵中烤出来的。在整个过程中，他们相互语言攻击。当然，他们之间也很有趣。

"你瞎了吗？这不是我让你买的那个牌子的肉桂！"

"我当然瞎了——瞎了眼才会娶你！"

几天的争吵过后，很多蛋糕做出来了，也送出去了。我并不总是记得吃它们，但是这些是我外祖父的最爱。他们会多做一些，在圣诞节结束之后很长时间，他还在吃着这些蛋糕。这是他下午喝咖啡时的点心，或者他会在吃夜宵喝牛奶时来上一块。她会告诉他这么晚吃东西对消化不好，但是他会一边答应着一边再吃一块。

他们结婚第53个年头的春天，我的外祖母去世了。没有了外祖母，外祖父完全地迷失了。他看见听见的每一件事都会使他想起她来。他再也吃不到她做的东西了，现在他的胃口也很不好。很快就到了她的生日、家庭大聚会、母亲节……这些都是她喜欢的日子。第一次度过这些日子对他来说几乎是无法承受的。

圣诞节快到了，我和我的表兄害怕他一个人在家里会孤单，想到这是他们一起做蛋糕的日子。我们决定为他带来一个新的习惯。我们烤蛋糕，让他来装饰蛋糕，再让他帮助把蛋糕送出去。他最后还是同意了，但是兴致不高。当然，家里再也没有了外祖母的身影，这也是他思念她的证明。

虽然，他和我的外祖母在圣诞节早上不会做什么特别的事，我也无法忍受他一个人孤孤单单的。我坚持在那天早上很早就到了那里。当我来到厨房的后门时，我看见他正在吃着一片水果蛋糕当早饭。我问他哪来的蛋糕，私心里希望他可不要给我吃。

他眼含热泪，看着我说："这是你外祖母做的最后一片水果蛋糕了。她去年把它放在冰箱里，我没吃掉。我很庆幸我没吃，因为这样，现在我在圣诞节的时候还能和她在一起。"

我外祖父在外祖母走后那些年的生活，让我明白了他们之间真正的爱。他一直处在对她的回忆当中，我明白了，他们的婚姻不仅仅是相互依靠。他们在一起是因为他们想在一起。他们彼此深爱对方。

——德娜·玛丽

My Special Angel
我特别的天使

Perhaps they are not the stars, but rather openings in heaven where the love of our lost ones pours through and shines down upon us to let us know they are happy.

~Inspired by an Eskimo Legend

The day I married my childhood sweetheart was the happiest day of my life. We had been friends since the third grade and had always assumed that one day we would marry and raise a family. Our dreams had come true.

Over the course of the next three years, we lived in a dream world. We loved one another from the very depths of our souls and treated each other with respect, kindness, and compassion. We never thought of ourselves and always put the other first. There was nothing we would not do for each other.

We were seldom apart. We had common interests that ensured that we enjoyed each other's company. We would walk to the store together, holding hands, just to buy a loaf of bread. As well as being husband and wife, we were lovers and best friends.

After three years of marriage, I discovered I was pregnant. We were both delighted. We spent hours in the stores, picking out clothes, furniture, and accessories for the newest addition to our family.

Our daughter was born on a bright, sunny day in February. Our area had been hit by a heavy snowfall the week before and the world was white and beautiful. It seemed that this was an omen. Our family would have a bright future.

For the next ten months we nourished our daughter, watched her grow, learn to walk, and say her first words. My husband's heart soared the first time she looked at him with her big brown eyes and uttered the word, "Daddy." The world had never been so perfect.

Christmas was a great joy. We dressed Michelle in a red Santa suit and hat, played Santa and watched with joy as her eyes lit up at the sight of her first Christmas tree. We lay together later that night and reminisced about the joys of the day. We were ecstatic and talked of Christmases to come.

In the wee hours of New Year's Eve, my world came crashing down. I awoke to find my husband sitting on the edge of the bed, clutching his chest and crying out in pain. Before I could throw back the covers and get to him, he began screaming. He stood, pushed me to one side and staggered into the living room. I followed, fear gripping me as I asked over and over what was wrong. He never answered. His screams rebounded off the walls of the small room and almost deafened me. Suddenly, he fell face first onto the hardwood floor. Then… silence.

The deadly sound of silence seemed to fill the room even more than the screams of a moment before. I scrambled for the telephone and called an ambulance. It seemed an eternity before it arrived. I later learned it was actually a little over four minutes.

After I made the call, I dropped to my knees beside my husband. I shook his shoulder, rolled him onto his back and called out his name as tears ran down my face and fell onto his. There was no response. As the ambulance pulled into the driveway, siren wailing, I already knew that he was dead.

The next few days were a nightmare. I picked out his casket, made funeral arrangements, and stood by his coffin shaking hands and accepting the sympathy of family and friends. I felt no emotion whatsoever at this time. It was as if I had turned to stone.

At the cemetery, my father stood beside me, his hand on my shoulder in a gesture of comfort. I knew his heart ached. He and my husband had gotten along splendidly. I couldn't bring myself to comfort him. When they began to lower my husband's casket into the ground, I began to sob, deep wracking sobs that seemed to tear away my soul. As far as I was concerned, my life was over. Not only had I lost a husband, but also my lover and best friend. It had all happened in the blink of an eye. I leaned against my father's chest while he smoothed my hair with his work-worn hand and crooned words of comfort. I remember wondering at the time how the world could be so cruel.

Over the next few weeks, I went through the normal grieving process. I was angry with my husband for leaving me, angry with God for taking him, and angry at the world in general. I didn't have the opportunity to go through the denial process. My husband had died right before my eyes and the reality of it was not to be denied.

For three weeks, I barely slept a wink. Each time I drifted off, my husband's screams revisited. Then, I would awaken, hoping it was all a bad dream and trembling uncontrollably. I couldn't eat, lost weight and wished that I had died with him.

During this period, I stayed at my parents' house, refusing to set foot in my own home. I couldn't bear the thought of entering the living room where my husband had died, and was afraid the bedroom would echo his screams of pain. I ignored my infant daughter, locked myself in the bedroom of my childhood where I remained for hours, and turned a deaf ear to my mother's pleas to come out and join the family. Though I continued to wish I had died with my husband on that fateful night, I never once contemplated suicide. I didn't realize it at the time, but this was a good indication that I was going to make it.

After a month, my father told me that I either had to go back to the house to live or give the landlord notice that I was moving. I understood the logic of this but wanted nothing more to do with that house. I wrote a notice to terminate my tenancy, asked Dad to deliver it and begged him to sell everything in the house with the exception of our personal belongings and a few mementos. At first Dad protested but finally he relented. He thought I should face my fears— my ghosts—so there'd be closure. Again, I refused.

• Dad made arrangements to meet a used furniture dealer at the house and one day, just after my daughter's first birthday, went to take care of things. It seemed like he was gone for hours and my imagination ran wild. Had something happened to him? In my sorry state of mind, I felt the house was cursed.

When I heard Dad's truck pull into the driveway, I breathed a sigh of relief. All of the reminders of that terrible night would now be gone. I would never have to step into that house again.

Dad entered the house looking haggard and drawn. He took off his coat and hat, hung them up, took a small package out of his pocket and handed it to me. He told me he had found it in the mailbox at the house.

The return address on the envelope was that of the jewelry store where my husband and I had purchased our wedding bands. I tore it open, curious to see what was inside. When I dumped the contents, I found an angel pendant about a half-inch high on the finest gold chain I had ever seen. Embedded in one of the angel's wings were three birthstones. An amethyst represented my daughter, a blue sapphire for me, and an emerald for my husband. I looked at Dad. He shrugged. Apparently he knew nothing about it.

It was then that I realized there was something left in the envelope. The letter inside was addressed to my late husband. It was a letter of apology, indicating that though they had promised Christmas delivery, there had been a delay and they were giving him a partial refund. A check was enclosed along with a handwritten note from my husband. The note read: "When you wear this beautiful angel, always know that I am near."

As I read, I could feel my husband's presence and almost see the smile on his face. I fastened the chain around my neck, knowing that he would be beside me always to guide me through the trials and tribulations of being a single parent. Peace enveloped me and in that moment, I knew that for his sake and that of my infant daughter, I must get on with my life.

Luckily for me, Dad had ignored all of my requests. The furniture was still in the small house where my husband and I had lived, loved, and laughed since the day we were married. The notice that I had told Dad to give to the landlord was still in his pocket. Michelle and I were going home.

The very next day, I bundled Michelle into her snowsuit and took her back to that house. I made a decision to pursue my lifelong dream of being a published writer. That fall, I enrolled in a writing class. Over the course of many years, my writing began to sell. How proud my late husband would have been.

The grief didn't leave overnight. Sometimes, I would awaken in a cold sweat, frightened and lonely. When this happened, I would hold my special angel between my fingers and rub her gently. Always, peace would envelop me and I would fall into a relaxed sleep.

I lost my special angel some years ago. At first, I was heartbroken. Then, I realized that I no longer needed to depend on her for peace and comfort. My only hope is that she brings peace and comfort into the life of the person who found her. She will always be my special angel and I will never forget the gift that my first husband sent me from beyond the grave. It truly was a gift of love.

~Mary M. Alward

可能天上的并不是星辰，而是我们失去的爱人在天堂闪烁着，照耀着凡间，让我们知道他们很好。

——由爱斯基摩的传说演化而来

　　我和我童年时就爱的人结婚的那一天，是我生命中最开心的一天了。我们从三年级开始就是朋友了，一直就确信，总有一天我们会结婚，成立一个家庭。我们的梦想终于实现了。

　　在接下来的三年里，我们生活在一个梦幻般的世界里。我们从心底深处爱着彼此，相互之间尊重、友好和相互同情。我们从来不会先想到自己，总是把对方放在第一位。我们为了对方什么都会做。

　　我们很少分开，且有着相同的兴趣，享受着对方的陪伴。我们手牵着手一起去商店，只为了买一条面包。我们既是丈夫和妻子，也是爱人和挚友。

　　结婚三年之后，我发现自己怀孕了。我们都很开心，去商店为我们家的新成员挑选衣服、家具和配件。

　　我们的女儿米歇尔降生在 2 月阳光明媚的一天。前一个星期下了一场大雪，整个世界都银装素裹，美丽动人。这就像是一个预兆一样。我们的家庭将会有一个光明的未来。

　　接下来的 10 个月里，我们抚育着女儿。看着她长大，学走路，第一次说话。当她用棕色的大眼睛看着他并且第一次叫他"爸爸"的时候，我的丈夫心花怒放。世界从来没有这么美好过。

　　圣诞节是一次大狂欢。我们给米歇尔穿上了一件圣诞老人的衣服，还戴了一顶圣诞老人的帽子，玩圣诞老人的游戏。当她睁大眼睛盯着她见到的第一株圣诞树时，我们真是开心极了。那天晚上很晚了，我们躺在一起，怀念着白天的欢乐时光。我们心中充满狂喜，期待着下一个圣诞节快些到来。

　　新年前夜的凌晨，我的世界崩塌了。我半夜惊醒，发现我的丈夫坐在床边，抓着胸口，痛苦地大叫着。在我掀开被子到他跟前之前，他又开始尖叫。他站起来，把我推到一边，跌跌撞撞地走到了起居室。我跟过去，一遍又一遍地问他到底怎么了，我惊恐万分。他没有回答我。窄小的房间里回荡着他的尖叫声，几乎把我震聋了。突然，他面部朝下，倒在了硬木地板上。一切……都安静了。

　　致命的安静笼罩在屋子里，这比刚才的尖叫还要可怕。我抓起电话，叫了救护车。在救护车到来之前，时间就好像静止了一样。后来我知道，实际上这过程只有 4 分多钟。

　　在我打完电话之后，我跪在我丈夫身边，摇晃着他的肩，把他翻过来，背部向下。我一边哭一边叫他的名字，泪水滴落在他的身上，但是毫无反应。当救护车开进车道，警报声呼啸而来的时候，我知道，他已经去世了。

接下来的几天就像一场噩梦一样。我收拾他的骨灰盒，安排葬礼，站在他的棺材旁边和来来往往的人握手，接受家人朋友的同情和安慰。此时的我没有任何感觉。我就好像变成了一块石头一样。

在墓地的时候，我爸爸站在我的身旁，他的手放在我的肩上，那是一个安慰的姿势。我知道他心痛。他和我的丈夫相处得非常好。我自己无法去安慰他。当他们开始把我丈夫的骨灰盒埋入地下的时候，我开始抽泣，极度痛苦地抽泣，好像我的灵魂都要被泪水冲走了一样。我所能想到的就是——我的生活结束了。我失去的不仅仅是丈夫，还是我的爱人和挚友。这一切都发生在顷刻之间。我靠在我爸爸的胸前，他用他粗糙的大手抚摸着我的头发，低声地安慰着我。在那个时候，我想知道世界为什么如此残酷。

接下来的几周时间里，我度过了一段悲伤的时日。我恨我的丈夫为什么离开了，我恨上天为什么要带走他，我恨整个世界。我没有那个拒绝接受的过程。我的丈夫就在我眼前死去，事实是无法否认的。

三个星期以来，我几乎没有合眼。每次我刚要入睡，我丈夫的尖叫声就在脑海中响起。然后，我就会惊醒，不可抑制地战栗，希望这一切不过是个噩梦而已。我吃不下东西，瘦了很多，真希望随他而去。

在这段时间里，我待在我爸妈家里，拒绝回我自己家。我无法承受再次走进我丈夫死去的那个起居室，而我也害怕那间卧室，那里回响着他痛苦的尖叫声。我无视我襁褓中的女儿，把我自己长时间地锁在我儿时的卧室里，对我妈妈叫我出去和家人待在一起的请求，我充耳不闻。虽然我一直希望在那个夜晚我已经随我丈夫而去，但是我从来没有考虑过自杀。那时我还没有意识到，但是很多迹象表明，我可能会这样做。

一个月之后，我爸爸跟我说，要么我回到那里去住，要么我给房东一个信儿，让他知道我要搬走。我知道这么做很有必要，但是我不想再和那所房子有任何瓜葛了。我写了一封信终止了我的租约，让爸爸递过去，并恳请爸爸把那间房子里的一切都卖掉，除了我的一些个人物品和一些遗物。起初，爸爸反对这么做，但是最终他还是同意了。他认为我应当面对恐惧——我心中的幽灵——这一切才能结束。我再一次拒绝了。

那天正好是我女儿1岁生日的第二天，爸爸安排了和一位买卖旧家具的商人在房子里见面，他过去处理一些事情。他好像走了好几小时，我胡思乱想起来。他发生了什么事情吗？我的脑子还处在悲伤的状态，我觉得那个房子被诅咒了。

当我听到爸爸的车开进车道的时候，我长舒了一口气，对那个可怕的夜晚的回忆才被驱散。我绝不会再走进那所房子。

爸爸走进来，看起来十分憔悴。他脱掉外套和帽子，挂起来，从口袋里拿出了一个小包裹，递给我。他告诉我这是在那个房子的邮箱里找到的。

回信的地址写的是一家珠宝店的名字，我和我丈夫在那家店买了我们的婚礼用品。我撕开信封，很好奇里面装了什么。我把里面的东西倒出来，发现了一个——三四厘米高的天使吊坠，挂在一条我看见过的最精美的金链子上。镶嵌在天使翅膀中的是三块诞生石。紫水晶代表我女儿，蓝宝石代表我，绿宝石代表我丈夫。我看了看我爸爸，他耸耸肩。很明显他什么也不知道。

我意识到信封里还有什么东西在。里面有封信是写给我已故的丈夫的。这是一封道歉信，商家表示说虽然他们许诺会在圣诞节寄到，但是延误了，于是他们给他一部分退款。里面还有一张支票，以及一封我丈夫的手写字条。上面写着："当你戴上这个美丽的天使项坠，就会知道我一直在你身边。"

读完了信，我仿佛感到丈夫就在身边，我几乎都能看见他在微笑。我把项链戴在脖子上，知道他一直就在我身边，他会带着我度过当一个单身妈妈的痛苦和磨难。那一刻，我重归平静。我知道，为了他，为了我们襁褓中的女儿，我必须继续我的生活。

幸运的是，我爸爸忽视了我的请求。家具仍然在那间小房间里，自从我们结婚后，我和我的丈夫曾经在那里生活过、相爱过、欢笑过。我让我爸爸给房东的信还在他口袋里。我要和米歇尔回家。

第二天，我帮米歇尔穿上厚厚的防雪装，带着她回到了那所房子。我决定追求我一生的梦想，要成为一名作家。那个秋天，我参加了一个写作培训班。在很多年的课程之后，我的作品开始出版了。我已故的丈夫该是多么骄傲啊。

悲痛不会留到第二天。有时候，我半夜惊醒，冷汗直流，惊恐万分，又是那么孤独。每当这样的时候，我就会把我特殊的天使放在我的指间，轻轻地摩挲着。我总是会平静下来，重新放松入睡。

我几年前弄丢了我特别的天使。一开始，我的心碎了。后来，我明白，我不再需要她来给我宁静和安慰了。我希望她会把这一切带给发现她的人。她将永远是我特别的天使，我将永远不会忘记我第一位丈夫在去世之后送给我的礼物。这是一个真正的爱的礼物。

——玛丽·M.奥尔沃德

The Last Valentine
最后的情人节礼物

The love game is never called off on account of darkness.
~Tom Masson

The day before Valentine's Day that year, I stared out at the bleak hospital parking lot from a small window for the hundredth time, wishing I could see something new, some sign of hope beckoning from an invisible horizon. Instead, all I could see was fading light over cars and concrete. It seemed to be fading inside too, temporarily softening the usually sterile setting in which my father now slept.

I turned toward his bed. Daddy breathed quietly, as though trying not to disturb anyone, maintaining a gentle dignity befitting his solitary nature. I was relieved that he appeared comfortable. This illness, stealthy and slow, had gone on so long that people no longer sent flowers or cards. They no longer knew what to say and, like the light in that room, simply faded away.

I was still young, and unused to the waiting

times so familiar to those who helplessly stand watch over a terminally ill loved one. My mind retreated to happier times and I reviewed images from memories of my father. In each picture he was with my mother; adoring her. He would give her flowers and she would clap her hands together and purr with her sweet southern voice, "Oh Dave! These are the loveliest ever!" Then a soft kiss on his cheek and he would blush with pleasure. She tucked his cards away in an old wooden box which after so many years became so filled to the brim that it would no longer shut properly.

And now, my mother, who had never left his side before, was at home, getting a few hours of desperately needed sleep. Without her the silence in this room felt threatening and ominous. The inevitability of death and impending grief hovered unseen, waiting. Prayers of petition for his recovery seemed useless and unwise. Why would I want my father to linger in pain? I closed my eyes and silently implored, "Father... Father..." speaking to both of them.

A nurse walked briskly into the room, stirring up the silence with her purposeful efficiency. Then, with customary, but oddly out-of-place cheeriness, she sang out, "How is our patient?"

I turned from the window and smiled but didn't reply to the obvious. As she held my father's limp wrist and listened for his faint pulse she chattered on. Only half listening I slid down into a chair in the corner of the room and looked up at the window. Dark now. Nothing to see.

A moment later snippets of her words nudged me out of my numbing thoughts. "Tomorrow... Valentine's Day... Have you bought your Valentine's cards yet?" The gift shop was open for another hour if I wanted to run down and get some and she would be happy to sit with my father until I came back. For the first time I looked at her, saw her soft pink sweater, her younger hands holding my father's old hands. I nodded gratefully and hurried to the elevator.

In the gift shop I looked at the rows of cards. I picked up the ones that said

"For my Father" and then unexpected tears slipped down my face. Why should I buy him a valentine when he might not live long enough to see it? Why would he care about Valentine's Day?

I was returning them to the rack when I realized I had picked up one that said, "To my wife on Valentine's Day." I remembered the cards in my mother's old box, representing almost forty years of marriage and then, without thinking about the impossibility of what I was preparing to do, bought the card and hurried back to my father's room.

After the nurse had left, I leaned over the bed, listened to his faint breathing, and whispered "Daddy, you have to do one more thing. Please Daddy. Just one more thing." There was no response.

I slipped a pen into his hand and laid the open card on his chest. He didn't move. "Please, Daddy. This is for Mom. A valentine. You've never forgotten." He seemed beyond my sense of urgency, beyond such a childish request and didn't move.

I stepped away from the bed, feeling a sense of shame that I had asked of him what he could no longer do and whispered a prayer of apology to God for being foolish. Time crawled slowly forward. Many more hours until sunrise. I pulled the chair closer to the bed, lowering myself slowly into it and closed my eyes. And I slept.

Hours later I awoke with a start, disoriented and alarmed that sleep had taken me away from my father's bedside. I rose from the chair and reached out to take the pen from his hand. The valentine had slipped to one side and as I reached for it, I saw my father's lips move. I leaned forward but I couldn't hear him. There was the tiniest trace of a smile on his face. The hand that had held the pen moved slightly. I picked up the card and looked inside. There, in shaky letters he had written, "Love, Dave."

"Thank you, Daddy." I whispered. "Mom will love this." He raised his fingers in a kind of benediction and I hugged his frail body one more time before releasing him to what had to be.

He died three hours later, as dawn was gathering light for this part of a waiting world. And when my mother entered the room, resting by the pillow was his last valentine for her, miraculously signed by him because love will always have the last word.

~Caroline S. McKinney

真爱绝不会因为黑暗而失效。

——汤姆·马森

那一年的情人节前一天，我从医院的小窗户里不下一百次地盯着荒凉的停车场，希望能看见一些什么新鲜的东西——从无形的地平线上能升起一些希望的标志。然而，我能看见的只有暗淡的车灯和混凝土。屋里的光线似乎也逐渐暗了下来，暂时使得无菌室柔和了许多，我父亲正在里面躺着。

我转向他的床边。父亲平静地呼吸着，好像试图不想要打扰任何人，保持着绅士般的尊严，就像他天生孤寂的本性。他看起来很舒适，这让我十分欣慰。这种疾病潜伏期长，发作慢，已经拖了许久。人们已经不再来送花和卡片了。他们不知道还能说什么，就像那屋里的灯光一样，他们的身影逐渐退去了。

我还很年轻，还不习惯等待的时光。有些人面对自己身患绝症的爱人，只能无助地眼睁睁地看着，他们对这样的日子已经很熟悉了。我的脑海里还是昔日快乐的时光，一遍又一遍地回想关于父亲的记忆。每一个场景里，他都是和母亲在一起，宠爱着她。他给她送花，妈妈会高兴地拍手，用她那甜美的南部嗓音欢呼道："啊！戴夫！这些最漂亮了！"然后会给爸爸一个轻吻，爸爸就会快乐得脸都羞红了。妈妈会把卡片抽出来，放在一个旧的木盒子里，这么多年过去了，装得已经溢出了边缘，都不能好好地盖上了。

现在，我妈妈正在家里补觉，她急需几小时的睡眠，在这之前她一直没有离开过爸爸身边。她离开了，这间屋子显得特别寂静，让人感到恐慌和不祥。死亡不可避免，悲伤总要到来，这一切就好像在周围徘徊着、等待着。为他的康复而祈祷似乎是无用的，也是不明智的。我为什么希望爸爸在痛苦边缘多加徘徊呢？虽然知道是无用的也不明智的，但我还是闭上眼睛，默默地恳求："爸爸，爸爸……"

一个护士轻快地走进房间，用她有目的高效率的行动打破了屋子里的寂静。然后，像往常那样，她大声问道："病人怎么样？"但是，奇怪的是，这一次语气里带着些不合时宜的欢快。

我从窗户那边转过脸，笑了笑，但是没有回答，一切都显而易见。她一边喋喋不休地说着话，一边举起我爸爸无力的手腕，听着他微弱的脉搏。我心不在焉地听着，窝到了角落里的椅子里，抬头望着窗户。天黑了。我什么也没看见。

过了一会儿，我听到了她话中的一些片段，把我从麻木的思考中拉回现实。"明天……情人节……你买了你的情人节卡片了吗？"礼品商店还开着门，如果我想去买一些的话，她很乐意陪我爸爸，直到我回来。我第一次观察她，她穿着粉色的毛衣，年轻的手正举着我爸爸苍老的手。我点了点头，急忙冲向电梯。

在礼品商店里，我看着一排排的卡片。我挑出一张，上面写着"送给父亲"，眼泪毫无预兆地滑落脸庞。为什么我要给他买情人节礼物，他有可能都活不到能看见它的时候了。他又怎么会在乎情人节呢？

我把卡片放回架子上，突然，我看见一张上面写着"送给我的妻子，情人节快乐"。我记得我妈妈的旧盒子里有这张卡片，代表了他们将近四十年的婚姻。我买下了这张卡片，匆匆赶回爸爸的病房，都来不及想一下我接下来想做的事情是多么不可能。

护士走后，我倚在床边，听着爸爸微弱的呼吸声，轻声说："爸爸，你还有一件事没做呢。爸爸，求你了，就一件。"没有任何回应。

我把笔塞到他手里，把卡片展开，放到他的胸前。他没有动。"爸爸，求你了，这是给妈妈的情人节礼物。你从来没有忘过的。"他似乎一点也感觉不到我的焦虑，不理会我这个孩子气的请求，一动也不动。

我从床边走开，想到我要求他做他不可能做到的事，就感到一阵羞愧。我轻声祈祷，请求上天原谅我的愚蠢。时间慢慢流逝，几小时过去了，太阳升起来了。我把椅子拉到床边，慢慢地陷到椅子里面去了，闭上了眼睛。我睡着了。

又过了几小时，我突然惊醒。迷糊不清地发现睡着的时候我离爸爸的床边越来越远了。我从椅子里起来，去把笔从他手里拿开。这个情人节礼物已经滑落到了一边，当我拿到它的时候，我发现爸爸的嘴唇动了动。我身子前倾，但是我听不见他在说什么。他的脸上有一丝最微弱的笑容。那只拿着笔的手轻轻地动了一下。我捡起卡片，看了看里面。那里有他歪歪扭扭写的几个字："我爱你。戴夫。"

我轻声说："谢谢你，爸爸。妈妈会喜欢的。"他动了动手指，做成一个祝福的姿势，我再次拥抱了他虚弱的身体，知道一旦松手他就会离开去他该去的地方。

三小时之后，他去世了。窗外，黎明正在为等待着的世界收集一束束阳光。当妈妈走进来的时候，他写给她的最后的情人节礼物，正静静地放在枕边。他奇迹般地写下了"我爱你"，因为爱永远不会没有最后一声道别。

——卡洛琳·S.麦金尼

The Perfect Gift
完美的礼物

If I know what love is, it is because of you.
~Hermann Hesse

Ten years ago in a fit of rage and intentional cruelty, my ex-husband David destroyed my family roots when he lit a match to my heirloom quilts that had been passed down to me from my grandmother. I stood by helplessly as her tangible legacy of love, courage, faith in God and hard work went up in flames.

Whenever I felt depressed, I had pulled out those quilts, carefully stored in her cedar chest, and wrapped myself up in them for comfort. They always gave me the courage to face my fears and future with hope. The quilts triggered fond memories because they were made from scraps of my hand-me-down school clothes. They transported me back in time to simple pleasures of snuggling beneath those "comforters" as Grandma tucked me into her four-poster bed and read me a bedtime story in her farmhouse. She told me there was a prayer in every stitch that God would bless me and keep me safe and secure as my guardian angels watched over me.

David even burned Grandma's quilting frames that I had planned on using to make legacy quilts for my two own daughters and future grandchildren.

I told my boyfriend Todd of David's numerous cruel acts and couldn't stop weeping when I lamented about my irreplaceable quilts. Over the past seven years that we've been dating, Todd has proposed to me many times and I've continually turned him down—the Queen of Excuses. In a heated argument, Todd asked me why I kept rejecting his proposals. Finally, I confessed that after my first experience, I didn't think I could ever get married. How could I possibly risk being hurt again? How could I learn to trust anyone again with my heart and what precious belongings I still had?

Then, one December day, Todd called, saying he was coming over to give me my birthday and Christmas present early. Little did I know that he had discovered the "perfect gift" that would melt the ice in my heart and set me free.

Todd shooed me out of my bedroom while he carefully arranged his gifts for maximum impact. Then he gently took my hands and whispered, "Before I let you see your presents, I want you to know that these are not intended to replace what you've lost. But if you can bring yourself to trust me, I hope they'll adequately express that I would give the world to make your life whole again."

Todd opened the door and I burst into tears of joy and screamed at the sight of three quilts of exquisite beauty spread out on my bed. I was amazed that Todd could be so caring, patient and compassionate in giving of himself to ease my pain. I didn't realize how angry and bitter I had become until his gift of love broke down the protective barriers I'd erected around my soul. Those quilts and his tenderhearted kindness and sensitivity toward me have restored my faith in people and given me the courage to love again.

~Judy Fox as told to Judy Howard

如果我理解了爱情，那也是因为你。

——黑塞

　　10 年前，我的前夫大卫被怒火冲昏了头脑，他故意残忍地摧毁了我家族根源的标志。他划着了一根火柴，点燃了我那床家传被子，那是我的祖母传给我的。那是我祖母的爱和勇气物化的遗留，是她对主的信仰的实化。我无助地站在旁边看着火焰在燃烧，什么也不能做。

　　每当我感到消沉的时候，我就把那些被子拉开，平时它们被仔细地收藏在雪松木的柜子里。我把我自己裹住，从中寻求安慰。它们总是能给我战胜困难的力量和面对未来的希望。那些被子总会触发我深情的记忆，因为它们是用我穿过的校服的碎片做成的，能把我带回那段时光，我偎依在这些"安慰"之下，体会着单纯的快乐，在她的乡间小屋里，祖母把我塞到她那有四个柱子的床上，为我读睡前故事。祖母告诉我，一针一线里都有着她的祈祷，上帝会祝福我，保佑我平安，就像我的守护天使一直在照看我一样。

　　大卫甚至把祖母做被子的架子都烧了。我本来是打算用它来为我的两个女儿和未来的孙子孙女做被子，让它们流传下去的。

我对我的男友托德说了大卫的种种恶行，在我回忆起我无可替代的被子的时候，我还是止不住地哭泣。在过去我们约会的七年里，托德已经向我求过很多次婚了，我一直拒绝他——用各种各样的借口。在一次热烈的讨论中，托德问我为什么我一直拒绝他的求婚。最后，我承认，在我的第一次婚姻之后，我觉得我自己再也不想结婚了。我怎么可能冒着再被伤害一次的风险呢？我如何才能学会再一次全心全意地信任一个人呢？上一次婚姻给我留下了什么珍贵的东西呢？

然后，在 12 月的一天，托德打电话给我，说他要过来给我生日礼物和提前的圣诞礼物。我一点也不知道，他发现这份"完美的礼物"可以融化我心中的寒冰，释放我以自由。

托德把我赶出了卧室，他要仔细地布置他的礼物，以达到最好的效果。然后他轻轻地牵着我的手，轻语道："在我让你看礼物之前，我想让你知道，这些不是用来代替你失去的东西的。但是如果你能信任我的话，我希望这份礼物足以表达：我将带给你一个世界，让你的生命重新完整。"

托德打开门，我喜极而泣，尖叫了起来。我看见三床精美的被子铺展在我的床上。我惊讶于托德是如此的在乎并耐心，是那样悲悯地奉献出自己，来缓解我的痛苦。直到他爱的礼物打破了我在心灵周围设置的重重防护，我才知道我以前有那么多的愤怒和仇恨。这些被子和他温厚善良的心灵，以及对我的无微不至，让我重树了对人的信任，也给了我再次去爱的勇气。

——朱迪·福克斯对朱迪·霍华德说的话

Timeless Love
永恒的爱

Love is not only some-thing you feel. It is something you do.
~David Wilkerson

My son-in-law, Chris, fiddled with his watch and tapped his finger on its glass until he had my daughter's attention. He had come to pick her up after a long day of work that had followed the short-sleep night of new parents and he was tired.

Hilary looked up from buckling their baby girl into her car seat and smiled at him.

Chris yawned and stretched his neck. He picked up Emily's car seat and waited for Hilary to make her rounds of hugs and thank you to all the loved ones who had come to celebrate their baby and shower her with gifts. Chris and Hilary had been married just over a year and in that time he had mastered the fine art of waiting and waiting and waiting and waiting….

But, after waiting for years to fall in love and start his family, this former confirmed bachelor counted these minutes of waiting among his blessings before finally waving goodbye and taking his wife and baby home.

I was happy for my daughter. Hilary had been through so much. Her first marriage had been painful and short, the happiness beginning to change just twenty minutes after leaving their large and elaborate wedding.

Hilary had worked hard to regain her confidence and equilibrium and then Chris came into her life and his love helped complete her healing.

My aunt and I were picking up after the shower when she said, "Cindy, I really like Chris, but I'm a little worried now."

That puzzled me. "What do you mean?"

"Didn't you see what he did when he got here? He no sooner came in the door then he was hurrying Hilary, pointing to his watch and tapping on it!"

"Yes, he does that a lot." I answered. "Isn't it sweet?"

That puzzled her until I explained.

Chris and Hilary were married in a small ceremony, with only their parents in attendance. After we had briefly rejoiced with them, Chris had scooped up his new bride and carried her off to his car. As they pulled out of the church parking lot and headed to his house to start their life together, he could feel Hilary tensing up. As they got farther from the church and closer to what would now be their home, her apprehension grew.

Chris reached over and took her hand. They drove like that for a few more minutes until his watch's alarm started beeping.

He dropped her hand and tapped on his watch. "Well, Hilary," he said, "we've been married twenty minutes and I still love you."

He smiled at her. Hilary slowly returned his smile and then teared up in her relief. Chris had given her the best wedding day gift of all, the reassurance of his kindness and love.

And these five years later, he continues to reassure her in their day to day life, through his love and care of their daughter and two-year-old son.

And when the words can not be spoken or the depth of his feelings can not be expressed, he gently taps on his watch, an intimate and personal reminder to Hilary of his timeless love.

~Cynthia Hamond

爱不仅仅在于你感受到了什么，而是在于你做了什么。

——大卫·威尔克森

我的女婿克里斯把弄着他的手表，手指轻敲表盘，直到引起了我女儿的注意。在一整天的工作之后，他来这儿接我女儿回家。他们刚有了孩子，晚上睡得很少，他已经十分疲倦了。

希拉里把他们的小女儿扣在她的座位上，抬起头来，对他一笑。

克里斯打着哈欠，伸了伸脖子。他收起艾米丽的小婴儿车，等着希拉里。她正在和周围的人——一一拥抱，向他们道谢，感谢他们来庆祝他们女儿的降生，并送给她礼物。克里斯和希拉里结婚才一年，原来，他掌握的最好的艺术就是等待，等待，等待，再等待……

但是，在等待了几年之后，他赢得了她的爱，并且成立了家庭。这时，这位以前坚定的单身汉在收到祝福时，正在看着时间，计算着还有多久就可以挥手说再见，把他的妻子女儿带回家。

Chapter 4 Gifts from the Heart
第四部分 心灵礼物篇

　　我为我的女儿高兴。希拉里经历了这么多事情。她的第一次婚姻痛苦而短暂。在他们盛大而精美的婚礼结束后仅仅 20 分钟，幸福就离她而去了。

　　希拉里努力地使自己重拾自信和平静，之后，克里斯就出现在她的生命中，他的爱帮助她完全地恢复了。

　　我的姑妈在送礼会之后，和我一起收拾，她说："辛迪，我很喜欢克里斯，但是我今天有点担心。"

　　她让我迷惑了："你这么说什么意思？"

　　"你难道没看见他在这里的时候在干什么？他一进门就开始催希拉里，指着他的表，还一直在敲它！"

　　我回答说："是的，他确实如此。这不是很甜蜜吗？"

　　这次轮到她迷惑了。我只得细细解释。

　　克里斯和希拉里的婚礼只举行了一场小的仪式，只有双方父母到场了。在我们简短地祝福了他们之后，克里斯就抱起了他的新娘，把她带到了车上。他们离开教堂停车场，驶向他们的新家，一同开始他们的生活，他能够感觉得到希拉里十分紧张。当他们离教堂越来越远，离他们现在的家越来越近的时候，她越来越忧惧了。

　　克里斯伸手握起她的手。他们像那样又开了几分钟，直到他的手表闹钟响了起来。

　　他放下她的手，指了指他的表，说："好了，希拉里，我们已经结婚 20 分钟了。我仍然爱着你。"

　　他对她笑了笑。希拉里逐渐地向他报以笑容，释怀之后开始哭泣。克里斯给了她最好的结婚礼物——他的保证和他的爱。

　　现在已经过去五年了，日常生活中，他仍然在用他的爱，以及对女儿和两岁儿子的照顾来让她安心。

当他们之间有什么不好说出口、或者是他深沉的爱无法用语言表达的时候，他就会轻敲手表，这是一种亲密而隐秘的提醒，告诉希拉里他对她的爱一直到永恒。

——辛西娅·哈蒙德

Gold Stars
金色的星星

Of all the shooting stars I knew, I never fell for anyone but you.

~Ozma

On August 7, 1999, I was on vacation in Red Lodge, Montana sitting on a bench watching a parade when my life changed forever.

It was a sunny, warm beautiful day and very possibly the entire population of 2,400 and all the tourists were crammed on the sidewalks. The town was full of excitement. But I saw nothing of it. My eyes were focused on something else. Behind my sunglasses, no one could see where I was really looking, especially the person I was watching.

Amidst all the people meandering about, I couldn't help but notice this one man who had walked back and forth in front of me at least four times. To be honest, I had noticed him a few days earlier. I was walking down the street. He was sitting outside a coffee shop surrounded by people chatting. He was just about to take a sip of coffee when we made eye contact. I smiled; he immediately lowered the cup and with a smile said, "Hello."

Now here he was again. I'm sure I wasn't the only woman watching this tall, handsome man. What aroused my interest the most was his sense of being very comfortable in his own skin. He was intriguing to say the least.

When the parade was over, almost instantly, the people disappeared, including the lady sitting beside me. I thought I should go, too, but because I had nowhere to go I stayed put. There he was standing in front of me. He said, "Is this your own personal bench or can anyone sit here?" I said, "It's not mine. Have a seat."

From the moment he sat down, we were both very at ease. It was like talking with a dear friend you hadn't seen in a long time. They say it happens when you're not looking. I wasn't and it did.

We talked for hours, each telling our life stories. Ed was fifty-three and I was forty-nine, so we had plenty to tell.

We were both honest right from the beginning. We spoke of our finest hours and confessed to our worst. There were no judgments. Neither of us was perfect and we were never going to be; we accepted each other just as we were.

On one occasion, I told him of a situation I encountered with a man from my past. I was explaining that what I wanted from a relationship was simply to be appreciated. The response I heard was, "Tena, I'm fresh out of gold stars." Several days after I told Ed this incident he asked me to get something out of the trunk of his car. To my surprise I found a card and just as I opened it a breeze rolled in and gold stars were flying everywhere. He wrote in the card, "You will never have to worry about being appreciated and I will never run out of gold stars." My heart leaped and tears of joy ran down my face.

We spent a glorious six weeks together until my vacation was over. In order to spend a little more time together, he offered to drive me home, as opposed to flying home alone. When I got in the car, he told me to look in the back. I couldn't believe my eyes. He had bought me the bench where we met. It sits in my backyard and is my most valuable possession.

That was ten years ago. Whether this relationship lasts until the day we die or ends tomorrow, I'll never forget him. No one has touched my life so profoundly.

He's taught me so many things. I can be in a relationship and still be myself—an individual on my own. Who knew? Not me.

He believes in me and has no doubts I can do anything I put my mind to. He's given me the joy of living with my best friend. I can tell him anything, no matter how stupid or profound. There is no need to keep my insecurities and fears to myself, or my triumphs.

We have fun together whether we are golfing, having a night out, or just hanging around at home. In addition, I've had great adventures with him, such as whitewater rafting, something I would never have considered before—way too scary.

He loves me without controlling or suffocating me. I wouldn't have missed sharing my life with him for anything in the world. I believe the greatest gift he's given me is to experience the depth and intensity of love I can feel for another person, while always aspiring to give more than I receive.

~Tena Beth Thompson

在所有的流星中，除了你，我不会为任何人陨落。

——奥兹玛

在 1999 年 8 月 7 日，我在蒙大拿的红客栈镇（蒙大拿的一个小镇）度假，我坐在长椅上看着一队游行队伍经过，这时我的生活永远地改变了。

那天阳光明媚，十分暖和。可能整个镇上的 2400 个居民和所有的游客都涌到了人行道上。整个小镇都沸腾了。但是我什么都看不见。我的注意力集中到了其他一些东西上。我戴着墨镜，没有人知道我在看什么，特别是我正在盯着的那个人。

在所有这些缓慢而曲折地前进着的人中间，我不由自主地就注意到了这个人，他来来回回在我面前走了至少四遍。坦白地说，我几天前就注意到他了。当时我正在街上散步，他坐在一个咖啡馆外面，周围的人都在聊天。当我们眼神交会的时候，他正要抿一口咖啡。我微笑了一下，他立即放下杯子，笑了笑，说："你好。"

现在他又出现了。我肯定不只我一个人盯着这个又高又帅的人看。最吸引我的在于他泰然自若的感觉。至少可以说，他是耐人寻味的。

等游行队伍完全通过，大部分人都四散而去，包括坐在我旁边的女士。我觉得我也该走了，但是因为我无处可去，所以我仍旧坐在那儿。他就站在我面前，说："这是你的私人长椅，还是说别人也可以坐在这儿呢？"我说："当然不是我的，请坐。"

他一坐下来，我们就都放松下来了。就好像你在和一位很久没见的好朋友聊天一样。所谓的不期而遇，大抵就是如此。

我们聊了几小时，两个人都在说自己生活中的故事。艾德 53 岁，我49 岁了，所以我们有很多可以聊的。

我们从一开始就十分坦诚。我们谈论今生最好的时光，也坦白最尴尬的时刻。彼此都不作评判。我们都不是完美的人，以后也不会是，我们接受彼此最真实的样子。

有一次，我告诉他我过去遇到过的那个人的情况。我对那个人说，我想从这份关系中得到的仅仅是被人欣赏。他回答说："特纳，我刚把金色的星星（相当于中国人说的幼儿园的小红花）都发出去了。"在我告诉艾德这个故事几天之后，他叫我去他车的后备厢里取些东西。让我惊讶的是，当我打开后备厢的时候，一阵风吹来，金色的星星到处飞舞。他在一个卡片上写道："你没必要为了得到赞赏而焦虑，我的金星永远都不会用完。"当时我的心怦怦直跳，喜悦的泪水流了下来。

直到我的假期结束，我们在一起度过了愉快的 6 个星期。为了和我多待一会儿，他提出要开车送我回家，而不是让我孤孤单单地飞回去。当我坐上车的时候，他让我看后面。我简直不敢相信自己的眼睛。

他买下了我们第一次见面时坐的长椅。现在它放在我的后院里，成了我最珍贵的收藏。

那是 10 年前的事了。无论这段感情是会一直持续到老，还是在明天就会戛然而止，我都不会忘记他。从来没有一个人这么深地触及过我的灵魂深处。

他教会了我这么多事情。我能够处在一段感情之中，并且仍然做我自己——一个独立的人。以前谁知道呢？反正我不知道。

他信任我，相信只要我认真去做了，就能做到任何事情。他给我一种和最好的朋友相处般的快乐。我可以和他谈论任何事情，无论是愚蠢的或者是深奥的。没必要把我的不安全感和恐惧感放在心里，当然成就感也要说出来。

无论是去打高尔夫、整晚在外面，还是仅仅在家附近散步，我们在一起都很快乐。我和他一起冒险，比如乘激流木筏，这是我从来都没有想过会去做的事情——这太可怕了。

他爱我，但是不会控制我或束缚我。我不会错过和他分享我生活中的任何事情。我相信，他带给我的最好的礼物就是：如果感受到了对另一个人深刻和浓烈的爱，就会永远渴望给予，而非索取。

——特纳·贝斯·汤普森

Secret Soup
秘密的《心灵鸡汤》

Love is the poetry of the senses.

~Honoré de Balzac

My husband Matt and I have a secret nighttime ritual. It's one that even our closest friends and relatives don't know about. To the rest of the world we probably seem just like any other average middle-class, mid-life couple. Our philosophy is that whatever happens between two consenting adults is okay, as long as no one is harmed. We have decided to come out from behind closed doors and share this glimpse into our private life. Our secret… Matt reads stories to me from the *Chicken Soup for the Soul* series.

To me, the most beautiful sound in the world is Matt's voice. It has a rich masculine resonant quality. Whenever he sings in church, his powerful baritone voice can be distinctly heard above the rest of the congregation. After the service is over, the ladies in our church often compliment him on his singing.

I believe it is the combination of his robust voice and boyish enthusiasm that captures their attention.

While we were dating, Matt and I would meet each other for coffee after I finished work at the hospital. We sat for hours in our favorite booth holding hands, sharing our dreams, and planning our future. Afterwards, he waited patiently for my call to let him know that I had arrived home safely. We then spent several more hours talking on the telephone. Matt's voice was the last sound that I heard before drifting off to sleep. It is amazing how little rest you need when you are falling in love. He still teases me, "I married you so that I could get some sleep at night."

Matt learned the art of reading aloud from his mother, as she read to each of her nine children. He continued the tradition with our own children. Danielle and Michael always enjoyed it when he read stories to them. His characters leapt off the page, as he brought them to life by varying the pitch and tempo of his voice. I loved listening as he read, treasuring this time together as a family. Gradually, as the nest emptied… I began to miss hearing Matt's stories.

Over the years Matt and I have shared the joys and challenges of life together. One of our most devastating setbacks was immediately following my back injury. A back injury is disastrous to the career of a bedside nurse. Along with severe pain, emotional and economic loss, there has been an extensive rehabilitation period with many relapses. Matt has been loving, supportive, and patient throughout my recovery.

One of the most troubling symptoms that I experienced during this stressful time was insomnia. I tried every known remedy including: establishing a regular bedtime, eliminating caffeine, drinking warm milk with nutmeg, lavender aromatherapy, and relaxing music. For a brief period, I resorted to taking sleeping pills. I hated the drowsy feeling the next morning and feared becoming dependent on them.

One particularly difficult night Matt suggested that I try reading a book. I was too tired to read and too restless to sleep. He offered to read to me. A natural choice seemed to be *Chicken Soup for the Nurse's Soul*. The book is a collection of encouraging uplifting stories about how nurses make a difference in the lives of their patients. This simple gesture combined the happy memories of hearing his voice over the telephone and listening to him read stories to our children. As he read, I began to feel more relaxed and after a few stories I was able to drift peacefully off to sleep. Thus began our nightly ritual of Matt reading stories to me from the *Chicken Soup for the Soul* series.

An added benefit has been the inspiration that we have both received from the stories themselves. As soon as we finish one book, we start another. Many of the volumes have been re-read several times. Others have been passed on to friends or family members. We select titles related to whatever is going on in our life. From time to time, the power of a story will cause Matt's voice to crack with emotion or a tear to roll down his cheek.

"That was a good one."

"You know… one of these days, one of my stories will be in *Chicken Soup for the Soul*."

"Yes, Laura, it will and I will read it to you."

~Laura Wisniewski

爱是感官的诗。

——奥诺雷·德·巴尔扎克

　　我和我的丈夫马特有一个秘密的夜间仪式。
这连我们最好的朋友和亲戚也不知道。对于其他
人来说，我们可能看起来和其他中产阶级般的中
年夫妻没什么两样。我们的理念就是，在双方都
认可的两个成年人之间，只要没有人受伤，发生
什么都无所谓。我们决定从紧闭的门后走出来，
把我们私人生活的一隅与大家分享。我们的秘密
就是……马特为我读《心灵鸡汤》系列故事。

　　对我来说，马特的声音堪称这个世界上最美
妙的声音。他的声音阳刚而洪亮。只要在教堂唱
诗，他强大的男中音总能被旁边的人清清楚楚地
听到。每次结束之后，我们教堂的女士们都会对
他的歌声大加赞赏。我相信，这是由于他美妙的
声音和孩子气的热情吸引了她们的注意力。

　　我和他的约会，往往安排在我医院的工作
结束之后，我和他会一起喝杯咖啡。在我们最喜
欢的摊子上，我们手拉手一坐就坐好几小时，聊
着我们的梦想，计划我们的未来。之后，他会耐
心地等待，直到我安全到家之后打电话给他报平

安。我们会在电话里再聊几小时。在我进入梦乡之前，马特的声音是我听到的最后的音符。这真的很奇怪，在你陷入热恋之后，你对其他的一切所求是那么少。他仍然嘲笑我说："娶了你，我晚上才能好好睡一觉。"

马特大声朗读的天分来自他的母亲，她为她的9个孩子读书。对于我们的孩子，马特坚持这一传统。当他为丹妮尔和迈克尔读书的时候，他们总是特别的享受。在他的声音里，故事中的人物跃然纸上，他变化着声音的节奏和腔调把这些故事讲得活灵活现。在他读书时，我也喜欢去听，珍惜这一家人在一起的美好时光。逐渐地当孩子们都长大并离开了家……我开始想念听马特讲故事了。

这么多年来，我和马特一同分享着生活中的快乐和挑战。在我背部受伤之后，我们遭受了生活中最严重的一次挫折。作为一名陪床护士，背部创伤对我的职业生涯不啻于一场灾难。我承受着严重的疼痛、情绪的波动和经济上的损失，我的康复期十分漫长，还多次复发。在我恢复期间，马特毫不厌烦，一直爱着我、支持着我。

在那段紧张的时间里，我所经历的最麻烦的症状之一就是失眠。我试过了所知道的各种疗法，包括：建立定时睡眠时间，戒掉咖啡因，喝放了肉豆蔻的温牛奶，用薰衣草香熏，听轻松的音乐。有一段不长的时间里，我还服用安眠药。我讨厌第二天早上昏昏欲睡的感觉，还害怕会对它们产生依赖。

有一天晚上我失眠特别严重，马特建议说让我试试读本书吧。我是太累了不想读书，又太焦躁了而睡不着。他主动读给我听。我们自然而然地选择了《心灵鸡汤：献给护士们》。这本书收集了一系列的励志故事来振奋人心，都是关于护士们如何改变了病人们的生活。他这一个简单的举动，勾起了我两段美好的回忆，一段就是通过话筒听他的声音，一段就是听他给孩子们讲故事。听他读着，我开始感到越来越放松，读了几个故事之后，我终于能够平静地进入梦乡了。从此开始了我们每天晚间的仪式：马特从《心灵鸡汤》系列中读故事给我听。

这样一个额外的好处就是：我们都从故事本身汲取了灵感。我们读完一本接着一本。好几卷都被反复读了好多次。其中的一些都被我们送给了亲戚朋友。我们会选那些标题和我们生活息息相关的篇目来读。一次又一次，故事的力量让马特的声音因感情波动而喑哑，让他的泪水滑落脸庞。

"那个故事不错。"

"你知道……总有一天，我的故事也会出现在《心灵鸡汤》里。"

"是的，劳拉，会的，那时我会读那个故事给你听。"

——劳拉·维希涅夫斯基

第五部分 爱情永恒篇

Chapter 5
Love Everlasting

We loved with a love that was more than love.

~Edgar Allan Poe

我们与爱人相爱，我们的感情超越了爱情。

——埃德加·爱伦·坡

Night Visit
夜间来访

Where love reigns the impossible may be attained.
~Indian Proverb

I woke up from a deep sleep.

I was enfolded in warmth. Howard's warmth. I could feel him, solid against my back. My head was pillowed on his left arm. His other arm was over me, his huge, rawboned hand holding mine against my breast.

"H-Howard? I thought you were dead," I said.

"Nah. I'm here. Go back to sleep," he whispered.

He hugged me closer and I went back to sleep, no questions, accepting.

But I remembered, in the morning.

I remembered the warmth, the love, even though the sheets behind me were cold.

~Evelyn L. Stringham

Author's Note: Howard was my husband of fifty-four years. He died of brain cancer three months before this occurred.

有爱的地方，万事皆有可能。

——印度谚语

我从熟睡中醒来。

我被温暖包围着。霍华德的温暖。我能够感受得到他，我背对着他。我的头枕在他的左臂弯里，他的另一只胳膊搂着我，他那消瘦的大手抚在我的胸前。

我说："霍华德？我以为你去世了呢。"

他小声说："没，我在这儿，睡吧。"

他把我抱得更紧了，我继续睡觉，毫无疑问，就是这样。

但是，早上醒来之后，我又记起来了。

我记得他的温暖，他的爱，哪怕我的身后只是一片冰冷的床单。

——伊芙琳·L.斯特林厄姆

作者注：霍华德是我的丈夫，我们一起生活了54年了。在我写这篇文章的三个月前，他死于脑癌。

The Girl Next Door
隔壁的女孩

Love is a symbol of eternity. It wipes out all sense of time, destroying all memory of a beginning and all fear of an end.

~Author Unknown

My father had always been healthy until he was stricken with Parkinson's Disease. He was slowly losing his motor skills and memory. He started telling me about a girl who lived next door who he really liked.

Week after week, he would tell me how much he liked this girl and how much he wanted to marry her. This went on for months. Each time I would see him, he told me that he loved her and was going to ask her to marry him.

He sometimes would not remember who I was, or he would confuse me with my sister. He would often tell me he saw people who were not in the room or he would ask me who that was with me even though there was no one there.

I did not know how to break the news to my

mother that after all these years of marriage my father was in love with another woman. I hoped he was imagining it until one day my mother told me (as she was laughing) that Dad asked her to marry him today.

All of a sudden it made sense. My mother lived next door to my dad when they met in 1945. He wasn't imagining it at all. He was reliving it. Dad taught me that true love is never ending. Thanks, Dad.

~Jean Hale

爱是永恒的标志。它能消除人们对时间的感知，能抹去最初的记忆，还能消除对死亡的恐惧。

——佚名

在我的父亲患了帕金森症之前，他一直都很健康。他逐渐丧失了运动能力和记忆。他开始给我讲述一个住在隔壁的女孩，一个他真正喜欢过的女孩。

一周又一周，他给我讲他有多么喜欢这个女孩，他有多么地想要娶她。这种情况持续了几个月。每次我去看他，他都会告诉我，他有多么爱她，他将要向她求婚。

有时候，他根本不记得我是谁，或者把我和妹妹弄混了。他经常跟我说他看见了一些根本不在这间屋子里的人，或者是问我和谁一块来的，哪怕我旁边根本没有人。

　　我不知道如何跟我妈妈说，说经过了这么多年的婚姻，我的爸爸还在爱着另外一个女人。我希望这只是爸爸的一个幻想，直到有一天，我妈妈告诉我说（就像她以前常取笑的那样）：你爸爸今天向我求婚了。

　　突然间，我一切都了然了。在 1945 年，我的爸爸妈妈相遇的时候，妈妈就住在爸爸的隔壁。这不是爸爸的想象。他在重新经历当年的一切。爸爸教会了我，真爱无止境。谢谢您，爸爸。

——珍·哈雷

特别的朋友，特别的爱

We are each of us angels with only one wing, and we can fly only by embracing each other.

~Luciano de Crescendo

The story of Louis and Deb began thirty-five years ago on the yellow minibus that drove them to and from the special school for the developmentally-disabled. Deb was a beauty, with a porcelain complexion and soft, brown hair. Her countenance was serene, a contrast to my brother's lively, never-ending encyclopedia of facial expressions. Deb was, for the most part, non-verbal. When Louis spoke, it was in halting phrases punctuated with his own brand of hand signals. Somehow, though, they understood each other.

After several years of sharing bus rides, their routine was predictable. Louis would exit the bus, call out, "Goodbye, Deb," from the curb, and watch his friend wave from her window seat as the bus rounded the corner. As the teen years sprinkled fairy dust over them, their friendship became more romantic. Deb lived nearby and Louis would sometimes walk to her house for an afterschool visit. Soon he began to ask if she could stop by our house on Saturday afternoons. Both mothers agreed, and Louis and Deb often sat at our dining room table, playing bingo or tic-tac-toe, or drawing pictures on large pieces of white paper with colored markers. They both enjoyed music, too, and Louis would sometimes play some of her favorite records on his stereo. I chaperoned these afternoons and frequently I noticed them sharing a starry-eyed gaze over a snack of cookies and milk or bowls of warm, homemade chocolate pudding.

Through the years their friendship continued to grow. At school and at afternoon recreation programs one could hardly be seen without the other. However, their bliss was soon to end. Louis announced that he had spotted a "For Sale" sign on Deb's front lawn as he approached her house one day. When Deb's mother dropped her off the next Saturday, my mother mentioned the sign and Deb's mother explained that she and her husband had put the house up for sale and were moving to a more pleasing southern climate. It had been arranged, she said, that Deb would remain in New York and live in a community residence for the developmentally-disabled run by a local organization.

"But she's so young," my shocked mother said. "You're placing her already?"

"She's twenty-one," Deb's no-nonsense mother explained. "It's time for her to move out."

Louis had also turned twenty-one and after graduation from school, he planned to attend a workshop program starting in the fall. That meant that Louis and Deb had only the remaining few days of school and eight weeks in summer camp together. My mother sat Louis down. "Deb is moving," she explained.

"Where?" Louis asked.

"She's going to a group home when camp is finished."

"No."

"Yes."

"Why?"

"Her family is moving and Deb needs a new place to live."

"Not me," Louis said as he pointed to the floor, "I'm staying right here."

"Yes, you can stay here, but do you understand that Deb is moving away?"

Louis looked down and nodded his head, "Yes."

That summer reports came from camp that Louis and Deb could not be separated. They held hands on the bus and during camp. They even held hands during lunch, maneuvering their respective sandwiches and juice boxes with their one free hand each. Deb's mother complained that despite the beautiful weather Deb was moody and though Louis made no mention of their looming separation my mother voiced her concerns about Louis' reaction on the last day of camp.

The final day arrived and friends and family were invited to a camp show given by counselors and campers. As always, it was a grand event and Deb danced a number with some other young ladies, after which Louis and his friends performed to a sassy tune from *A Chorus Line*. Then the camp director came to the stage and announced that this year there would be a very special final event. Louis' counselor entered from behind the curtain wearing a black plastic garbage bag and white clerical collar over his T-shirt and shorts. Louis followed him dressed in his green camp shirt and a makeshift cardboard top hat. Then strains of the wedding march began and Deb walked on adorned with a paper veil, carrying a bouquet of white paper flowers.

The counselor addressed the crowd, "Everyone here knows these two special people and everyone knows that they belong together. By the power vested in me I pronounce them Louis and Deb, friends forever." He lifted his right hand over their heads and gave his benediction, "Live long and prosper."

Louis faced the cheering group and took a bow as Deb looked on, smiling sweetly. Polaroid photos were taken and each member of the mock wedding party was presented with a picture as a memento.

That afternoon they rode the bus home together as they had for more than fifteen years. When it reached his stop, Louis exited, stood at the curb, waved, said "Goodbye Deb," and watched her tear-streaked face pressed to the bus window until it faded out of sight. For weeks after, he would take out that Polaroid photo of them, shake his head and simply say, "No more Deb."

Twenty-one years later, at the age of forty-two, Louis moved into a community residence also. Although our mother had died four years earlier, my father still maintained the family home and Louis preferred to spend weekends with his dad to remaining at the residence and participating in their recreational activities. One weekend, however, Louis was convinced by the staff to forego a home visit to attend the monthly dance held at a local church to which all other group home residents were invited.

That Saturday night at 11:00 P.M., I was startled from my sleep by my ringing phone. I ran to the kitchen, picked up the receiver and before I had the chance to say "Hello," I heard Louis cry out from the other end, "I danced with Deb tonight!" He went on with the details of his evening and after the call ended I returned to bed with my heart bursting.

A few days later, the staff member who had escorted Louis' group to the dance relayed to me the details of the two friends' reunion. When they spotted each other across the room, they ran to each other, clasped hands and could not be pried apart for the rest of the evening. "I swear," she said, "I never saw anything like it in almost twenty years in this business."

She may have never seen anything like it before, yet the pure, innocent love between two special friends can be witnessed every third Saturday of the month in the activities room of St. Mary's Church where the dances are held. Just ask for Louis and Deb.

~Monica A. Andermann

我们都是单翼的天使，只有紧紧相拥，才能一同飞翔。

——卢西亚诺·德·科里森多

路易斯和黛布的故事开始于 35 年前，那时，他们一起乘坐接送残疾人来去特殊学校的黄色小巴士，那所学校是为具有发育性残疾的人们建立的。黛布是一个漂亮的女孩子，有着瓷娃娃一般的肌肤和柔软的棕色头发。她的性格宁静安详，与我弟弟的活泼好动形成了强烈的反差，我弟弟的面部表情就是一部永无止境的百科全书。黛布在大部分的时间里都是不说话的。每当路易斯说话的时候，他都会用磕磕绊绊的语言再加上他独特的招牌手势来强调。虽然如此，他们就是能够相互理解。

在一起坐了几年巴士之后，他们对对方的路线都已相当熟悉。路易斯下了车，往往会在马路边叫一声："再见，黛布。"他会看见好朋友从靠窗的座位对他挥着手，直到巴士在街角转弯不见。少年时光就像童话中的梦境一样，他们的友情也变得更加的浪漫。黛布和路易斯住得不远，有时放学后，路易斯会步行去她家拜访。很快，他开始邀请黛布在周六下午来我们家做客。双方的妈妈都同意了，于是路易斯和黛布就经常坐在我们餐厅的桌子边，玩宾果游戏和一字棋，或者是在一张大白纸上用彩色的马克笔画画。他们也都喜欢音乐，路易斯有时会用他的立体音响放黛布最喜欢的唱片。在这些下午，我陪护着他们。我发现，面对饼干、小点心、牛奶，或者是热气腾腾的家里做的巧克力布丁，他们会两眼放光地盯着，馋涎欲滴。

这么多年来，他们的友情更加稳固。无论是在学校还是在下午的娱乐活动中，他们都几乎形影不离。然而，他们的幸福生活很快就要结束了。路易斯说，他在路过黛布家的时候，发现她家的草坪上有一个"此房出售"的标志。在下一个周六，黛布的妈妈来接她的时候，我妈妈提到了这件事，黛布的妈妈解释说她和丈夫准备把这座房子卖掉，迁居到气候更加宜人的南方。她说这些都安排好了，黛布还会留在纽约，住在一个由当地组织开办的专门为发育性残疾人服务的社区里。

我妈妈十分震惊，她说："但是她还小啊，你们就准备让她搬出去了吗？"

黛布的妈妈直截了当地说："她 21 岁了，是时候搬出去了。"

路易斯也 21 岁了，在他毕业之后，他计划去参加一个秋天开始的工作室项目。那就意味着，路易斯和黛布可以待在一起的时间，只剩下几天的学校生涯和 8 周的夏令营了。我妈妈让路易斯坐下，她解释说："黛布要搬家了。"

路易斯问："搬到哪里去？"

"夏令营结束后，她要去团体之家生活。"

"不。"

"是的。"

"为什么？"

"她的家人要搬走了，黛布需要一个新的地方来生活。"

路易斯指着地板说："我不搬走，我就要待在这儿。"

"是的，你可以继续待在这里。但是我说黛布要离开了，知道是什么意思吗？"

路易斯低着头，点点头说："明白。"

从那次夏令营传递出的信息看来，路易斯和黛布无法被分开。他们在巴士上和夏令营期间，一直手牵着手。甚至在吃午饭的时候，他们也手牵着手，他们分别用另一只手来演习做三明治和调果汁。黛布的妈妈抱怨说，尽管天气晴朗，黛布的情绪仍然很低落。虽然路易斯没有提到过他们即将到来的分别，但是鉴于路易斯的反应，夏令营的最后一天我的妈妈仍然表达了她的担忧。

夏令营的最后一天到了，朋友们和家人们被邀请观看夏令营的表演，辅导员和营员们都会参加演出。一如既往，这是一次盛会，黛布和其他几个年轻女孩子跳了几支舞，然后路易斯和他的朋友们表演了《歌舞线上》里一首活力四射的歌曲。然后，夏令营的指导员走上舞台，宣布今年有一个特别的结束仪式。路易斯的辅导员从帘子后面出来，在他的 T 恤衫和短裤外面，穿了件黑色塑料袋做成的服装，以及一副白色的教士才会穿的硬白领。路易斯紧随其后，穿着他的绿色的夏令营 T 恤，带着一个临时做的纸糊的高帽子。婚礼进行曲的音乐响起，黛布走了出来，戴着纸做的面纱，捧着纸做的白色花束。

辅导员向人群宣布："大家都知道，在这里有两个特别的人，他们属于彼此。在此，请允许我宣布：路易斯和黛布，是永远的朋友。"他举起右手，放在他们的头上方，送上了他的祝福："友谊地久天长。"

路易斯面对着欢呼的人群，鞠了一躬，而黛布则看着他，甜甜地笑着。他们用宝丽来的一次成像照相机留了影，这个模拟婚礼派对的每一个成员都收到了一张照片作为纪念。

那天下午，他们乘坐巴士回家，就像他们15年多来一直做的那样。当路易斯到站的时候，他下车，站在路边挥手，对黛布说："再见，黛布。"然后，他看见她泪流满面，扒着车窗，直到汽车驶离了视线。后来的几周里，他会拿出他们的照片，摇着头只是说："黛布走了。"

21年之后，路易斯已经42岁了，他也搬到了一个社区里居住。虽然我们的母亲在4年前去世了，我们的父亲仍然住在家里，路易斯也更喜欢和爸爸一起过周末，在老房子里住着，参加他们的娱乐活动。然而，一个周末，工作人员劝说路易斯放弃了回家的机会，去参加了一个每月一次在当地教堂举办的舞会，那次，所有团体之家的住户都被邀请了。

那个周六晚上11点，我在睡梦中被电话铃声惊醒。我跑到厨房，接起电话，在我有机会说出"你好"之前，就听见路易斯在电话的那一头大叫："我今晚在和黛布跳舞！"他继续讲了那一晚的细节，放下电话，我回去睡觉，心突突直跳。

几天之后，在舞会上，路易斯所在的社区负责照看他的一位工作人员来了，他向我讲述了两个好朋友重逢的细节。当他们隔着一间屋子认出对方的时候，他们跑向对方，紧握双手，在那天晚上接下来的时间里，谁也不能再分开他们。她说："我发誓，在这行里，我近20年都没有见过这样的事。"

她以前可能从没见过这样的事，然而，从那时起，每个月的第三个星期六，在圣玛利亚大教堂的活动室里举办的舞会上，人们都会见证这两位特殊的朋友间纯洁纯真的爱。问问路易斯和黛布，这是什么样的感受吧。

——摩尼卡·A. 安德曼

Chapter 5 Love Everlasting
第五部分 爱情永恒篇

Letting Go
放手

Across the years I will walk with you—in deep, green forests; on shores of sand: and when our time on earth is through in heaven too, you will have my hand.

~Robert Sexton

My parents lived by themselves until about six months ago, when my dad became sick with congestive heart failure. He had a stroke and a slight heart attack. It was then that we discovered Mom's Alzheimer's was much worse than we thought. Dad had been "covering" for her.

As my dad's health continued to decline, it became obvious that they could no longer remain in their home alone. We tried so hard to find people to stay with them and help. The final straw was when Dad had a short hospital stay and developed Mercer's. The help we had for them quit on the spot when he came home. Four months after Dad's stroke, we were forced to admit that they needed to be "placed" in a facility. We were fortunate to get them placed together, and they even got to share a room.

Mom and Dad adjusted fairly well to being there, and the nurses developed a special relationship with Dad, who was one of the few patients there who did not have Alzheimer's. He joked with them, teased, and just won their hearts. Soon my parents became the darlings of the facility. Mom did not understand that Dad was sick, and she became more and more confused. The nurses were wonderful about bringing her back to her room when she became lost, helping her with the daily tasks that she could no longer perform, and reassuring Dad that Mom was alright. Many times, although they had twin beds, Mom would be found in Dad's bed with him when morning came.

Unfortunately, Dad's condition worsened. There were many times that the family was called in, but Dad somehow rallied through whatever crisis he was facing. We would leave shaking our heads, with the nurses apologizing for the false alarm. I cannot tell you how many times this happened. His feet became so swollen because of the congestive heart failure that they considered amputation, but Dad's heart was not strong enough to withstand surgery. We decided that Dad just was not going to leave Mom until he was absolutely forced to. This was his biggest fear, and he talked to all six of his children many times about Mom and what would happen to her when he was gone. We tried to reassure him that we would always be there for her, but still he did not want to leave her. Theirs was a relationship that had survived many years, six children, financial problems, sickness, and many more hardships, and had only gotten stronger through the years.

Finally Dad began to get worse. We were called to the facility. Dad was very weak, had not eaten, and could barely talk. At least Mom didn't realize what was going on. She just followed her normal pattern, spending much time wandering the halls, rearranging clothes in her closet, etc. It was almost as if she just didn't realize Dad was there.

This continued for the next four days. Dad's condition steadily worsened. One of us tried to be there most of the time, and each of us held Dad's hand and told him to just let go. It hurt so badly to see him suffering, and suffering he was! Hospice kept him on pain medication, and even with that, he was not comfortable. On the fourth day, I went to work, planning to sit with Dad right afterward. About noon, I just had a feeling that I should go right away. I left work, went to the facility, and found my sister Jo already there. She said she had been on her way to work and just got a feeling that she wanted to see Dad, so she turned her car around and headed for the facility. Jo and I spent the day listening to Dad's horrible breathing and talking to him. The nurses would come in every two hours, change him, turn him and try to make him comfortable. He had not opened his eyes or communicated for the past four days except to moan in pain.

About 5:00, Jo had to leave. Another sister was coming in around 6:30, so I settled down to wait. Soon the nurses brought Mom back to the room. I said, "Come sit down and talk to me, Mom." She came over, sat beside me and I got ready to hear the same things over and over. Instead, Mom looked at me and then looked over to Dad. She said, "Jack's dying, isn't he?" I told her he was dying, and that he was in a lot of pain. Mom said, "I don't want him to hurt." I suggested that she go over and tell him that, wondering what would happen.

All of a sudden, this Alzheimer's patient became my mom again! She walked over to Dad, took his hand, and started talking to him. "Jack, I love you so much and you have been such a good husband and father. I have so many memories of things we have done. I don't want you to leave me, and I will miss you so much, but I don't want you to hurt anymore." She continued to talk to him for about thirty minutes. During this time, my dad opened his eyes and just stared at his wife. He tried so hard to talk to her.

A couple of the nurses joined us around Dad's bed. All three of us were crying and watching this miracle! Mom steadily held Dad's hand, kissed him and talked to him. A lot of what she said was said only to him, and we couldn't hear. This was a precious, private talk between a husband and wife. Things I'm sure that my dad needed to hear from the only person who mattered at that time to him.

The nurse said that Dad's lungs were quickly filling up with fluid and perhaps everyone should be called in. I went outside and made the dreaded calls once again. Within an hour, everyone was there. Mom was back in her regular state, not paying any attention to Dad. We got her dressed in her pj's and she went to bed and straight to sleep. Finally, a couple of hours later, nothing had changed. We all left for the night, except my sister Tammy, who was spending the night.

About an hour after arriving home, the phone rang. Tammy, between her sobs, said, "Daddy's gone."

I know in my heart that God gave my father a special gift... the ability to have Mom give him permission to go.

~Teresa Keller

这么多年来，我们携手走过——走过幽深的丛林，走过银色的海滩；当我们在人间的时光用尽，我们依旧会携手走向天堂。

——罗伯特·塞克斯顿

大约六个月前，我的父亲得了充血性心脏衰竭，在那之前，我的父母都一直自己生活。他患有中风和轻微的心脏病。也就是从那时起，我们发现母亲的老年痴呆症比我们想象的要严重。父亲一直在"照顾"着她。

由于我的父亲健康状况持续恶化，很明显，他们不能够再单独住在自己的家里了。我们努力地找人去陪他们，帮助他们。直到有一次，父亲病情恶化，短期住院。他出院回家之后，我们决定轮流看护应该到此为止了。于是，在父亲中风四个月之后，我们不得不承认，他们需要被"安置"到疗养院去住了。很幸运，他们搬到了同一家疗养院，甚至还被安排在同一个房间。

爸爸妈妈在那里适应得很好，护士和爸爸的关系尤为不错，因为他是那里为数不多的没患有老年痴呆症的病人之一。他和他们聊天、开玩笑，和护士们打成一片。很快，我的爸爸妈妈在疗养院里大受欢迎。妈妈并不知道爸爸也生病了，她的脑子越来越不清楚了。护士们都很好，他们会把迷路的妈妈带回她的房间，帮她做一些日常琐事，他们还安慰爸爸说妈妈一切都好。虽然他们的房间里有两张床，但是很多次，一早醒来，他们会发现妈妈在爸爸的床上依偎着他。

不幸的是，爸爸的情况持续恶化。很多次，疗养院都通知了家属，但是爸爸总是能够度过他面临的危机。我们走的时候总是摇着头，护士们在一旁为发出错误的通知而道歉。我都不记得这样的事发生多少次了。爸爸的双脚因为充血性心脏衰竭而肿胀，医生们认为应该截肢，但是爸爸的心脏是那么脆弱，无法承受一次手术了。我们认为，直到爸爸不得不离开的时候，他是不会丢下妈妈的。这是他最害怕的事，他和他的六个儿女都说过很多次妈妈的事，他不知道如果他走了，妈妈会怎么样。我们试图安慰他说我们会一直陪着妈妈的，但是他依旧不舍得离开。他们一起走过了这么多年，经历了我们六个孩子的成长，经历了经济困难、生病，还有那么多磨难，这么多年来感情已经越来越浓烈了。

　　最终，爸爸的病越来越糟糕。我们被叫去了疗养院。那时的爸爸已经十分虚弱，不能进食，也几乎不能说话了。只有妈妈不知道这是怎么回事。她只是像往常一样，花很多时间在大厅里散步，在衣橱里重新整理她的衣物等，就好像她根本不知道爸爸在旁边一样。

　　这种情况持续了四天。爸爸的情况继续恶化。我们保持至少一个人一直陪着爸爸，我们都握着爸爸的手，告诉他，让他放心地去吧。看着他受苦，我们是那么心疼！他一直用着止痛药，但是即使那样，他仍然很不舒服。在第四天的时候，我去上班了，准备在下班的时候去爸爸那坐坐。大约在中午的时候，我突然间觉得我必须马上到那里去。我丢下工作，立即去了疗养院。到那时，发现我妹妹乔已经在那里了。她说她在上班的路上，觉得自己自己必须得来看爸爸一眼，于是她就掉转车头，来了疗养院。我和乔陪了爸爸一天，跟他说话，他一直都在痛苦地呼吸。护士两小时进来一次，给他翻个身，试图让他更舒服点。在这四天里，他一直都没有睁开过眼睛，也无法交流，只能痛苦地呻吟。

　　大约5点的时候，乔不得不离开了。另一个妹妹在6点半的时候会过来，于是我静下心来等着。很快，护士把妈妈带回了房间里。我说："妈妈，来这儿坐下，我们聊聊天。"她过来坐在我旁边，我已经准备好了她会把一些事情一遍又一遍地说。但是，妈妈看了看我，然后把目光投向了爸爸。她说："杰克快死了，是吗？"我告诉她是的，而且他很痛苦。妈妈说："我不想让他痛苦。"我让她过去，对爸爸说些话，并且想知道会发生什么。

　　突然，这个患有老年痴呆症的病人一下子又变成了我的妈妈！她走过去，抓着爸爸的手，对他说话："杰克，我是这么爱你，你是那么好的一个丈夫和父亲。我们之间有着那么多的回忆。我不想让你离开我，我是多么想念你，但是我不想你继续痛苦了。"她对着爸爸继续讲了大约半小时的话。在这期间，爸爸睁开了他的眼睛，凝望着他的妻子。他努力地想要说话。

两个护士也过来围在了爸爸的床边。我们三个人默默地哭泣着，看着这奇迹般的一幕！妈妈一直抓着爸爸的手，亲吻他，和他说话。她的很多话都是只说给他听的，我们都听不到。这是丈夫和妻子之间的珍贵而且私密的对话。我相信，这些话是我爸爸在人生的那一刻需要听到、也只有妈妈说才管用的话。

护士说爸爸的肺里已经充水，可能每个人都得叫进来了。我走出去再次宣布了噩耗。一小时之内，每个人都来了。妈妈又回到了她一贯的状态，不再注意到爸爸。我们给她换上了睡衣，她回到床上一会儿就睡着了。最终，几小时之后，一切还是如常。除了我妹妹塔米，我们晚上都离开了，她在那守着爸爸。

在我们回家大约一小时之后，电话响了。塔米抽泣着说："爸爸走了。"

我在心里一直认为，上天给了我爸爸一份特别的礼物……让他在得到我妈妈的允许之后，才步入天堂。

——特里萨·凯勒

The Most Glorious Vacation
最辉煌的假期

For death is no more than a turning of us over from time to eternity.

~William Penn

When Dad was diagnosed with terminal lung cancer, the journey that he took was not alone. Family and friends were with him the entire way. Chemotherapy could possibly put the stage four cancer into remission but we all knew it was ultimately incurable and the prognosis of six months to live could very well be the reality.

Watching Dad lose his hair and suffer was heartbreaking. But along with the pain and tears there was such beauty, so many miraculous gifts that we, his family and friends, were blessed with. As the months passed into years, we all knew how precious each day we had with him was. The memories and lessons learned are forever in my heart.

During the last two and a half years of his life Dad taught me about hope, how to fight, and when to surrender. He taught me about trust. Not only that he trusted in God, but also the most amazing trust between a husband and a wife. During the last few weeks of his life, Mom would sit by his hospital bedside, sleeping most nights in a hospital recliner. She truly showed me the sacredness of the Sacrament of Marriage and what "in sickness and in health" meant. Dad trusted in her and the commitment they made to each other forty-eight years ago. It was evident to me that he was so grateful for her love and devotion just by the way he looked at her.

One hot, muggy August day, the world seemed to go on as usual. But for me it was anything but usual—it was an unforgettable moment in time. A day in which I was blessed with experiencing one of the most amazing examples of the devotion my parents had for each other. Seventy-two hours earlier, Dad had a near-death experience after he unexpectedly stopped breathing. Now, he sat surrounded by machines, in the intensive care unit after just coming off the ventilator. He had survived, but if it were to happen again we had to know what he wanted.

As Mom started talking to him about his wishes on being resuscitated, I wasn't sure if I could keep my composure. It was so difficult for her to ask him. She started and stopped several times but, finally, after several deep breaths and many tears, she asked what he wanted regarding resuscitation. Dad grew quiet. For the first time ever, he was at a loss for words. The minutes seemed like hours as I sat there trying to avoid sobbing, I began to focus intently on the small wooden cross hanging in the center of the wall. "Please God, help me be strong," I prayed silently, over and over again. The he broke the silence with his old, familiar voice.

Tears glistened in his eyes as he looked lovingly at Mom. He slowly said, "I don't want to be a burden to you, but I don't want to leave you."

My mom gently reached for his hand and stroked his hair back. "Jerry, let's think of it as if you are going on one of the most glorious vacations ever, and I will catch up to you later."

With a simple nod of the head, my dad accepted this, and as tears streamed down our faces, a sense of peace filled the room.

His charts were marked, and he wore a band around his wrist designating him as a "do not resuscitate" patient. Even with this, he worked diligently for weeks trying to regain strength to return home. He was anxious for Thursday, September 6th, to arrive. We all were. This was the date the doctors and nurses had set for him to go home. He proudly let his many visitors know that he was going home then.

After their nightly ritual of praying together, Mom left his hospital room to go home and make the final preparations for his homecoming the next day. Shortly after midnight, the phone startled Mom, abruptly waking her. A nurse from the hospital called to let her know that Dad was having difficulty breathing and was being taken to the emergency room. With urgency in the nurse's voice, she told Mom she needed to come to the hospital right away.

When Mom arrived at the emergency room, Dad's eyes were open. He had been asking for Mary—my mom—over and over again. The nurses advised he had minutes, maybe hours left.

God had planned their final goodbye so perfectly. Mom stroked his hair back one last time, and with love in her voice, she courageously said, "Jerry, it's okay. Go ahead. It's time to take that vacation."

A tear fell down his cheek, and he closed his eyes. It was time to surrender. His fight was over. He had so diligently prepared for his return home. To his eternal home, where he now waits for his loved ones to join him on the most glorious vacation ever.

~Susan Babcock

死亡仅仅是一个转折，让我们从短暂走向永恒。

——威廉·佩恩

当爸爸被诊断出肺癌晚期之后，他走过的路程并不孤单。家人和朋友一路都和他在一起。化疗也许可以把癌症分成四个阶段来缓解，但是我们都知道，这最终是不可治愈的，现实情况是，他可以预见的生命最长还有六个月的时间。

看着爸爸头发脱落，遭受痛苦，我们是那么心痛。但是在这痛苦和眼泪的过程中，我们家人和朋友们也感到了那么多的美好，上天恩赐给了我们这么多的奇迹。时间日积月累，我们都知道相聚的每一天都是那么珍贵。这些记忆和体会到的道理，我一生都不会忘记。

在他生命最后两年半的时间里，爸爸教会了我什么叫做希望，如何去抗争，什么时候要投降。他教会我信任，不仅仅是他对上天的信任，还在于夫妻之间令人震惊的绝对信任。在他生命的最后几周里，妈妈就在医院里，坐在他的床边，大部分的时间就在医院的躺椅上过夜。她充分地诠释了什么叫做婚姻誓言的神圣，什么叫做"无论生老与病死"的相守。爸爸信任她，信任他们在 48 年前立下的誓言。我也知道，仅仅从爸爸看妈妈的眼神中就可以看出，他对于妈妈的爱心存感激、不悔而忠实。

8 月闷热的一天，似乎一切如常。但是对我来说，那一天却惊心动魄——那是我永远无法忘怀的一刻。那天，我经历了最令人震惊的一幕，看到了我的父母之间的奉献和忠诚。72 小时之前，爸爸出乎意料地屏住了呼吸，几乎濒临死亡。现在，由于刚刚脱离了呼吸器，他坐在一堆机器中间，被重症监护系统包围着。他活下来了，但是不知这样的事是否还会再次发生，我们必须知道他想要干什么。

妈妈和他聊天，问他想这样被抢救一次是为了什么，我不知道我是否能保持镇静。对她来说，问出这样的话是那么困难。她吞吞吐吐很多次，但是，最终在几次深呼吸和流了无数眼泪之后，她问他：想要被抢救的目的是什么。爸爸沉默了。他史无前例地不开口说话。我坐在旁边，努力不去抽泣，每一分钟都像一小时那样长，我开始把我的注意力放到屋里墙上挂的木头十字架上。我一遍又一遍地默默祈祷："上天啊，请给我力量。"然后，他用他那苍老熟悉的声音打破了沉默。

他泪光闪闪，深情凝视着妈妈。他缓缓说道："我不想成为你的负担，但是我也不想离开你。"

妈妈轻轻地握了握他的手，抚摸着他的头发："杰瑞，让我们把这想象成你就要去度一个最辉煌的假期，我以后会追上你的。"

爸爸只是点了下头，就接受了这种说法。我们的泪水流了下来，屋子里宁静安详。

他的病历被做了标记，手腕上戴了一个带子，那表示他是"不必抢救"的病人。即便这样，他还是努力地治疗了几周，想要积聚力量回到家里去。他急切地希望那一天快点到来，那一天是 9 月 6 日，星期四——

我们也很期待——那是医生护士准许他出院回家的日子。他骄傲地让探望者都知道，他要回家了。

在他们每晚例行的祈祷仪式后，妈妈离开医院先行回家，为他第二天回家作准备。午夜时分，妈妈被手机铃声惊醒。医院的护士打电话来说爸爸呼吸困难，已经送到了抢救室。护士焦急地告诉妈妈，她要马上来医院。

当妈妈赶到抢救室的时候，爸爸正睁着眼睛一遍又一遍地叫着玛丽——妈妈的名字。护士说，他可能只有几分钟、最多几小时可活了。

上帝完美地设计了他们的人生告别。妈妈最后一次抚摸他的头发，言语间深爱流露，她鼓励他说："杰瑞，这没什么。放心去吧。到了要度假的时候了。"

一行清泪从爸爸脸上滑落，他永远地闭上了眼睛。这是投降的时候了。他的抗争结束了。他是那么费心费力地准备回家。他步入了他永恒的归宿，在那里等着他的挚爱来和他一起度过这最辉煌的假期。

——苏珊·巴布科克

A Paradigm Shift
模式转变

What do we live for, if it is not to make life less difficult for each other?

~George Eliot

Peg lay prostrate on the wooden floor, unable to lift her head or move her body. Five minutes passed… ten… fifteen. All because she'd reached for their wedding picture and fallen out of her wheelchair.

What a day for John to be late, Peg thought, as her immovable position grew more and more uncomfortable. It had been years since Peg could remember what it had been like to have control over her body. The multiple sclerosis had come on slowly, but in the last few years it had attacked viciously.

Out of the corner of her eye, she saw the photo that had fallen on the floor beside her, a picture of a bride and a groom, each with blue eyes and dark hair. Friends told her that raising three children hadn't aged either of them one bit, that in fact she was still as beautiful as ever and John as handsome.

John's car tires crunched in the snowy driveway. Her heart pounded as she heard her lover leap the eight stairs of their split-level home two at a time, eager to see his wife. Stunned to find her on the floor, John dropped to his knees, covered her body with his arms, pressed his cheek against hers—and wept with her.

Not out of sympathy. Peg's quips disarmed any of that maudlin stuff. Out of love—the deepest kind.

At that almost sacred moment, I intruded. "Oh I'm sorry," I said, standing in the half-open doorway, peeking through the stair railing.

According to my custom as Peg's physical therapist, I had knocked and let myself in. I walked up and stood beside them not knowing what to say. Concern for Peg's welfare occupied my mind, but my heart, wounded from a recent divorce, felt rather uncomfortable around such tangible expressions of marital devotion.

John dried his tears, scooped up her thin, paralyzed body, and carried her to the bathroom. This was his habit every lunch hour.

"I'd do the same for you if things were reversed," Peg told him, her pluck restored, her smile broad as she winked at me over his shoulder.

"No, you wouldn't. I'm too big for you," he said with an equally broad smile. He fixed Peg lunch and returned to his work at the phone company. As she ate using a therapeutic spoon strapped to her wrist, I sat at the kitchen table, my mouth open in amazement at what had just transpired before my eyes.

How could I be divorced when I had had such an easy life compared to Peg and John? When they had married "for better or for worse," they had no idea what would befall them. Yet they seemed to truly love each other and their lives. What was wrong with me?

"Do you hurt today after the fall?" I asked Peg, wanting to change my thoughts.

"No, I'm just a little stiff. Go ahead and do the exercise routine," Peg said, adding, "I went to the counselor yesterday." Peg was a good conversationalist.

"How did that go?" I stretched her arm.

"Okay, until he asked, 'How's your intimate life?' I answered him, 'Fine, how's yours?' That quieted him right down." She had that familiar twinkle in her eye.

I chuckled within. No one tampered with this lady's love life, or for that matter, with her willingness to persevere. When therapy was over, she asked me to place a puzzle on her lap tray so she could arrange it. She knew her fingers were useless, but hey, why not give it a try?

I shook my head in wonder. My life in my former marriage had health, adequate wealth, two wonderful kids, and no big challenges—except finding happiness. I always thought it was a husband's responsibility to create his wife's happiness. When he hadn't met my expectations, I became increasingly irritable until finally things fell apart. The truth about happiness in marriage had eluded me until, around Peg and John, something warm and wonderful and puzzling stirred in my heart.

One lonely evening, I decided to call on them. I baked cookies, not because that was my custom, but because I wanted an excuse to be around those who understood love, to try to discover their secret. A friend and I drove to their house and I peeked through their family room window to see Peg seated in her wheelchair in front of the TV. John stood behind her like a tall, protective sentinel.

John opened the door, welcomed us, and retreated to the back of the room where Peg sat. They both smiled but said very little. All of a sudden, I saw a side of them I hadn't seen before—a certain shyness. They weren't used to outsiders intruding into their sanctuary. After some small talk, I moved towards the door, my friend following. They thanked us for the cookies and as we walked away, I glanced back through the picture window at Peg's forever smile. Like a framed photo, her husband had resumed his attentive stance—her guardian, lover, friend for life. Oh, sure, Peg and John were pleased we had thought of them. But their happiness came not from others but from another source.

Inspired to discover it, I searched through resources for insight and found one mundane quote after another. Finally a saying by Elbert Hubbard stood out. "The love we give away is the only love we keep."

That was it! Just then a paradigm shift took place in my divorce-weary soul. I realized happiness in love came from giving not from receiving, from sacrifice not ease, from putting another person's interests first not second. Old selfish habits had to go and I hoped a new me… in time… would come forth. Happiness was worth a try.

~Margaret Lang

如果不是为了让彼此的生活少些苦难，我们活着是为了什么呢？
——乔治·艾略特

佩格俯卧在木质地板上，不能抬头也不能动。5 分钟……10 分钟……15 分钟……过去了。一切都是因为她想拿她的结婚照片，从轮椅里摔了下来。

佩格想，今天约翰还迟到了。她僵硬的姿势已经越来越难受了。已经很多年过去了，佩格几乎记不起能控制自己的身体是什么样的感觉了。

多发性硬化症发展得很缓慢，但是在最后几年间，它凶猛地侵蚀了她的身体。

她用眼角瞟到照片就在地板上，掉在她的身边，照片里是一对新郎和新娘，都是蓝色的眼睛、黑色的头发。朋友们都说虽然他们已经有了3个孩子，但是岁月一点也没在他们身上留下痕迹，实际上，她还是那么漂亮，约翰也还是那么帅。

约翰的车在落满雪的车道上行驶着，车轮摩擦嘎吱嘎吱地响。当她听见约翰在他们有错层的房间内，一步两级地跃上了8层台阶，急切地想看见他的妻子，她心跳加速。约翰震惊地看见她正趴在地上，他俯身下来，用双臂搂住她，紧紧地贴着她的脸颊——陪着她哭泣。

这不是出于同情。佩格的妙语连珠驱散了现在感伤的气氛。这是出于爱——最深的爱。

在这最神圣的一刻，我却闯入了。我站在半开的门前面，通过楼梯扶手瞟到了里面，我连忙说："哦，对不起。"

作为佩格的物理治疗师，我的习惯是敲门然后再进入。我走上前去，站在他们身边，不知道说什么好。对佩格的关注占据了我的脑海，但是看见一对夫妻之间的挚爱这么真实地出现在我的面前，对于才离婚的我，心里感到相当的不舒服。

约翰才擦干了他的眼泪，抱起她单薄瘫痪的身体，把她抱到盥洗室里。这是每次中餐时间，他都会有的习惯。

佩格平复一些后，告诉他："如果倒过来的话，我也会为你做同样的事情。"她趴在他的肩膀上，对我眨眨眼，露出了一个大大的笑容。

约翰也同样地笑着对她说："不，你不行，我太重了。"他把佩格的午餐放好，回去工作，他在一家电话公司工作。她用一种配合治疗之用的勺子吃饭，勺子柄绑在她的手腕上。我坐在厨房的桌子边上，惊奇地看着刚才发生的一切。

我的生活要比佩格和约翰轻松得多，我为什么要离婚呢？当他们结婚的时候说"无论好坏"，他们并不知道将要遇到什么。他们真的爱着彼此和他们的生活。我究竟是怎么了？

"你今天跌倒摔伤了吗？"我问佩格，想要改变自己的想法。

佩格说："没有，我就是行动有点僵硬。像往常一样做康复练习吧。"她又加了一句："我昨天去见了咨询师。"她十分健谈。

我伸展她的胳膊，问她："怎么样？"

"还不错。直到他问我：'你的亲密生活怎么样？'我回答说：'挺好的。你的怎么样？'那让他立即就沉默了。"她眼神中掠过一丝熟悉的狡黠。

我呵呵笑了。没有人能改变她的爱情生活，这件事情也不能，只要她自己愿意守护这份爱情。治疗结束之后，她让我在她的腿上摆一盘棋，她想玩一玩。她知道自己的手指没有用了，但是为什么不试一试呢？

我迷惑地摇了摇头。我的前一段婚姻中，我们健康、富有，还有两个很棒的孩子，没有遇到什么大风大浪——除了寻找幸福。我总是认为让妻子幸福是丈夫的责任。当他没有达到我的预期要求时，我开始变得易怒，直到我们最后分手。婚姻中幸福的真相一直困扰着我，直到今天我看见了佩格和约翰，温情和美好在我的心中涌动。

在一个寂寞的晚上，我决定去拜访他们。我烤了一些饼干，这并不是我的习惯，我只是想要找个借口去接近这些懂得爱的人，去发现他们的秘密。我和一个朋友驾车前往他们家，透过窗户可以看到，佩格坐在轮椅里看电视。约翰站在她身后，像一个高大的守护神。

约翰打开门欢迎我们进来，然后又退到了佩格坐的旁边。他们一直微笑，但是很少说话。突然，我看见了以前从没注意过的一面——他们都很羞涩。他们不习惯外人侵入自己的生活空间。聊了一会儿天之后，我和我朋友告辞离开。我们走的时候，他们感谢我带来了饼干。我透过窗户回头看了一眼，佩格依然在微笑着，就像一幅定格的画一样，她的丈夫保持着他那照料的姿势——他是她的卫兵、爱人和一生的朋友。哦，当然，佩格和约翰很高兴我们想着他们，但是他们的快乐不是来自于别人，而是另有源泉。

为了找到这个源泉，我收集了很多材料，发现有很多平凡的谚语。最终，我发现了艾尔伯特·哈伯德的一句话。他说："我们付出多少爱，就会得到多少爱。"

原来如此！在我离过婚的疲惫内心里，原来的模式改变了。我明白了爱和幸福来自付出而不是索取，来自奉献而不是享受，来自把另一个人的事放在第一位而不是自己的。我要摒弃旧的自私的模式，我希望得到一个全新的我……很快地，那个我就要出现了。为了幸福，值得一试。

——玛格丽特·朗

Saying Goodbye
说再见

I may wear the glass slippers... but my hero wears combat boots.

I clutched the car's door handle as I watched him walk away. He was my soulmate, my lover, my best friend, and the father of the baby asleep in the infant seat within the car.

He had told me that he didn't want to part in the terminal, so we said our goodbyes in the parking lot next to the car. "I'll call you tonight from San Francisco," was all that he said before he turned away. I frantically tried to think what I could do to hold him there a few more minutes, but the pragmatist in me knew that I had to restrain myself from running after him, putting my arms around him, and kissing him one more time. Sobbing, I stood and watched as his image become smaller. Not once did he turn back to look at me. I closed my eyes and wiped away the tears. When I opened them again, he had completely disappeared.

He had told me to go home, but I couldn't tear myself away. If the plane had mechanical problems and the flight was canceled, he would have no way to call me back.

For more than an hour, I sat in the car, tormented by knowing he was in the terminal a few hundred feet away. I knew we had said our goodbyes, and there was nothing more to say. We had made the break; it would hurt even more to see each other again. I concentrated on the airplane sitting on the tarmac and waited for it to leave but, at the same time, I dreaded seeing it lift off. In my mind, being able to hold the image of the plane in front of me was paramount. As long as it sat there, we had a small chance for our fortunes to change. A miracle might happen to keep him from leaving. Once the plane pulled away from the gate, I would have to recognize that we might never be a couple ever again.

He and I had met nine years earlier at a resort where we were both summer employees. From the beginning, we were friends. One evening he asked me to go along when he found himself without a date after his plans had been finalized for an evening with another couple. From then on, we were drawn to each other. We had much in common and enjoyed our time together. An affectionate and caring courtship led to recognition of an enduring love for each other. During the ensuing years, we married, finished college, moved across the country, and taught school. Then the war years descended on us in a black, choking cloud. In a matter of weeks, his teaching deferment was canceled, and he was told to report for duty. We had to sell our home, and in the next two years, we moved five times. Then the orders came that he was to be sent to a war zone for a year. Completely understanding the full essence of the orders for deployment was realizing that he might not come back, that he might die in combat.

The night before he left, we stopped by his parents' home where we had dinner and then with strained voice he said goodbye to them. That night we couldn't sleep. We held each other and talked until there were no words left to say. Our thoughts were full of anguish.

In the morning, we went about doing ordinary things that took on new meaning. I watched him take out the trash and check the oil in the car. He gave me instructions about lighting the furnace and hot water heater. We were going into winter, and he worried that we might not be warm. He talked about care of the car. I didn't want to know about those things; I wanted him to be with us and to take care of us as he always had. My heart ached, and my brain was exhausted. The hours we could still be together were bleeding away.

The wait was over when the plane roared down the runway and lifted into the sky. As I watched it disappear into the clouds, I felt devastated. What was I going to do? I had no picture in my mind of how to live without him. I did realize I could not go on feeling as I did at that moment. It was too painful, and I had a baby to love and care for. I had to get busy. I had to be optimistic that he would come back to us. It was the only way not to be eaten by despair.

Many months later, I was at the airport and watched the plane land. With me was the little fellow who had learned to turn over, sit up, and walk—events in a child's development that his father had missed. We stood in the terminal at one of the gates. Somehow, it seemed all right to express our joy in public, when earlier our grief had been too personal to share. Passengers walked down the plane's steps and onto the tarmac. Finally, he emerged. We were no longer waiting. He was home. We could go on with our lives. It meant that we could be ordinary people doing ordinary things. I ran to meet him, to hold him, and to be with him for all of our years to come.

~Suzanne Waring

我穿着水晶鞋……而我的英雄穿着战靴。

——逸名

我紧紧地抓着车门把手，看着他离开。他是

我心心相印的人，是我的爱人，我最好的朋友，还是车里婴儿座中孩子的爸爸。

他对我说不想在航站楼告别，于是我们在停车场的车旁边说再见。他走前唯一说的一句话就是："我今晚会从洛杉矶给你打电话。"在几分钟之内，我疯狂地想了很多次我要怎么留住他，但是理智告诉我要控制住自己，不要去追着他跑，不要去抱住他，不要去再一次地亲吻他。看着他的背影越变越小，我默默地抽泣着。他一次也没有回过头来看我。我闭上眼睛，擦掉泪水。当我再次睁开眼睛的时候，他已经完全不见了。

他让我回家，但是我一动也动不了。如果飞机出现故障，或者是航班取消了，他回来找我就找不到了。

我在车里坐了一个多小时，一想到他在不远处的航站楼里我就心痛。我知道我们已经说过再见了，再也没有什么可说的了。我们已经分手了，再见面只会伤害更深。我注意着停机坪上的飞机，等着它起飞，但是我又害怕看着它真的离开。只要它停在那里，我们还有一丝机会改变现在的一切。也许会发生奇迹，他不走了。一旦飞机起飞，我就不得不承认，我们再也不是一对夫妻了。

他和我九年前在一个景点相遇，我们都是那里的暑期工。一开始，我们只是朋友。一天晚上，他让我陪他。因为他和另一对情侣订了一个计划，但是他发现自己没有女伴。从那时起，我们相互吸引。我们有很多相似之处，享受待在一起的时光。之后是深情和温馨的求爱，这是不渝的爱情的必经旅程。在接下来的几年里，我们结婚了，上完了大学，走过了很多地方，在学校里教书。后来，发生了战争，这就像一朵黑暗窒息的云压在我们头顶。在几个星期的时间里，他的教学延期计划被取消了，他被告知要立刻回到岗位。我们不得不卖掉房子，在接下来的两年里，我们搬过五次家。随后他被派到了一个战乱地区，为期一年。我们完全理解这道命令的实质，我们都意识到他可能一去不回，在战争中牺牲。

他离开的前一晚，我们在他父母家吃晚饭，他用一种紧张的声音和他们说再见。那一晚我们都没有睡。我们紧紧相拥，说了很多话，直到没什么可说。我们都充满了悲伤。

早上的时候，我们做着往常一样的事情，但是又都有了新的意义。我看着他倒垃圾，检查油箱。他告诉我照明炉和热水器怎么用。冬天要来了，他怕我会冷。他讲着怎么养护汽车。我不想知道这些事情；我想让他陪着我，像原来那样照顾我们。我的心那么痛，感觉已经筋疲力尽了。我们还能待在一起的时间在一点点地流逝。

当飞机在跑道上呼啸起飞的时候，我的等待结束了。我看着它消失在云层里，感到无比绝望。我要怎么办？我一点都不知道，没有他我要怎么生活。我知道我不能一直像刚刚那一刻那样。那太痛苦了。我还有个孩子需要照顾。我要忙起来，并保持乐观的心态，相信他会回来和我们在一起。这是唯一的方式，能让我自己不沉浸在绝望中。

很多个月过去了，我在机场看着飞机着陆。我后面跟着一个正学着翻身、坐起和走路的小家伙——他的父亲错过了他生命中的好多第一次。我们站在航站楼的门边。我们先前的悲伤太过私人，不适合分享，但是现在我们可以公开地表达喜悦了。乘客们走下旋梯，步入停机坪。最终，他出现了。我们无须等待，他回家了。我们的生活可以继续了。那意味着我们可以像普通夫妻那样过普通的生活。我向他跑过去，拥抱他，在接下来的时光里，再也不分开。

——苏珊·华林

Meet Our Contributors
见见我们的撰搞人

Mary M. Alward lives in southern Ontario. Her work has been published in both print and online venues. When Mary isn't writing, she enjoys spending time with her family, reading and blogging. Mary can be reached via e-mail at malward2002@yahoo.ca.

玛丽·M.奥尔沃德 现居安大略省南部。她的作品已经出版了印刷版和网络版。当玛丽不写作的时候，她喜欢享受和家人在一起的时光，还喜欢阅读、写博客。她的电子邮箱地址：malward2002@yahoo.ca。

Monica A. Andermann is an essayist and prize winning poet whose work has appeared or is forthcoming in various literary journals and anthologies. When she is not writing, she enjoys reading or spending time with friends and family.

摩尼卡·A.安德曼 是一位随笔作家，也是一位获过奖的诗人。她的作品已经或是即将在多种文学期刊和文选上发表。当她不写作的时候，她喜欢阅读或者是享受和家人朋友在一起的时光。

Susan Babcock is a devoted wife and mother. Her three children and husband have been her greatest joys and the best job she could have ever hoped for. She has been a stay-at-home mom for the past fifteen years and has always found time to do volunteer work. Her hobbies include traveling, reading and spending many hours at her children's various sporting events.

苏珊·巴布科克 是一位全心全意的妻子和母亲。照看她的三个孩子以及丈夫是她最大的乐趣所在，也是她所能想到的最好的工作。在过去的十五年中，她一直待在家里，并且经常去做志愿服务。她的兴趣包括旅行、阅读，以及参与她的孩子们的各种体育活动。

Linda Baskin is a stay at home mom and loves spending every day with her son and daughter. She enjoys reading and journaling. She loves to golf with her husband and is working on getting her score under 100! Linda plans to continue writing as inspired. She thanks God for all the wonderful blessings in her life.

琳达·巴斯金 是一位全职母亲，她最爱每一天都和自己的儿子女儿待在一起。她喜爱阅读、写日记，还喜欢和丈夫一起去打高尔夫，正努力使自己的杆数低于 100！琳达计划在灵感到来时继续写作。她对于生活中的一切美好充满了感恩。

Martha Belknap is a teacher and the author of *Stress Relief for Kids: Taming Your Dragons,* and *Mind-Body Magic.* She has been married for twenty-six years and hopes that the Snitterfield story will inspire others to find creative, original, and humorous ways to handle challenges in their relationships.

玛莎·贝尔纳普 是一名老师，也是《孩子如何缓解压力：驯服心中的龙》，和《体验身心的魔法》的作者。她结婚已经 26 年，希望斯尼特菲尔的故事可以激励人们找到有创造性的、独创的和幽默的方式来处理人与人之间关系中的挑战。

Cynthia Bilyk joined the Army at nineteen and then became a Border Patrol

Agent at twenty-four. She lives in Quemado, Texas with her husband, and two children. Cynthia enjoys leading a Girl Scout Troop and spending time with her family and friends.

辛西娅·比利克 19 岁参军，24 岁成为了一名边界巡逻员。她和丈夫以及两个孩子居住在得克萨斯州的克马多。辛西娅喜欢领导一小队女童子军，喜欢享受与家人朋友待在一起的时光。

Sheryl Brownlee has published a local parenting magazine, penned a weekly humor column in a local newspaper and produced radio commercials. She also has twenty years experience selling radio and television advertising. She is currently working on a novel. Her favorite position is being a wife and mother.

雪莉·布朗利 出版了一份当地的关于父母养育子女的杂志，在一份当地报纸上为一个每周幽默专栏执笔，并制作过收音机商业广告。她在销售收音机和电视的广告方面有 20 年的经验，最近在写一部小说，最喜欢的角色是做一名妻子和母亲。

Beth Cato resides in Buckeye, Arizona with her husband and son. Her work has appeared in publications such as *Niteblade Fantasy and Horror Magazine, Crossed Genres, Six Sentences*, and the book *The Ultimate Cat Lover*. Information regarding her current projects can always be found at www.bethcato. com.

贝丝·卡托 现在和丈夫和儿子一起居住在亚利桑那州的七叶树（亚利桑那州地名）。她的作品已经发表于《荧光之刃幻想恐怖杂志》《交叉类型》《六句话》《终极猫咪情人》上。有关她最近的工作可以参见 www.bethcato. com。

Stefani Chambers lives in New York City where she is a writer of creative non-fiction and personal essays. She received her Masters of Journalism from the University of North Texas and has taken courses from Gotham Writers'

Workshops. Her dream is to publish a collection of short essays. Contact her via e-mail at stefiwefi@yahoo.com.

史蒂芬妮·钱伯斯 居住在纽约，她是一名富有创造力的纪实类文学作家和个人随笔作家。她在北得克萨斯大学取得了新闻学硕士学位，并且在纽约哥谭作家工作坊上过课。她的梦想是出版一部短篇随笔集。她的电子邮箱地址：stefiwefi@yahoo.com。

Jennifer Colvin is a marketing manager and freelance writer. Her stories about travel and misadventure have been published in numerous anthologies. These days, bike rides with her husband Bob take place much closer to their home in the San Francisco Bay Area, with their daughter in tow.

珍妮·科尔文 是一位市场经理人，也是一位自由作家。她写的旅行故事和灾难故事在很多选集中都发表过。这些天来，她和丈夫鲍勃骑着自行车，拖车里还带着他们的小女儿，在旧金山湾区骑行，这使得他们的家庭关系更加亲密了。

Harriet Cooper is a freelance writer, editor and language instructor. She specializes in writing creative non-fiction humor and articles, and often writes about health, exercise, diet, cats, family and the environment. A frequent contributor to *Chicken Soup for the Soul*, her work has also appeared in newspapers, magazines, newsletters and websites.

哈瑞特·库伯 是一位自由作家、编辑和语言教师。她擅长于写富有创造力的纪实类幽默文学作品和文章，还经常写关于健康、锻炼、饮食、猫、家庭和环境的文章。她经常为《心灵鸡汤》供稿，其作品也经常发表于一些报纸、杂志、时事通讯和网站上。

Debra A. Crawford lives in Florida with her husband, John. Diagnosed with SPS in 1994, Debra has a personal outreach with her website: www.livingwithsps. com. She enjoys family, church, outdoors, and reading. Future plans include writing short stories and autobiographical non-fiction.

黛布拉·A.克劳福德 与丈夫约翰居住在佛罗里达。在 1994 年被诊断出患有不孕不育症，更多有关黛布拉的情况，可以参见她的个人网站：www.livingwithsps.com。她享受家庭生活，喜欢教堂、户外运动和阅读。未来的计划包括写短篇故事和自传式的纪实类文学作品。

Jean Davidson resides in Pocatello, Idaho. Her greatest writing interests are family stories and historical fiction stories about colorful individuals of the Old West. Her greatest joys are her family members, particularly her grandchildren and her cat Simba.

吉恩·戴维森 现居爱达荷州的波卡特洛。她最喜欢写的文章类型是家庭故事，还有有关古老的西方那些丰富多彩的人物的历史虚构故事。她最大的快乐来自于她的家庭成员们，特别是她的孙子孙女们和猫咪辛巴。

Jamie Driggers writes about marriage and family issues whenever possible. The rest of the time she shares her thoughts about life at www.jamiedriggers. com. Her children and husband provide plenty of fodder and she counts herself fortunate that they give her something to laugh at and write about every single day.

杰米·德里杰斯 一有机会就会写写关于婚姻和家庭的文章。她的业余时间会在 www.jamiedriggers.com 网站与大家分享一些关于人生的感想。她的丈夫和孩子为她提供了大量的素材，她认为自己很幸运，有他们为她带来欢笑。她每天都会把这些写下来。

P. A. Flaherty earned degrees from Barnard College of Columbia University and Smith College. She writes and edits fiction and creative non-fiction as well as grants. She recently planned her wedding. Follow her adventures in food writing at www.examiner.com/x-12601-Cheese-Examiner.

P. A. 弗莱厄尼 取得过哥伦比亚大学巴纳德学院和史密斯学院的学位。她撰写并编辑小说和富有创造性的纪实类文学作品。她最近正在筹备婚礼。

她有关饮食的作品见于网站：www.examiner.com/x-12601-Cheese-Examiner。

Jackie Fleming, a native Californian, grew up in the Bay Area and raised three boys on an Island in the California Delta. Her hobby is traveling the world by freighter, Yoga, reading and writing. For six years, she wrote columns for two weekly newspapers. She now lives in Paradise, California.

杰姬·佛莱明 是一名土生土长的加利福尼亚人，在海湾地区长大，在加利福尼亚三角洲地区的一个小岛上抚养着三个儿子。她的爱好是乘船周游世界、瑜伽、阅读和写作。六年来，她一直为两份周报写专栏。她现居于加利福尼亚的天堂镇。

Kimberlee B. Garrett spends most of her time caring for her wonderful husband and three children Emalee, Michael and Doug. When she does get a minute to herself, she enjoys reading, writing, and dreaming of being the first woman to win the Tour de France!

金伯里·B. 加勒特 生活中大部分的时间都用来照顾她的好丈夫和三个孩子：伊美里、迈克尔和道格。当她自己一有空闲的时候，她就喜欢去阅读和写作，还会梦想成为赢得环法自行车赛的第一位女选手！

Jean Hale graduated from the University of Tennessee with a Bachelor of Science degree in Business. She is a licensed Property and Casualty Insurance Agent. She is currently working part time as an Assistant Manager in retail. Her primary job is at home with her twin boys.

珍·哈雷 毕业于田纳西大学，获得了商科专业的理学学士学位。她是持有执照的财产和意外伤害保险代理人。她现在在零售业兼职做一名助理经理。她最基本的工作还是在家里照顾她的双胞胎儿子。

Melissa Harding lives in Colorado Springs with her husband and three small children. She loves to travel and has lived in New Zealand and Costa Rica. When she's not changing diapers or breaking up fights, she enjoys hiking, boating, camping, and writing. She is currently working on an inspirational non-fiction book.

梅利莎·哈丁 和丈夫以及三个很小的孩子居住在科罗拉多斯普林斯。她喜欢旅行，曾经在新西兰和哥斯达黎加居住过。在她不用给小孩换尿布或是拉架的时候，她喜欢远足、划船、露营和写作。她现在正在创作一部励志的纪实类文学作品。

Wes Henricksen is an author, attorney, and frequently-consulted expert on academic success. With his wife and young son, he travels to Argentina every chance he gets, and enjoys Malbec wine and engaging conversation. You can find out more about Wes at weshenricksen.com.

韦斯·里克森 是一名作家和律师，他作为一名专家，经常被咨询有关学术上的成功。他和妻子以及年幼的儿子一有机会就会去阿根廷，享受马尔贝克葡萄酒、参与聊天。关于他的更多信息参见：weshenricksen.com。

Jennifer Hofsommer currently resides with her husband in Chicago, Illinois where she is pursuing her Masters in Spanish Linguistics from the University of Illinois at Chicago. She has a passion for traveling, with her favorite destinations being in South America. Contact her via e-mail at jennifer.hofsommer@gmail.com.

珍妮弗·郝夫索莫 现在和她的丈夫居住在伊利诺伊州的芝加哥，她正在位于芝加哥的伊利诺伊大学攻读西班牙语言学的硕士学位。她热衷于旅行，最喜欢的目的地是南非。她的电子邮箱地址：jennifer.hofsommer@gmail.com。

Cara Holman worked for several years in the computer industry before making the easy decision to stay home full-time and raise her three children. She currently lives in Portland, Oregon with her husband and their youngest son.

Her writings have appeared in various online journals and on her blog: http://caraholman.wordpress.com.

卡拉·霍尔曼 在计算机行业工作了几年，之后决定生活得轻松一些，就辞职在家，全职照看她的三个孩子。她现在和丈夫以及最小的儿子居住在俄勒冈州的波特兰。她的作品已经发表于很多在线期刊和自己的博客上：http://caraholman.wordpress.com。

Pamela Humphreys received her Bachelor of Science in Clinical Dietetics from the University of Oklahoma in 1978. She is a freelance writer, Bible teacher and registered dietitian. She enjoys traveling, cooking, reading and writing short stories and poetry. Please e-mail her at DelandPam1@sbcglobal.net.

帕梅拉·汉弗莱斯 于 1978 年在俄克拉何马大学获得了临床营养学的理学学士学位。她是一个自由作家，圣经教师和注册营养师。她喜欢旅行、做饭、阅读、写短篇故事和诗歌。她的电子邮箱地址：DelandPam1@sbcglobal.net。

Sheila Sattler Kale believes words have the power to change lives. She owns and manages The Closer Walk Christian Bookstore as well as writes and speaks encouragement to groups of all sizes. Her devotions can be viewed at www.thecloserwalk.com. Please e-mail her at closer@austin.rr.com. See her profile on Facebook.

希拉·萨特勒·卡尔 相信文字具有改变生活的力量。她持有并经营着亲密同行基督教书店，同时也写作和演讲，鼓舞人们。她的贡献参见：www.thecloserwalk.com.。她的电子邮箱地址：closer@austin.rr.com。欢迎参观她在 Facebook 的主页。

Teresa Keller has been a social worker for the past twenty years for Department of Social Services. Teresa has written poetry for pleasure for years but this is only her second short story. She lives in Virginia with her husband and two Golden Retrievers. Please e-mail her at nugsmom@yahoo.com.

特里萨·凯勒 在过去的 20 年中一直在社会服务部做一名社会工作者。特里萨多年来写诗，只为自己娱乐，但是这是她的第二篇短篇小说。她和丈夫以及两只黄金猎犬居住在弗吉尼亚州。她的电子邮箱地址：nugsmom@yahoo.com。

Marylane Wade Koch has over twenty-five years of experience in writing, editing, speaking, consulting, publishing, and coaching. She home schools her daughter and serves as adjunct faculty at the Loewenberg School of Nursing, University of Memphis. Contact her via e-mail at mwkoch@att.net.

玛丽·韦德·科赫 在写作、编辑、演讲、咨询、出版和辅导方面有超过 25 年的经验。她在家教育她的女儿，并在孟菲斯大学的鲁文贝格护理学院担任兼职教师。她的电子邮箱地址：mwkoch@att.net。

Margaret Lang loves to draw from her life experience to write poignant true stories, having had about forty published. She is a speaker at women's and children's meetings, and a planter of afterschool Good News Clubs in the public schools. Her favorite role is that of grandma of three.

玛格丽特·朗 喜欢提炼生活中的经历来写心酸的故事，已经发表了约 40 篇文章。她在妇女和儿童会议上是一名演讲者，也是在公立学校成立课后好消息俱乐部的先行者。她最爱的角色还是三个孙子孙女的祖母。

Dina A. Leacock lives in Southern New Jersey with her husband, her two sons and her cat. She is a founding member and past president of the Garden State Horror Writers, a multi-genre writing organization and past president of the Philadelphia Writers' Conference. Visit her at www.dinaleacock.com.

迪娜·A. 里柯克 和丈夫、两个儿子，还有一只猫居住在新泽西州南部。她是"花园州"恐怖作家协会的创建者之一和前任主席，该组织是一个混合多种元素的写作团体。她还是费城作家联盟的前任主席。她的主页：www.

dinaleacock.com。

Linda Leary, mother, grandmother, and business owner for twenty years until she decided to transition at midlife to pursue her writing, which includes short stories, poetry, editing, ghost writing and magazine articles. She is involved in the international alternative justice movement called Restorative Justice and is a member of eWomen Network. siouxlu@comcast.net.

琳达·利里 是一位母亲，还是一位祖母，她从事商业 20 年，直到中年之时，她才决定改变生活，追寻自己的写作梦，其中包括短篇故事、诗歌、编辑、代笔和杂志文章。她参与了叫做恢复性司法的国际替代司法运动，还是互联网妇女组织的一员。她的电子邮箱地址：siouxlu@comcast.net。

Delia Lloyd is an American writer/journalist/blogger based in London. Her essays have appeared in *The International Herald Tribune*, *The Christian Science Monitor*, and Mothering.com. She blogs about adulthood at www.realdelia.com.

迪莉娅·劳埃德 居住在伦敦，是一名美国作家、记者和博客写手。她的随笔发表于《国际先驱论坛报》《基督教科学箴言报》和网站 Mothering.com。她的博客内容多为成年故事：www.realdelia.com。

Gary B. Luerding is a retired army NCO and high school administrator and lives in Southern Oregon with his wife of forty-seven years. He has contributed numerous stories to the *Chicken Soup for the Soul* and *Cup of Comfort* anthologies and several magazines and newspapers. He can be reached at garyluer@frontiernet.net.

加里·B. 努尔丁 是一名退休军士，也是一名高中管理人员，和他的妻子居住在俄勒冈州南部 47 年了。他在《心灵鸡汤》《一杯安慰》选集和一些杂志报纸中发表过很多文章。他的电子邮箱地址：garyluer@frontiernet.net。

David Martin's humor and political satire have appeared in many publications including *The New York Times, the Chicago Tribune* and *the Smithsonian Magazine*. His humor collection, *My Friend W,* was published in 2005 by Arriviste Press. David lives in Ottawa, Canada with his wife Cheryl and his daughter Sarah.

大卫·马丁 的幽默和政治讽刺作品已经发表于很多出版物上，包括《纽约时报》《芝加哥论坛报》和《史密森学会杂志》。他的幽默故事集《我的朋友 W》在 2005 年由阿瑞韦斯特出版社出版。大卫和妻子谢莉尔、女儿萨拉居住在加拿大的渥太华。

Dena May is an elementary Special Education teacher in Texas. She teaches Sunday School and plays the piano at her church, is on the local Child Welfare Board, and volunteers in the local Rainbow Room for CPS. Her first priority is being a wife and mother.

德娜·玛丽 是得克萨斯州的一名基础特殊教育教师。她在星期日学校（指星期日对儿童进行宗教教育的学校）教书，在教堂里弹钢琴，隶属于当地的儿童福利委员会。她还是当地 CPS（儿童保护服务组织）彩虹屋的志愿者。她最基本的责任还是作为一个妻子和母亲。

Caroline S. McKinney teaches in the School of Education at the University of Colorado at Boulder where she earned her PhD. She enjoys spending time with her children and grandchildren, hiking Colorado's mountains and traveling in Italy. She has written numerous articles for educational journals, and poetry for spiritual publications.

卡洛琳·S.麦金尼 是科罗拉多大学波尔德分校教育学院的一名老师，她在那里取得了博士学位。她喜欢和她的孩子以及孙子孙女在一起，也喜欢在科罗拉多的山间徒步，还喜欢去意大利旅行。她为教育类期刊写过很多的文章，还为教会出版物写诗。

Lynn Maddalena Menna is happily married to her one true love, Prospero. They live in Hawthorne, NJ, with their cat, Toonsie. A retired educator, Lynn has been doing some freelance writing. She and Prospero enjoy sports cars, motorcycles, and traveling Europe and Hawaii. Friends can contact them at prolynn@aol.com.

林恩·玛塔莲娜·门纳 很高兴嫁给了自己的真爱普罗斯帕罗。他们和宠物猫同希一起居住在新泽西州的霍索恩，作为一名退休了的教育工作者，林恩会做一些自由撰稿的工作。她和普罗斯帕罗喜欢跑车、摩托车、去欧洲和夏威夷旅行。她的电子邮箱地址：prolynn@aol.com。

Toni-Michelle Nell lives with her husband Martin in Metro Atlanta. She enjoys being with those she loves and sharing in laughter, something the world needs more of. Toni-Michelle is currently enrolled at the University of Phoenix where she maintains a 4.0 GPA and is working on her AA in Psychology with the hopes of continuing on to get her Master's degree. Please e-mail her at tmnell@comcast.net.

托尼·米歇尔·内尔 和丈夫马丁居住在亚特兰大中心地区。她喜欢和她爱的人在一起分享快乐，她觉得这个世界需要更多的欢声笑语。托尼·米歇尔现在凤凰城大学上学，她的平均学分达到4.0。她正在争取拿到心理学的文科准学士学位，希望能继续攻读硕士学位。她的电子邮箱地址：tmnell@comcast.net。

Laurie Ozbolt received her B.A. in Psychology from the University of Virginia and her M.B.A from the College of William and Mary. She works in HR and is training to be a Spiritual Director. She enjoys gardening, dancing and spending time with her family. Please e-mail her at laurie_ozbolt@hotmail.com.

劳里·奥兹波特 在弗吉尼亚大学取得了她心理学学士学位，并从威廉玛丽学院取得了 MBA 学位。她从事人力资源行业，现在她正在接受培训成为一名身心灵导师。她喜欢园艺、跳舞以及与家人相聚。她的电子邮箱地址：

laurie_ozbolt@hotmail.com。

Saralee Perel is an award-winning nationally syndicated columnist and novelist. She is honored to be a multiple contributor to *Chicken Soup for the Soul*. Saralee welcomes e-mails at sperel@saraleeperel.com or via her website: www.saraleeperel.com.

萨拉莉·佩雷尔 是一个屡获殊荣的国家级的专栏作家和小说家，她的专栏在多家报纸杂志上同时发表。她为《心灵鸡汤》系列贡献了很多文章。她的电子邮箱地址为 sperel@saraleeperel.com，个人主页地址为：www.saraleeperel.com。

Jill Pertler writes a weekly syndicated column, "Slices of Life," which is printed in newspapers throughout her home state of Minnesota and beyond. She also dabbles in short fiction and photography. She lives in a cozy house with her husband, four children and assorted critters. Visit her website at: http://marketing-by-design.home.mchsi.com.

吉尔·佩特勒 所撰写的专栏每周在多家报纸上同时发表，"生活碎片"在她的家乡明尼苏达州及其他报纸上都有发表。她在短篇小说和摄影方面也有所涉猎。她和丈夫、四个孩子和很多家畜生活在一座舒适的房子里。她的个人主页：http://marketing-by-design.home.mchsi.com。

Kay Conner Pliszka and her "unromantic hubby" were both teachers in the Milwaukee public school system. They met in 1972, were married a year later, and have enjoyed life together for thirty-six years. They are now retired and living in a fantastic retirement village in Florida. For speaking engagements e-mail kmpliszka@comcast.net.

凯·康纳·普里斯卡 和她丈夫都是密尔沃基公立教育体系的教师，她觉得她的丈夫"一点也不懂浪漫"。他们在 1972 年相遇，一年后结婚，已经在一起快乐地生活了 36 年。现在他们退休了，住在佛罗里达州的一个极好的退休村里。她的电子邮箱地址：kmpliszka@comcast.net。

Gayle Danis Rinot is an experienced journalist, copywriter, columnist and editor. She is a 1987 graduate of Emerson College in Boston, where she majored in Broadcast Journalism. Gayle lives in central Israel with her charming husband and three beautiful and talented daughters. You may contact her at gaylerinot@gmail.com.

盖尔·丹尼斯·瑞诺特 盖尔是一名经验丰富的记者、广告文案撰稿人、专栏作家和编辑。她 1987 年毕业于波士顿的艾默生学院，专业是广播新闻学。盖尔和她帅气的丈夫、以及三个美丽聪慧的女儿居住在以色列。她的电子邮箱地址：gaylerinot@gmail.com。

Jay Rylant graduated from Mountain View College in Dallas, TX, after which he went on to spend fourteen years as a freelance musician. He now pursues a career as a writer and novelist. He has served the last year as editor for *Different Strokes*—a weekly newsletter for golfhelp.com, and he was published in *Chicken Soup for the Soul: The Golf Book*.

杰·瑞兰特 毕业于得克萨斯州达拉斯的山景城学院，毕业之后，他做了 14 年的自由音乐人。他现在追求的事业是成为一名作家和小说家。他去年成为了"各有所好"的一位编辑——那是 golfhelp.com 网站的一个每周时事通讯栏目，他曾经在《心灵鸡汤：献给高尔夫》上发表过文章。

Arthur Sanchez hails from the sunny state of Florida. Primarily a Fantasy writer he loves telling the story of how he met his wife. For more information on Arthur's work, links to free stories on the web, or to find out about his books, visit his website: www.ArthurSanchez.com.

亚瑟·桑切斯 来自阳光明媚的佛罗里达州。他是一名奇幻作家，但他最喜欢写的故事是他遇见他妻子的过程。想要了解更多关于亚瑟的信息，或者想要免费阅读他写的故事及查阅他出版的书，可参见他的个人网站：www.

ArthurSanchez.com。

Elizabeth Schmeidler is happily married and a mother to three wonderful sons. She is an author of poetry, children's stories, novels, short stories, and is an inspirational speaker. Elizabeth has composed/recorded three CDs of original music. She is working on her newest CD, "*Believe*." Contact her at www. elizabethshop.org.

伊丽莎白·施迈德勒 的婚姻美满幸福，现在已经是三个儿子的母亲了。她写过诗歌、儿童故事、小说、短篇故事，还是一位鼓舞人心的演讲家。伊丽莎白现在已经自己作曲并录制了三张原创唱片。她现在正忙于她的最新唱片《相信》。她的个人网站：www.elizabethshop.org。

Toni Somers is a retired photographer and drawing teacher. She has a Bachelor of Arts in Studio Art from Columbia College. She enjoys drawing and playing classical guitar and hammered dulcimer. Toni lives on the Texas Gulf Coast with her husband of fifty-four years. Please e-mail her at txlaughinggull@yahoo.com.

托尼·萨默斯 是一位退休的摄影师和绘画老师。她在哥伦比亚学院获得了摄影艺术的学士学位。她喜欢画画、弹奏经典吉他曲目，还喜欢弹奏德西马琴。托尼和她的丈夫在得克萨斯海湾已经生活了 54 年了。她的电子邮箱地址：txlaughinggull@yahoo.com。

Deb Stanley lives in Michigan with her husband and three daughters. She teaches 6th grade Special Education. Deb's hobbies include spending time with family, inspirational writing, singing, and working with children with special needs, especially those with autism. E-mail her at dstanley64@gmail.com.

戴坡·斯坦利 和她的丈夫和三个女儿生活在密歇根州。她教特殊教育六年级的课程。黛波喜欢和她的家人在一起，喜欢富有灵感的写作、唱歌、照顾需要特殊看护的孩子，特别是那些有孤独症的孩子。她的电子邮箱地址：

dstanley64@gmail.com。

Susan Staunton received her BA in Elementary Education and her Master's in Guidance Counseling. She taught for nine years in Maryland and now home schools in Minnesota. Susan hopes to continue writing stories that teach and inspire in addition to writing home school curriculums. Please e-mail her at s.staunton@comcast.net.

苏珊·士丹顿 获得过基础教育的文学学士学位，还获得了指导咨询专业的硕士学位。她在马里兰教过九年书，现在在明尼苏达州的家庭学校教书。苏珊想要继续写故事，希望不仅可以用来作为家庭学校课程的材料，还可以鼓舞她的学生。她的电子邮箱地址：s.staunton@comcast.net。

Jean H. Stewart writes and edits from her home, where she lives with her husband of forty-nine years and stays involved with their twin daughters and families. An award-winning writer, her stories can be found in numerous *Chicken Soup for the Soul* books as well as other anthologies, magazines and newspapers. You can reach her at jeanstewart@cox.net.

珍·希瑟·斯图尔特 在家里写作和编辑。她和丈夫一起生活了 49 年，她的两个双胞胎女儿已经成家，他们生活得很甜蜜。她是一位屡获殊荣的作家，她的作品多次发表在《心灵鸡汤》系列图书中，也发表在很多其他的选集、杂志和报纸中。她的电子邮箱地址：jeanstewart@cox.net。

Anji Limón Taylor is a writer and poet. She is currently working towards a BS degree in Digital Communications and Media at New York University. She enjoys reading, running and laughing. Her future writing projects include a very unique children's book series. Feel free to e-mail her at anji@anjiwrites.com.

安吉·利蒙·泰勒 是一位作家和诗人。现在，她正在纽约大学攻读她的数字通信和新闻传媒专业的学士学位。她喜欢阅读、跑步和大笑。她未来的写作计划里包括一个非常独特的儿童图书系列。她的电子邮箱地址：anji@

anjiwrites.com。

Lisa Tiffin is a freelance writer from Upstate New York, where she lives with her husband and twin sons. Her essays and articles have appeared in a variety of magazines. She is the author of *The Eagle Ridge Prep Technological Adventure* series for children. Find out more at www.lisatiffin.com.

丽莎·蒂芬 和她的丈夫和两个儿子一起居住在纽约州的北部，是一位自由作家。她的随笔和文章发表在很多杂志上。她是《鹰岭探险技术准备》儿童系列图书的作者。她的个人网站地址：www.lisatiffin.com。

Christine Trollinger took up writing as a hobby after retiring from the insurance business in 1991. She has been published in several magazines and books of inspiration. She enjoys painting, gardening and has two great granddaughters, who are the love of her life. Please e-mail her at gabby_trolly@yahoo.com.

克里斯汀·托灵格 在 1991 年从保险行业退休之后，一直把写作当成爱好。她的作品已经发表在多种杂志和励志图书上。她喜欢画画和园艺。她的两个孙女是她一生的钟爱。她的电子邮箱地址：gabby_trolly@yahoo.com。

A retired college teacher and administrator at Montana State University in Great Falls, **Suzanne Waring**, Ed.D., is now a freelance writer. Recently celebrating their forty-fifth wedding anniversary, Suzanne and her husband, Leonard, have two adult sons. Please e-mail her at swaring7@yahoo.com.

苏珊·华林 教育学博士，她是大瀑布城的蒙大拿州立大学的一名退休教师和管理人员。现在，她是一名自由作家。最近，她和她的丈夫莱纳德度过了他们 45 周年的结婚纪念日。他们有两个儿子。她的电子邮箱地址：swaring7@yahoo.com。

Meet Our Contributors
见见我们的撰搞人

Meet Our Authors
见见我们的作者

Jack Canfield is the co-creator of the *Chicken Soup for the Soul* series, which Time magazine has called "the publishing phenomenon of the decade." Jack is also the co-author of many other bestselling books.

Jack is the CEO of the Canfield Training Group in Santa Barbara, California, and founder of the Foundation for Self-Esteem in Culver City, California. He has conducted intensive personal and professional development seminars on the principles of success for more than a million people in twenty-three countries, has spoken to hundreds of thousands of people at more than 1,000 corporations, universities, professional conferences and conventions, and has been seen by millions more on national television shows.

Jack has received many awards and honors, including three honorary doctorates and a Guinness World Records Certificate for having seven books from the *Chicken Soup for the Soul* series appearing on the New York Times bestseller list on May 24, 1998.

You can reach Jack at www.jackcanfield.com.

杰克·坎菲尔德是《心灵鸡汤》丛书的创作者之一,《时代》杂志把《心灵鸡汤》系列称为"近十年来出版界的神话"，杰克也是许多其他畅销书的合著者。

　　杰克是加利福尼亚州桑塔芭芭拉市坎菲尔德培训集团的首席执行官，也是加利福尼亚州卡尔弗市自尊心基金会的创立人。他在二十三个国家为超过一百万人举行了成功原理的个人专业发展讲座，在一千多家公司、大学、专业会议和国际大会上的成千上万的人面前发表过演讲，还上过无数的电视节目。

　　杰克获得过很多奖项和荣誉，包括三项荣誉博士称号以及一份吉尼斯世界纪录证书，以表彰他编辑的七本《心灵鸡汤》系列丛书于 1998 年 5 月 24 日登上《纽约时报》的畅销书榜单。

　　你可以登录 www.jackcanfield.com 与他取得联系。

Mark Victor Hansen is the co-founder of *Chicken Soup for the Soul*, along with Jack Canfield. He is a sought-after keynote speaker, bestselling author, and marketing maven. Mark's powerful messages of possibility, opportunity, and action have created powerful change in thousands of organizations and millions of individuals worldwide.

Mark is a prolific writer with many bestselling books in addition to the *Chicken Soup for the Soul* series. Mark has had a profound influence in the field of human potential through his library of audios, videos, and articles in the areas of big thinking, sales achievement, wealth building, publishing success, and personal and professional development. He is also the founder of the MEGA Seminar Series.

Mark has received numerous awards that honor his entrepreneurial spirit, philanthropic heart, and business acumen. He is a lifetime member of the Horatio Alger Association of Distinguished Americans.

You can reach Mark at www.markvictorhansen.com.

　　马克·维克多·汉森和杰克·坎菲尔德一起创办了《心灵鸡汤》。马克是一名受欢迎的主题发言人、畅销书作家、市场专家，他的有关可能性、机遇和行动方面的强有力的信息已经使得全球成千上万的组织和个人产生了强有力的变化。

马克是一个多产的作家，除了《心灵鸡汤》，他还有很多畅销书。通过自己收藏的音频、视频资料和有关大胆思考、销售业绩、财富累积、成功出版、个人职业发展方面的文章，马克已经对人类潜能领域产生深刻的影响。他还是米加讲座系列的创始人。

马克曾被授予无数的奖项，以表彰他的创业精神、博爱的心和敏锐的商业眼光，他是霍雷肖杰出美国人协会的终身会员。

你可以登录 www. markvictorhansen.com 与他取得联系。

Amy Newmark is the publisher and editor-in-chief of *Chicken Soup for the Soul*, after a thirty-year career as a writer, speaker, financial analyst, and business executive in the worlds of finance and telecommunications. Amy is a magna Cum laude graduate of Harvard College, where she majored in Portuguese, minored in French, and traveled extensively. She and her husband have four grown children.

After a long career writing books on telecommunications, voluminous financial reports, business plans, and corporate press releases, *Chicken Soup for the Soul* is a breath of fresh air for Amy. She has fallen in love with *Chicken Soup for the Soul* and its life-changing books, and really enjoys putting these books together for Chicken Soup's inspiring readers. She has co-authored more than two dozen *Chicken Soup for the Soul* books and has edited another two dozen.

You can reach Amy through the webmaster@chickensoupforthesoul.com.

艾米·纽马克是《心灵鸡汤》的出版人兼主编，她在财务和电信领域工作了三十年，身兼数职，如作家、发言人、财务分析和商业主管。艾米以优异的成绩毕业于哈佛大学，她主修葡萄牙语，副修法语。她喜欢到处旅游。她和丈夫有四个孩子。

Meet Our Authors
见见我们的作者

　　长期撰写有关电信的书籍、长篇财务报告、商业企划和公司新闻发布稿，《心灵鸡汤》令艾米耳目一新。她爱上了《心灵鸡汤》和改变人生的书籍，很喜欢为受到《心灵鸡汤》启发的读者们编写这些书籍。她已经与人合著了超过十二本的《心灵鸡汤》，还编辑了其他十二本。

你可以通过 webmaster@chickensoupforthesoul.com 联络艾米。

Thank You
感谢词

We owe huge thanks to all of our contributors. We know that you pour your hearts and souls into the thousands of stories and poems that you share with us, and ultimately with each other. We appreciate your willingness to open up your lives to other *Chicken Soup for the Soul* readers.

We can only publish a small percentage of the stories that are submitted, but we read every single one and even the ones that do not appear in the book have an influence on us and on the final manuscript.

We want to thank *Chicken Soup for the Soul* Assistant Publisher D'ette Corona for reading the thousands of stories and poems that were submitted for this book. She shaped the initial manuscript and this book is as much hers as it is ours. We also want to thank our editor and webmaster Barbara LoMonaco and editor Kristiana Glavin for their expert editorial and proofreading assistance.

We owe a very special thanks to our creative director and book producer, Brian Taylor at Pneuma Books, for his brilliant vision for our covers and interiors. Finally, none of this would be possible without the business and creative leadership of our CEO, Bill Rouhana, and our president, Bob Jacobs.

我们向所有的投稿者致以最真诚的感谢。我们知道，你们把最真实的情感投入到了数以千计的故事和诗歌中去，你们与我们分享，最终会与大家一起分享。我们感谢您愿意把您的生活展示给所有《心灵鸡汤》的读者。

我们只能在收到的故事中择取一小部分发表于书中，但是我们阅读了每一个故事，包括那些没有出现在书里的故事。它们也深深地影响了我们，也影响了最终的书稿。

我们想要感谢《心灵鸡汤》发行社副社长狄爱特·科罗拉，她阅读了向本书投稿的数以千计的故事和诗歌。她完成了最初的书稿，与其说这本书是我们的，不如说是她的。我们也要感谢我们的编辑和网站管理员芭芭拉·洛摩纳哥，以及编辑克里斯蒂安娜·格拉文，他们为本书提供了专业的编辑和校对。

我们要特别感谢我们的创意总监和书的生产监督，精神书屋的布莱恩·泰勒，他对书籍的封面和内里都具有杰出的眼光。最后，如果没有商业和创意领导人、我们的首席执行官比尔·鲁哈纳和我们的主席鲍勃·乔布斯，就没有《心灵鸡汤》系列。

Chicken Soup for the Soul
Improving Your Life Every Day

Real people sharing real stories—for fifteen years. Now, Chicken Soup for the Soul has gone beyond the bookstore to become a world leader in life improvement. Through books, movies, DVDs, online resources and other partnerships, we bring hope, courage, inspiration and love to hundreds of millions of people around the world. Chicken Soup for the Soul's writers and readers belong to a one-of-a-kind global community, sharing advice, support, guidance, comfort, and knowledge.

Chicken Soup for the Soul stories have been translated into more than forty languages and can be found in more than one hundred countries. Every day, millions of people experience a Chicken Soup for the Soul story in a book, magazine, newspaper or online. As we share our life experiences through these stories, we offer hope, comfort and inspiration to one another. The stories travel from person to person, and from country to country, helping to improve lives everywhere. Ehebem pulere condacchus.

心灵鸡汤
每天改善你的生活

这十七年来，真实的人们分享他们真实的故

Improving Your Life Every Day
每天改善你的生活

事。现在,《心灵鸡汤》已经超越其书本的本身价值,成为改善生活的世界领导者。通过书本、电影、DVD、在线资源以及其他合作关系,我们将希望、勇气、灵感和爱心带给全世界千千万万的人们。《心灵鸡汤》的作者和读者都是全球独一无二的社区中的一员,他们分享建议、相互扶持、接受引导、安慰彼此、共享知识。

《心灵鸡汤》里的故事已被翻译成四十几种语言,在一百多个国家出版发行。每天都有成千上万的人通过书本、杂志、报纸或是网络阅读《心灵鸡汤》的故事。我们通过这些故事来分享自己的人生经历,给予人们希望、安慰和灵感。这些故事口口相传,不分国界,它们在世界的每一个角落帮助人们改善生活。

Share with Us

We all have had *Chicken Soup for the Soul* moments in our lives. If you would like to share your story or poem with millions of people around the world, go to chickensoup. com and click on "Submit Your Story." You may be able to help another reader, and become a published author at the same time. Some of our past contributors have launched writing and speaking careers from the publication of their stories in our books!

Our submission volume has been increasing steadily—the quality and quantity of your submissions has been fabulous. We only accept story submissions via our website. They are no longer accepted via mail or fax.

To contact us regarding other matters, please send us an e-mail through webmaster@chickensoupforthesoul.com, or fax or write us at:

Chicken Soup for the Soul

P.O. Box 700

Cos Cob, CT 06807-0700

Fax: 203-861-7194

One more note from your friends at *Chicken Soup for the Soul*: Occasionally, we receive an unsolicited book manuscript from one of our readers, and we would like to respectfully inform you that we do not accept unsolicited manuscripts and we must discard the ones that appear.

与我们一同分享

我们的人生中都经历过"心灵鸡汤"一刻，如果你愿意和世界各地的人们分享你的故事或是诗歌，请登录 chickensoup.com，点击"提交你的故事"。或许你在帮助另一名读者的同时，自己也能成为一名作者。我们过去的一些撰稿人在我们的书中发表了自己的作品后，开始了写作和演讲的职业生涯。

稿件递交量在稳步上升，你们提交的稿件的质量和数量都令人难以置信。我们只接受网络作品递交，邮件或是传真方式恕不接纳。

有关其他事项，请发邮件至 webmaster@chickensoupforthesoul.com，或传真或给我们写信，联系方式如下：

心灵鸡汤

P.O. Box 700

Cos Cob, CT 06807-0700

传真号码：203-861-7194

你的"心灵鸡汤"朋友的另一个特别提醒：偶尔我们会收到读者主动提供的书稿，我们在此郑重地提醒您，这些书稿是不被接受的，一旦收到，我们只能弃置不用。

Share with Us
与我们一同分享